VOLUME TWO

Messages for Building Up

NEW

BELIEVERS

WATCHMAN NEE

Living Stream Ministry
Anaheim, California • www.lsm.org

First Edition, March 1997.

ISBN 0-87083-813-X (3 volume set)
ISBN 0-7363-0977-2 (volume 2)

Published by

Living Stream Ministry
2431 W. La Palma Ave., Anaheim, CA 92801 U.S.A.
P. O. Box 2121, Anaheim, CA 92814 U.S.A.

Printed in the United States of America

05   06   07   08   09   10   11   /   10   9   8   7   6   5   4   3

CONTENTS

PREFACE

After Watchman Nee resumed his ministry in 1948, he fellowshipped several times with the brothers about the critical need to provide believers with a spiritual education. As a goal, he wanted to provide basic teachings to every brother and sister in the church so that they could have a solid foundation of the truth and express the same testimony among the churches. *Messages for Building Up New Believers,* Volumes 1—3, contains fifty-four lessons for new believers, which Watchman Nee released during his workers' training in Kuling. These chapters are rich in content and all-inclusive in scope. The truths are basic and crucial. It was Watchman Nee's intention that every local church use this material to build up its new believers, finishing all the lessons in the course of one year and then repeating the same lessons year after year.

Four of the fifty-four lessons appear as appendices at the end of Volume 3. These four messages were delivered by Watchman Nee as part of the "New Believers" series at Kuling mountain but were later removed from the final, published version. We have chosen to include them as appendices. In addition to these four messages, Volume 1 begins with a message given by Watchman Nee at a co-workers' meeting in July 1950 concerning the meeting for the building up of new believers. It covers the importance of this type of training, the main points to take care of, and some practical suggestions.

CHAPTER EIGHTEEN

WITNESSING

Scripture Reading: Acts 9:19-21; 22:15; 1 John 4:14; John 1:40-45; 4:29; Mark 5:19

I. THE MEANING OF WITNESSING

How long will the light of a candle last? Of course, the light will go out when the candle burns out. But if we light another candle with this one, the light will double in intensity. Will the light of the first candle diminish because it has lit the second? No. If we use the second to light a third, will the light of the second diminish? No. The light of each candle will last until the candle burns out. But when the first light goes out, the second will still be burning. When the second light goes out, the third will still go on shining. If we keep on lighting more candles—ten, a hundred, or a thousand candles—the light will never go out. This explains the testimony of the church. When the Son of God was on earth, He lit the first candle. After that, more candles were lit one after another. For the past nineteen centuries, the church has been like candles; when one candle burns out, it is continued by another one. This goes on and on even today. The church has never ceased shining on this earth, just as salvation has never stopped. Some have lit ten candles; some have lit a hundred. Candle after candle has been lit, and the light continues on.

Brothers and sisters, do you want your light to continue, or do you want to see it end when your candle is extinguished? You have been lit by someone. He does not expect the light to end with you. Every Christian must try his best to bring salvation to others. He must do his best to testify to others and lead others to the Lord so that the testimony may continue on this earth from generation to generation. It is unfortunate that with some people their light ends and their testimony ceases. This is most pitiful! The church has been propagating itself for generations. Some people find their testimony continuing, while others have unfortunately gone without posterity. The light of a candle can only shine while it is still burning. Likewise, a man's testimony continues only while he is still alive. In order for the light of a candle to go on, other candles must be lit before the first one burns out. In this way the second, the third, the hundredth, the thousandth, and even the ten thousandth candle will carry on the light. This light will continue forever and spread to all parts of the world. Such spreading will not diminish the light of each candle. We suffer no loss when we witness. But by witnessing, the testimony goes on.

What is witnessing? In Acts 22:15 the Lord sent Ananias to speak to Paul: "For you will be a witness to Him unto all men of the things which you have seen and heard." From this we see that the basis of witnessing is what we have seen and heard. You cannot be a witness to what you have not seen with your own eyes or heard with your own ears. Paul saw something with his own eyes and heard something with his own ears. God charged him to be a witness of what he had seen with his own eyes and heard with his own ears. First John 4:14 tells us what witnessing is: "We have beheld and testify that the Father has sent the Son as the Savior of the world." A person is a witness to what he has seen. Thank God, you have believed in the Lord. You have met Him, believed in Him, received Him, and gained Him. You are saved. You have been delivered from sins, received forgiveness, and obtained peace. Now that you have believed in the Lord, what joy you possess. This joy is something which you did not have before. Formerly, how heavy was the load of sin upon you! But now, thank God, this load of sin is gone. You have seen and heard something. What should you do today? You should testify of your experience. This does not mean that you have to leave your job to be a preacher. It means that you should witness to your friends, relatives, and acquaintances of what you have seen and heard, and bring them to the Lord.

The gospel will stop with you if your testimony does not continue. It is true that you are saved; you have the life of the Lord and you are lit. But if you do not light others, you will be finished when your candle burns out. You should not meet the Lord empty-handed. You should bring many with you when you meet the Lord. New believers must learn from the very beginning to witness to people and bring them to the Lord. Never be lazy in this matter. If a believer does not open his mouth from the very beginning, after a few days he will form a habit of keeping his mouth closed, and then it will take much effort to turn the matter around. You have believed in the Lord. For the first time you have tasted so great a love, received so great a Savior, obtained so great a salvation, and experienced so great an emancipation. Yet you do not testify for the Lord or light others with your light! You really owe the Lord something!

II. EXAMPLES OF WITNESSING

Let us consider four portions of the Word. They are good examples of witnessing.

A. Going into the City to Tell Others

In John 4 the Lord told the Samaritan woman about the living water. By this she realized that no one on earth can find satisfaction without the living water. Everyone who drinks of the water from the well will thirst again. No matter how many times man drinks of that water, he will thirst again; he is never satisfied. Only by drinking the Lord's water will we not thirst again, because there is a spring that will flow out of us and satisfy us continuously. Only this inner satisfaction can give us true satisfaction. The Samaritan woman had been married five times. She married one man after another; she had changed her husband five times, yet she was still not satisfied. She was a person who drank again and again but was never satisfied. Even the man who was with her at that time was not her husband. She, undoubtedly, was not a satisfied person. But the Lord had the living water that could satisfy her. When the Lord showed her who He was, and when she had Him, she left her waterpot and went away into the city, saying, "Come, see a man who told me all that I have done. Is this not the Christ?" (v. 29). Her first reaction was to testify to others. What did she testify? She testified Christ. Perhaps the people in the city knew something about her, but there were probably many things which they did not know. Yet the Lord told her everything. She testified to others, saying, "Is this not the Christ?" The moment she saw the Lord, she opened her mouth to invite others to find out whether He was the Christ. As a result of the woman's word, many believed in the Lord.

Every Christian has an obligation to be a witness and to introduce the Lord to others. The Lord has saved a great sinner such as me. If He is not the Christ, who else can He be? If He is not the Son of God, who else can He be? I have no choice but to open my mouth. I have to open my mouth to testify. Although I may not know how to give a message, at least I know that He is Christ. I know He is the Son of God, the God-appointed Savior. I have seen that I am a sinner, and I know that the Lord has saved me. I cannot explain what has happened to me, but I can ask others to come and see what a great change has occurred in me. I do not know how it came about. Formerly, I considered myself a good man. Now I see myself as a sinner. The Lord has shown me my sins, things which I did not realize were sins. Now I know the kind of person I am. I committed many sins in the past which others did not know about and which even I myself may not have known about. I committed many sins, yet I did not realize that they were sins. Here is a man who told me everything I have done. He told me what I already knew, and He also told me what I did not know. I can only confess that I have touched Christ and have met the Savior. Here is a man who told me that the "husband" I had was not my husband. He told me that if I drank of this water, I would thirst again and come back for more. How true were those words! Come and see. Is He not the Savior? Is He not the Christ? Is He not the only One who can save us?

All those who have seen that they are sinners surely have a testimony to give. Those who have seen the Savior also have a testimony to give. This woman gave her testimony within a few hours after she had met the Lord. It was something that happened on the same day, not something that happened a few years later when she returned from a revival meeting. She witnessed to others immediately after she returned to the city. Once a person is saved, he should tell others what he has seen and understood immediately. Do not speak what you do not know, and do not give a long discourse. Just tell them what you know. This is all you need to testify; you only have to tell others how you feel. Some can say, "I was so depressed before I believed in the Lord. But now that I have believed in the Lord, I have become so happy. In the past I pursued many things but was never satisfied. Now there is an unspeakable sweetness within. Before I believed in the Lord I could not sleep at night. But now I can sleep well. I used to be full of anxiety and bitterness. But now I feel peace and joy wherever I go." You can tell others what you have experienced. You do not need to tell them what you cannot say. You do not need to tell them what you do not know. Do not speak anything beyond what you know or beyond your present situation. That may stir up arguments. Present yourself to others as a living witness. They will have nothing to say.

B. Going Home to Tell Others

In Mark 5:1-20 we see a person who was demon possessed. It is the most severe case of demon possession recorded in the Bible. A legion of demons was within this man. He dwelt among the tombs, and no one was able to bind him, not even with a chain. Night and day, he would cry out among the tombs and in the mountains and gash himself with stones. When the Lord commanded the demons to come out from him, they did and entered into about two thousand hogs. They all rushed down the steep slope into the sea and drowned. After the demon possessed man was saved, the Lord said to him, "Go to your house, to your own people, and report to them what great things the Lord has done for you, and how He has had mercy on you" (v. 19).

After you are saved, the Lord wants you to tell your family, neighbors, relatives, friends, and colleagues that you are now a saved person. You should tell them not only that you have believed in Jesus but also what great things the Lord has done for you. The Lord wants you to tell others what He has done for you. He wants you to confess and witness to others what has happened to you. Others will be lit when you do this, and salvation will continue on; it will not stop with you.

What a pity that many souls in Christian families are on the way to eternal perdition. Some of our parents, children, relatives, and friends have not heard the gospel of Christ from our own mouths. They have only the blessing and happiness of the present age, without the hope of the coming age. Why should we withhold from telling them what the Lord has done for us? These are the ones who are right next to us. If they cannot hear the gospel from us, who else can?

In order to witness to our family, we must show them the great change in our conduct. We must show our family what a wonderful change has been wrought in our lives since we believed in the Lord. Only then will they listen to us. They will not have confidence in anything less than this. We must be more righteous, more self-sacrificing, more loving, more diligent, and more joyful than before. They will not believe us if there is no change in our conduct. At the same time, we need to witness to them the reason for this change.

C. Proclaiming in the Synagogue

Acts 9:19-21 says, "He was with the disciples in Damascus for some days. And immediately he proclaimed Jesus in the synagogues, that this One is the Son of God. And all who heard him were amazed and said, Is this not the one who ravaged those who call upon this name in Jerusalem and came here for this, that he might bring them bound before the chief priests?"

Saul was on his way to Damascus to bind the believers of the Lord. But he met the Lord on the way and the Lord spoke to him. The moment light came, he fell on his face and became blind. The men who journeyed with him led him by the hand and brought him into Damascus. He was there three days without seeing, eating, or drinking. The Lord sent Ananias to lay his hands upon him, and he received sight, rose up, and was baptized. After he had taken food, he was strengthened.

After a few days he immediately went into the synagogues to proclaim that Jesus is the Son of God and to witness to others. It was obviously difficult for him to do this because he had been persecuting the Lord's disciples all along. He could have been a member of the Sanhedrin. The Jewish Sanhedrin was comprised of seventy-one persons, and he could have been one among the seventy-one. He had secured a letter from the high priest and was on his way to bind the believers of the Lord and to bring them before the high priest. What should he do now that he had believed in the Lord? Originally, he was going to bind those who believed in the Lord. Now he himself was in danger of being bound. Humanly speaking, he should have escaped or hidden. Instead, he went into the synagogues, not just one but many, to prove that Jesus is the Son of God. This shows us that the first thing a person should do upon receiving the Lord is testify for Him. After Paul received his sight, he went at the first opportunity to testify that Jesus of Nazareth is the Son of God. Every believer of the Lord should do the same thing.

Everyone in this world knows that there is a Jesus. But they only know Jesus as one among millions of men in this world. In other words, Jesus is considered merely as one man among many. Although they regard Him as being a little more special than others, He is still an ordinary man to them. But one day light and revelation came to you; the eyes of your heart were enlightened, and you discovered something. You discovered that this Jesus is the Son of God. You discovered that God has a Son! Jesus is the Son of God! What a great discovery! You discovered that there is one man among all men who is the Son of God. This is truly tremendous! When a person receives the Lord Jesus as his Savior and confesses Him as the Son of God, he is doing a great thing, a tremendous thing. He cannot let the occasion pass by lightly, because it is a momentous event. Of the millions of men in this world, he has discovered One who is the Son of God. What a great and tremendous discovery this is! Among the billions of men throughout history, he has suddenly found out that Jesus of Nazareth is the Son of God. This is indeed a great matter. We would marvel if someone were to discover an angel among us.

How much more marvelous is it when someone discovers the Son of God? We do not know how many million times more superior the Lord is than the angels. There is no comparison between the two. The angels are far, far inferior to our Lord.

Here was a man on his way to bind all those who believed in the Lord's name. But after he fell and rose up, he went into the synagogues and proclaimed that Jesus is the Son of God. He either was mad or had received a revelation. He was not mad. Indeed, he had received a revelation. He actually had met the One among millions of men who is the Son of God. Like Paul, you also have met this Man among men, the One who is the Son of God. If you realize how great the discovery you have made is and how important and wonderful your discovery is, you surely will tell others immediately, "I have met the Son of God." You surely will proclaim aloud, "Jesus is the Son of God!" How can a person sit still and act as if nothing has happened when he has believed in the Lord Jesus and is saved? If a person has believed in the Lord Jesus and yet does not feel anything, if he considers this to be nothing marvelous or special, we doubt whether he has believed at all. Here is something great, marvelous, extraordinary, special, beyond all imagination—Jesus of Nazareth is the Son of God. This is too crucial a matter! It is not too much for a man who has seen such an important matter to knock on the door of his friends' house after midnight to tell them of his discovery. A marvelous thing has happened in the universe—Jesus of Nazareth is the Son of God!

Here was a man who had just recovered from his illness; he had just had his sight restored. We see him running immediately into the synagogues and proclaiming, "Jesus of Nazareth is the Son of God!" Every believer who has seen the same should go to the synagogues and shout, "Jesus of Nazareth is the Son of God!" Every time we consider how Jesus of Nazareth can be the Son of God, we feel that this is the greatest discovery in the whole world. No discovery can be more amazing and more crucial than this. What a tremendous thing for us to discover that this man is the Son of God! When Peter told the Lord, "You are the Christ, the Son of the living God," the Lord Jesus told him, "Flesh and blood has not

revealed this to you, but My Father who is in the heavens"
(Matt. 16:16-17). While He was among us in disguise, no one
knew Him except those who had the Father's revelation.

Brothers and sisters, never consider your faith to be a
small thing. You need to realize that your faith is a wonderful
thing. Saul had to go into the synagogues to speak because he
knew that his discovery was too wonderful. You will do the
same if you realize how wonderful the things you have seen
are. Jesus of Nazareth is the Son of God. This is a most wonderful and glorious fact.

D. One on One

A person needs not only to go to the city, to his home, and
to the synagogues to witness to others about his faith in the
Lord, but also to bear a special testimony—to lead others to
the Lord one on one. Such is the testimony in John 1:40-45.
The moment Andrew believed in the Lord, he led his brother
Peter to the Lord. Although Peter later became more gifted
than Andrew, Andrew was the one who led Peter to the Lord.
Philip and Nathanael were friends; Philip first believed in
the Lord and later led his friend to receive the Lord. Andrew
led his brother to the Lord, and Philip sought out his friend.
Both are examples of leading men to the Lord one on one.

About a hundred years ago, there was a believer named
Harvey Page. Although he did not have any special gift and
did not know how to lead many people to the Lord, the Lord
was gracious to him and opened his eyes to realize that he
could lead at least one person to the Lord. He could not do
many great works, but he could concentrate on one person.
He could only say, "I am saved. You also need to be saved."
Once he laid hold of one, he would not let go. He would pray
and talk to his friend until he was saved. Through this practice he solidly gained more than one hundred persons for the
Lord by the time he died.

In a certain country there was a believer named Todd, who
was very good at leading people to salvation. He was sixteen
when he was saved. It was a holiday and he was in a village.
An older couple from a church took him in for hospitality.
They were experienced workers, and they led him to the Lord.

The young man had lived a wanton life, but on that day he knelt down to pray and was saved. In the course of their conversation, the young man found out that the gospel could not prevail in that place because a certain Mr. Dickens would not repent. When Todd heard this, he asked, "Who is this Mr. Dickens?" They told him that he was a retired soldier over sixty years old. He kept a gun at home and vowed to shoot whoever came to preach the gospel to him. He regarded every Christian in the world as a hypocrite, and he called them all by such a name. Whenever he came across a Christian, he would behave in a violent way. No Christian dared to preach the gospel to him or even walk past the street where he lived. If he knew that a Christian was walking past his street, he would curse vehemently and fiercely. When Todd heard this, he prayed, "O Lord! I have received Your grace today. You have saved me. I must go and testify to Mr. Dickens." Even before he finished his tea, he said, "I am going." He had been saved less than two hours earlier, yet he wanted to witness to Mr. Dickens. The older couple advised him, saying, "Do not go. Many of us have failed. He has chased some away with a rod. Others fled when he threatened them at gunpoint. Even though he has beaten up so many people, we do not want to take him to court because we want to maintain a proper gospel testimony. This has given him the excuse to become more fierce." Todd said, "I feel that I should go."

He arrived at Mr. Dickens's door. As soon as he knocked, the man came to the door. He had a stick in his hands, and he asked, "Young man, what do you want?" Todd said, "Is it all right for me to speak a few words to you?" The man nodded, and both of them went into the house. The moment they were in the house, Todd said, "I would like you to receive the Lord Jesus as your Savior." Mr. Dickens lifted up his rod and said, "I suppose you are new here. I will let you go and not beat you up. But have you not heard that no one is allowed to speak the name of Jesus here? Get out! Get out right away!" Todd said again, "I would like you to believe in Jesus." Mr. Dickens became furious. He ran upstairs and returned with a gun in his hand. He shouted at him, saying, "Get out or I will shoot!" Todd responded, "I am asking you to believe in Jesus. If you want to shoot, you can shoot. But just let me pray before you shoot." He immediately knelt down in front of Mr. Dickens and prayed, "O God! This man does not know you. Please save him." Then he prayed again, "O God! This man does not know you. Please have mercy on him. Have mercy on Mr. Dickens." Todd knelt there and would not rise up. He continued praying, "O God! Please have mercy on Mr. Dickens! Please have mercy on Mr. Dickens!" After praying five or six times, he heard a groaning near him. A little while later, he heard Mr. Dickens lay down his gun. Soon Mr. Dickens was on his knees next to Todd, praying, "O God! Please have mercy on me." Within a few minutes, that man had accepted the Lord. He took the young man by the hand and said, "In the past I have only heard the gospel. Today I have *seen* the gospel." Later, the young man told others, "The first time I saw his face, it was truly a face of sin. Every wrinkle spoke of sin and evil. Later, light shone through the wrinkles, and every wrinkle seemed to be saying, 'God is merciful to me.'" The next Lord's Day, Mr. Dickens went to church, and later he led dozens of people to salvation.

In the first two hours after his salvation, Todd led a notoriously difficult person to the Lord. The sooner a new believer opens his mouth, the better it is. We should not waste any time in leading others to Christ.

III. THE IMPORTANCE OF WITNESSING

A. Being a Great Joy

The two happiest days in every believer's life are the day he believes in the Lord and the day when, for the first time, he leads another person to Christ. The first one, of course, is a particularly happy day. However, the joy of leading another person to the Lord for the first time may be greater than the joy experienced on the day of his own salvation. Many Christians do not have much joy because they have never spoken anything for the Lord; they have never led a person to the Lord.

B. Learning to Be Wise

Proverbs 11:30 says, "He that winneth souls is wise." From

the very beginning of our Christian life, we should learn to win souls by various means. We should learn to be wise. This will make us useful persons in the church. I am not talking about delivering a gospel message on the platform. Platform preaching can never replace the personal work of leading people to the Lord. A person who knows only to preach from the platform may not know how to lead people to the Lord. We are not exhorting you to give a message on the platform. We are asking you to save men. Many people are good at preaching, but not at saving men. They do not know what to do when a person is brought to them. They are of little use. The really useful ones are the ones who can lead men to Christ one by one.

C. Begetting Life

No tree will sprout without further growth. Likewise, no one can have God's life without begetting more life. Those who never witness to sinners are probably in need of others witnessing to them. Those who have no desire or interest in leading others to repentance unto the Lord are probably in need of repentance themselves. Those who are silent for the Lord in front of others probably need to listen again to the voice of God's gospel. No one can be so advanced that he no longer needs to save others. No one can advance to the degree that he no longer needs to witness to others. New believers need to learn to witness to others from the very beginning. This is something we have to do for the rest of our lives.

When you become a little more advanced in the spiritual life, others may tell you, "You have to be a channel of living water. You should be one with the Holy Spirit so that the living water—the Holy Spirit—can flow into you." However, a channel has two ends. This channel of the Holy Spirit, this channel of life, also has two ends. One end is toward the Holy Spirit, toward life, and toward the Lord, while the other end is toward man. The living water will never flow if the end toward man is closed. No one can be so wrong as to assume that just opening to the Lord is enough. The living water does not flow through those who are opened just to the Lord. One end must be opened to the Lord, and the other end must be opened to man. The living water will flow out only when both ends are opened. Many people are powerless before God because the end toward the Lord is not open. But many more people are powerless because the end for witnessing and leading others to Christ is closed.

D. Experiencing the Misery of Eternal Separation

Many people have not heard the gospel because you have not yet testified to them. The consequence of this is eternal separation; it is not merely temporal parting. This is too crucial. A brother was once invited to another person's home for dinner. As he was very learned and eloquent, he spoke quite much on intellectual subjects. Another elderly friend who lived nearby was also present at the dinner. Since both were very intellectual, they talked for a long time. It was getting late, and the host invited them to stay overnight. The elderly friend's room was directly opposite to this brother's room. Not long after they retired to their rooms, the brother heard the sound of something falling to the floor. When he went to the other room, he saw the friend lying on the floor, dead. Other people started rushing into the room. The brother said sadly, "If I had known that this was going to happen, I would not have spoken what I spoke two hours ago! I would have pointed out eternal matters. I did not spend even five minutes speaking to him about salvation. I did not give him an opportunity. If I knew what I now know, I would have tried my best to tell him about the Lord's crucifixion for him. But it is too late! If I had told him these words at dinner time, you would have laughed at me for speaking at an inopportune time. But it is too late for him. I hope that you will listen now. Every person needs to believe in the Lord Jesus and in His cross!" There is an eternal separation; this separation is not just temporary. What a tragedy! Once the opportunity is gone, a man will be eternally barred from heaven! We must seek out every opportunity to testify to others.

D. L. Moody was very good at leading men to salvation. He once made up his mind to preach the gospel to at least one person a day, whether or not he was giving a message on that day. One day he went to bed, and then he remembered that he had not preached the gospel to anyone yet. What should he do? He changed his clothes and went out again to look for someone he could speak to. It was already midnight when he looked at his watch; the streets were empty. Where could he find anyone at such an hour? The only person he could speak to was a policeman who was on duty: "You must believe in the Lord." The policeman was in a bad mood over something at that moment, and he scolded Moody angrily, saying, "Do you not have something better to do than persuade me to believe in Jesus in the middle of the night?" Moody went home after sharing a brief word with him. But the policeman was touched by Moody's word. A few days later he visited Moody and was saved.

As soon as a person believes in the Lord, he should make a resolution before the Lord to lead men to the Lord. Everyone should have a record of how many souls he will save in a year. He may resolve to save ten or twenty a year. He should then begin to pray for them. General prayers are useless prayers. If you go to the Lord and say, "O Lord! Please save sinners," it is too general a prayer. You must have a specific goal in mind. If you want ten, aim for ten. If you want twenty, aim for twenty. You can prepare a book in which you write down the names of the ones you have gained for the Lord. As you gain one, write his name down. At the end of the year, you can count the number of those who were saved and the number who remain unsaved. Continue to pray for those who are not yet saved. Every brother and sister should practice this. It is not too much to gain thirty or fifty souls a year; ten or twenty is common. We must ask the Lord for a specific number in our prayer. The Lord wants to hear our specific prayers. We should pray to the Lord every day and should testify whenever there is opportunity. If all of us preach the gospel and lead people to the Lord this way, our spiritual life will advance quickly in a few years.

We must uphold the torchlight of the gospel and must light everyone around us. Let every Christian go forth to light others. The testimony of the gospel needs to go out from us until the Lord's return. We should not be lit ourselves without lighting others. We should light more and more candles. So many souls before our eyes are in need of salvation. We must try our best to testify to them and lead them to Christ.

Chapter Nineteen

LEADING MEN TO CHRIST

Scripture Reading: Rom. 1:16; 10:14; 1 Tim. 2:1, 4; Mark 16:15

In the previous chapter we said that once a person believes in the Lord, he has to witness for the Lord. In this chapter we want to talk about the ways to lead men to Christ. If we do not know how to lead people to Christ, I am afraid that much of our witnessing will be in vain. There are several things which we must do and learn if we want to lead men to Christ. We can group them into two categories: First, going to God on man's behalf, and second, going to man on God's behalf. In addition, we would also like to say something about passing out tracts.

I. GOING TO GOD ON MAN'S BEHALF

A. Prayer Being the Foundation of Leading Men to Christ

There is a foundational work in leading men to Christ. Before one opens his mouth before man, he first must open his mouth before God. We need to first ask God and then talk to men. We always need to talk to God first, not man. Some brothers and sisters are very zealous to lead men to Christ, but they do not pray for them. A man may have great interest in people, but if he has no burden to pray before the Lord, his work of saving souls will be ineffectual. A person must have a burden before the Lord before he can witness to men.

The Lord Jesus said, "All that the Father gives Me will come to Me, and him who comes to Me I shall by no means cast out" (John 6:37). According to Acts 2:47, the Lord added to the church daily those who were being saved. The first thing that we must do is ask God for people, asking Him to give men to the Lord Jesus and to add them to the church. In order for men to be saved, we need to ask God and implore Him. It is very difficult to deal with man's heart. It is not easy for us to turn a heart toward the Lord. We must first go to God and pray for these people, asking God to bind the strong man (Luke 11:21-22). Afterwards, we can talk to them at length. We have to present these people one by one to the Lord and pray for them fervently before we can effectively lead them to Christ.

Those who are good at leading men to Christ are good at prayer. If you have trouble getting answers to prayer, you will have trouble witnessing for the Lord. If you have no confidence in prayer, you will have no confidence in leading men to Christ. Hence, you must learn to pray in a practical way and not let this matter slip by.

B. Preparing a Record Book

In order to pray for people in a proper way, you should keep a record book. Allow God to put the names of those whom He wishes to save in your heart. When you were first saved, how did you know to whom you should go to make restitution? How did you know whom you should repay? It was the Lord who put the person's name in your heart and who reminded you of particular things. This reminder compelled you to make restitution with others. One day you suddenly thought of something. Another day something else came to your mind. As a result of this enlightening, you dealt with these things one by one. The same principle holds true in leading men to Christ. Allow the Lord to put some names in your heart. When these names are in your heart, spontaneously you will be burdened to pray for them. The Lord may put a few people or a few dozen people in your heart. In writing these names down, the most important thing to remember is to take the names that the Lord has put in your heart. Do not sit down and simply make out a list at random. You will be wasting your time if you mindlessly write down something. Your success will be dependent upon how good your start is.

You have to ask God specifically for a few names. Out of all your family members, friends, colleagues, schoolmates, and those whom you know, a few names will spontaneously come to your mind. You will have a feeling for them, and you will want them to be saved first.

A record book should have the following columns: The first column should be a number; the second column, the date; and the third column, the name. This will remind us of the number we have assigned to a person and the date we began to pray for him. The fourth column should also be a date—the date when the person is saved. If the person unfortunately dies, we can put the date of death in this column. One should persist and not give up once a name is in the book. The prayer for a person should follow him until he dies. If the person is alive and not saved, you should keep on praying for him until he is saved. One brother prayed for his friend for eighteen years before his friend was saved. It is not certain when a person will be saved. Some are saved in a year, and some in two to three months. Perhaps one or two of them may prove to be very difficult, but in the end they will still be saved. You should not relax but relentlessly pursue in prayer for their salvation.

C. The Greatest Obstacle to Prayer Being Sin

Prayer is a test; it exposes your spiritual condition before the Lord. If your spiritual condition is proper and normal, others will be saved one by one. As you intercede continuously before the Lord, you may find one or two persons saved after a few days or half a month. After a while, another three or five may be saved. People should be saved regularly. If your prayers are not answered for a long time, it must mean that you are sick before the Lord. You should go to the Lord for light and find out where your problem lies.

The greatest obstacle to prayer is sin. We must learn to live a holy life before the Lord. We must reject all known sins. The moment we take sin lightly or tolerate it, our prayers will be hindered.

Sin has both an objective aspect and a subjective aspect.

The objective aspect has to do with God, while the subjective aspect has to do with us. On the objective side, sin obstructs God's grace and promises. Isaiah 59:1-2 says, "Behold, Jehovah's hand is not so short that it cannot save; / Nor is His ear so heavy that it cannot hear. / But your iniquities have become a separation / Between you and your God, / And your sins have hidden His face / From you so that He does not hear." Psalm 66:18 says, "If I regard iniquity in my heart, / The Lord will not hear." If a person does not take care of the problem of sin properly, he will find hindrance to his prayer. Unconfessed sins, sins which are never dealt with by the blood, are a big obstacle before God; they are the cause of unanswered prayer. This is on the objective side.

On the subjective side, sin damages man's conscience. When a person sins, no matter what he says to himself, how much he reads the Bible, how many promises there are in the Word, how much grace God has, and how much He accepts him, his conscience will be weakened and bound. First Timothy 1:19 says, "Holding faith and a good conscience, concerning which some, thrusting these away, have become shipwrecked regarding the faith." A ship may be old or small, but it cannot leak. Similarly, our conscience must not have a leak. As soon as the conscience is not at peace, many prayers cannot be uttered. Thus, there are obstacles not only before God but even within man himself. The relationship between faith and conscience is just like that between a ship and its cargo. Faith is like the cargo, and the conscience is like a ship. When the ship has a leak, the cargo will be damaged. When the conscience is strong, faith will be strong. But when there is a leak in the conscience, faith will be gone. If our heart blames us, God is greater than our heart and knows all things (1 John 3:20).

If you want to be a man of prayer, you must deal with sin thoroughly. You lived in sin for a long time in the past. If you are not careful with it now, you will not be totally free from it. You have to deal with sin seriously; you have to come before God to confess every sin, putting every sin under the blood, refusing it, and coming out from it. Then your conscience will be recovered. As soon as the blood cleanses, the conscience is recovered. There will be no condemnation, and spontaneously you will see God's face. Never give in to sin. This will weaken you before the Lord. If you are weak before the Lord, you will not be able to intercede for others. As long as sin remains, you will not be able to utter anything in your prayer. Sin is the number one problem. You should pay attention to it all the time, even daily. If one deals with sin properly before the Lord, he will be able to offer proper prayers, and others will be brought to the Lord through him.

D. Praying with Faith

Another important thing is to have faith in our prayers. If the conscience is blameless, it is easy for faith to be strong, and if faith is strong, spontaneously our prayers will be answered.

What is faith? Faith is freedom from doubt. It is to accept God's promises in our prayers. It is God who asks us to pray and who wants us to pray. God said, "Concerning the work of My hands, command Me" (Isa. 45:11). If we pray, God has to answer us. Jesus said, "Knock and it shall be opened to you" (Matt. 7:7). It is impossible for Him not to open after we have knocked. Jesus said, "Seek and you shall find." It is impossible for us not to find after we have sought. Jesus said, "Ask and it shall be given to you." It is impossible for us to ask and yet not receive. If we do not believe this, what kind of God do we think our God is? We must see that God's promises are faithful and dependable. Faith is based on our knowledge of God. The more we know God, the stronger our faith will be. We are saved already; we know God already. Therefore, we can believe; there should not be any difficulty at all for us to believe. When we believe, God will answer our prayers. Learn to be a person full of faith from the very beginning. We should not trust in our feelings or our mind. Instead, we should believe in God's word. God's promises are like cash; they work. In fact, God's promises are God's work. The promises tell us of God's work, while His work is the manifestation of His promises. We have to accept God's promises in the same way we accept His work. When we believe God's word, abiding in faith rather than in doubt, we will see how real God's words are and we will find answers to our prayers.

E. Aspiring to Be a Praying Person

We need to have the ambition to be a praying person, a person with power before God. Some people are powerful before God, while others are not. When some people speak, God listens. When others speak, He does not listen. What does it mean to be powerful before God? It simply means that God listens to the person when he speaks. It is as if God is happy to be influenced by such a one. Some people can influence God. Being powerless before God means that God does not listen to the person when he speaks. Such a one may spend much time before God, but God ignores him. We must have the desire and the aspiration to see that God often answers our prayers. No blessing can be greater than God answering our prayers all the time. We have to pray to Him, "May every request of ours be pleasing to Your ears." It is a most glorious thing for God to incline His ear to us. It is a tremendous thing for God to trust us to the extent that He can give us whatever we ask.

You have to present to the Lord the names that you are burdened with and pray for them one by one. See how long it takes for God to save them. If your prayers are unanswered after a long period, you have to deal with yourself and with God. In order for your prayers to be answered, it is often necessary to go through specific dealings. Unanswered prayer means that there is sickness somewhere. If you do not mean business in this matter, you will always fail.

This is why you need a record book. The record book will show you whether or not your prayers are answered. Many people do not know whether their prayers are answered because they do not have a record of anything. Newly saved brothers and sisters should learn to have such a record book. Then they will know whether or not their prayers are answered. They will know whether there is a problem between them and the Lord. They will know also when they have to deal with themselves and when they have to deal with God.

If you have prayed for a long time and there is still no

answer, you should realize that there must be some hindrance. The hindrances always occur because there is sin in your conscience or there is a problem with your faith. New believers need not worry about the deeper aspects of prayer. They need only to pay attention to their conscience and their faith. Before the Lord, we have to confess, deal with, and refuse our sins. At the same time we have to genuinely and fully trust in God's promises. If we do this, we will see people being saved one by one, and our lives will be full of answers to prayer.

F. Praying Daily

You have to pray for those around you. Is there no one who needs your prayers? How many colleagues do you have? How many neighbors do you have? How many relatives and friends do you have? Always ask the Lord to place one or two special persons in your heart. When the Lord places a person in your heart, He intends to save this person through you. You should write down his name in your record book and continually bring him to the Lord through prayer.

You need to set aside a fixed time daily for this work of intercession. Whether it be an hour, half an hour, or a quarter of an hour, it must be a fixed time. If there is no fixed time for prayer, there will not be definite prayer. As a result, there will not be any prayer at all. Hence, always fix a time for prayers, whether it is a quarter of an hour or half an hour. Do not be too ambitious; do not plan for two hours and end up not being able to carry it out. It is more practical to set aside one hour, half an hour, or a quarter of an hour. Always fix a time to pray for those who need your prayer. Do not relax. Do this every day. After a while, you will see sinners saved one by one.

G. A Few Examples of Intercession

We will mention a few stories here to show you how others have done this work.

1. A Boiler Worker

Once a boiler worker in a ship was saved. He asked the

brother who led him to Christ, "Please tell me the first thing that I must do for the Lord?" The brother replied, "The Lord will choose a few of your companions and put them in your heart. You will have to pray for them." There were more than ten persons working together at his place. He remembered one person in particular and prayed for him daily. That person found out about this, and he became angry. Later, an evangelist came by and preached the gospel to the men there. After the meeting he stood up and said, "I want to believe in Jesus." The evangelist asked, "Why do you want to believe in Jesus?" He said, "A person has been praying for me for some time. I have to believe in Jesus." The boiler worker had been praying for this man. Although he did not like this in the beginning, the power of prayer overcame him, and in the end he accepted the Lord.

2. A Sixteen-year-old Youth

A sixteen-year-old youth was working as a copy writer in a construction firm. The chief engineer of the company had a very bad temper and almost everyone was afraid of him. After the youth was saved, he started to pray for the chief engineer. He was afraid of the engineer and dared not open his mouth, yet he prayed earnestly for him daily. After a short while, the engineer asked him, "I have over two hundred people in the company, but I feel that you are different. Can you please tell me why you and I are so different?" The engineer was about forty to fifty years old, and the youth was only sixteen. The young man answered, "I have believed in the Lord, and you have not." The engineer immediately said, "I also want to believe in Him." The youth brought him to the church, and the engineer was saved.

3. Two Sisters

In Europe there are guest houses which are open to strangers. They are not hotels, but they receive travelers. Once there were two Christian sisters whose house was open to travelers. Sometimes, as many as twenty or thirty would stay at their place. They noticed the luxury of the travelers' attire and the vanity of their conversation. The sisters were bothered and wanted to win them over to Christ. However, there were many guests and only two of them. How could they win them over? They decided to sit at the two ends of the room during the conversation and pray for the guests from each end.

On the first day during the after-dinner conversation, each sister sat at one end, praying for the guests one by one. One prayed from one end, and the other prayed from the other end. They prayed for each and every one of them. This stopped the guests' jesting and chatting on that first day. They asked themselves what had happened. On that day, one person was saved. The next day, another lady was saved. One by one they were gradually all brought to the Lord.

Prayer is indispensable. The first condition in bringing people to the Lord is intercessory prayer. We must pray systematically, orderly, daily, and relentlessly, until our friends are saved.

II. GOING TO MAN ON GOD'S BEHALF

Merely going to God on man's behalf is not enough. We also have to go to man on God's behalf. We have to tell men about God. Many people have the courage to speak to God, but they have no courage to speak to man. We have to exercise boldness to speak to men. We have to tell them the kind of Lord our Lord is. When we speak, we need to pay attention to a few things.

A. Never Engaging in Useless Arguments

First, never engage in useless arguments. This does not mean that there should never be any arguments. Acts tells us of a few arguments. Even Paul argued (cf. Acts 17:2, 17-18; 18:4, 19). However, useless arguments do not save people. Sometimes it is all right to engage in arguments. But this is mainly for the benefit of other listeners. Try to avoid arguing with the ones you are trying to save because arguments often drive people away instead of bringing them in. If you argue with them, they will run away.

Many people think that arguments can touch men's hearts. Actually, this never happens. At the most, arguments can convince men's minds. Their mouths may be shut, but their hearts will not be won over. Arguments produce little result. Try to say less in the way of argument and more in the way of testimony. You have only to tell others that you felt happy and peaceful after you believed in the Lord Jesus, that you sleep well now, and that even meals are becoming tastier. No one can argue with you about these things. They can only wonder. You have to show them that they do not have your kind of peace and joy and that they should therefore believe in the Lord.

B. Keeping to the Facts

The key to leading men to the Lord is to emphasize the facts, not the doctrines. Just recall what it was like when you were saved. You did not believe because you understood the doctrines. Many people understand the doctrines, but they do not believe. It is impossible for any brother to try to lead others to Christ through arguments and doctrines. The key to leading men to Christ is to keep to the facts. This is why simple ones often are more effective in leading others to the Lord; those who are good at doctrines may not lead others to the Lord. Some people can give wonderful messages. But what use is there in winning the minds of others, if one cannot help them be saved?

Once there was an old man who considered going to church a good habit. He was not saved, yet he would go to church every Sunday and also make his whole family go. But when he returned home, he would lose his temper, and all kinds of bad words would come out of his mouth. The whole family was afraid of him. One day his daughter, who was a believer, came to visit him. She brought her little daughter with her. The old man brought the little granddaughter to the church. When they came out of the church, the little granddaughter looked at her grandfather and felt that he did not look like a believer. She asked him, "Do you believe in Jesus?" The grandfather said, "Children should keep their mouths shut." After walking a few steps, she said to her grandfather again, "You do not look as if you have believed in Jesus." Again the old man said, "Children should keep their mouths shut." After a while she asked her grandfather, "Why do you not believe in Jesus?" This little child saw a fact—the way her grandfather attended church was different from the way other believers attended church. The old man, who was otherwise wild and hard to deal with, became soft after his little granddaughter's probing questions. On that day he accepted the Lord.

The preaching of the gospel requires skill. One must know the way God works before he can preach the gospel. A person may preach the right doctrines, and crowds of people may come for his messages, but the same crowds may walk away unsaved. You will not get any fish with a straight hook. The fishing hook must be curved before one can catch fish. Those who lead others to the Lord need to know how to use a hook. Use only the words that can catch people. If your words cannot catch people, try to change the way you speak. Facts are words that catch; they are words that can touch others.

C. Being Sincere in Attitude

Do not delve into many teachings. Try to speak more facts. At the same time, be sincere in attitude. Saving a man's soul is not a light matter. I once saw a person who wanted to lead others to the Lord. He was willing to pray, but his attitude was wrong. He joked around as he spoke about the Lord. Whatever spiritual power he might have had was lost through his jokes. As a result, he could not lead anyone to the Lord. One has to be very sincere in his attitude. He must not be flippant or funny in his attitude. He has to let others see that this is the most serious matter in the whole world.

D. Praying for the Opportunity to Speak

You also need to pray unceasingly for God to provide you with the right opportunity to speak. When you pray, God will give you the opportunity.

One sister gathered a group of women together once a week and led them in a Bible study. The women all worked in the same company, and none of them believed in the Lord. One of them was very particular about her dress. She was very proud and would not listen to anything the sister said. The sister took notice of her and prayed for her. She asked God to give her the opportunity to speak to the woman. One day she felt a desire to invite the woman over for tea. Since this woman loved to socialize, she accepted the invitation. When she came, the sister encouraged her to believe in the Lord. She replied, "I cannot believe. I like to gamble, and I love pleasure. I do not want to lose these things. I cannot believe in Jesus." The sister said, "If a person wants to believe in the Lord Jesus, she has to stop gambling. Anyone who wants to believe in the Lord Jesus must give up vainglory. You have to give up these things if you want to believe in the Lord Jesus." The woman said, "The price is too high. I cannot afford it." The sister said, "I hope you will go back and consider it." After she said this, she continued to pray for her. The woman returned home and knelt down to pray. After she prayed, she suddenly said, "I have decided to follow the Lord Jesus today." She changed suddenly. She could not explain it, but her heart just turned. She changed her attire; she no longer dressed the same as before. Wonderful things followed one after another. Within a year many of her colleagues were brought to the Lord one by one.

You may think that it is difficult to talk to someone, but if you pray for him, the Lord will give you the opportunity to speak to him, and he will change. The sister who was having Bible studies had been afraid to speak to the woman because the woman behaved as though she knew everything and could do everything. She appeared to be very arrogant, but the Lord gave this sister the burden to pray for her. One day the Lord told the sister to speak to her. She put aside her considerations and spoke to her. You have to pray on the one hand and learn to open your mouth on the other. After you have prayed for a person for some time, the Lord will impress you to speak to him. You will have to tell him about the Lord's grace and the things that He has done for you. He will not be able to resist you because he cannot oppose the things that the Lord has done for you. The newly saved brothers and sisters must pray daily for the Lord to provide opportunities to speak to others. What a pity that some people have been saved for several years already, yet they dare not open their mouths to speak to their relatives and friends! Perhaps your fear has caused you to miss many opportunities that were waiting for you.

E. Speaking in Season and out of Season

We mentioned earlier that you must pray before you speak to a person. This, however, does not mean that you cannot speak if you have not prayed. You have to speak to men even if you are seeing them for the first time. Always grasp the opportunity to speak, whether in season or out of season. You never know who you are missing. Speak whenever there is the chance. Always be prepared to open your mouth. Of course, first and foremost, you have to pray for those whose names appear in your record book. But you have to pray for those whom you do not know. You should pray, "Lord, please save the sinners. Whoever they may be, please save them." Whenever you meet someone and have an urge in your heart to speak, you should speak to him.

If we do not heed this urging, we may let a soul slip away from us. We should not let so many souls slip through our hands. We hope that all the brothers and sisters will testify faithfully for the Lord and bring many to Christ.

F. Studying Carefully

Each time you lead someone to the Lord, you have to do a detailed analysis, just like a doctor who studies each patient's case in detail. The doctor cannot prescribe the same medicine to everyone. Certain sicknesses require certain drugs. He administers a particular drug to a particular patient. The same is true in leading men to Christ. No one can be a doctor without studying medicine. In the same way, no one can lead men to the Lord without studying. Some brothers and sisters are good at bringing people to the Lord because they have studied the ones whom they brought to the Lord. At the beginning of the work of leading men to Christ, a new believer has to work hard to study each case. You should always study why a particular person accepted the Lord. Why did a particular word open him up? Why did another person not believe after hearing a particular word? Why did a person shy away after listening attentively for a while? Why did a person accept when he earlier had opposed? Why are there no fish after waiting for a long time? We always have to find the reason that the Spirit is working, and we also have to find the reason that the Spirit is not working.

If you fail to lead men to Christ, do not put all the blame on others. Those who are good at leading people to the Lord always look for problems within themselves. We cannot wait by the seaside and hope that the fish will jump to the shore. Leading people to the Lord is not so simple. We have to spend time to study and learn where the problems lie. Leading people to the Lord is a skill, and this skill is acquired through working with people. There is always something we can learn, whether through failure or success. Through failure, we learn the reason for our failure. Through success, we learn the reason for our success. In every situation, we need to study the reasons behind the results.

If you do this conscientiously, you will learn many lessons. Eventually, you will discover an interesting thing—as far as believing in the Lord is concerned, there are only a few types of people in the world. If you meet a certain type of person, you will need only to speak certain words to him, and he will receive the Lord. If you speak something else to him, he will oppose you and not believe. If you know how to handle these few types of people, you can handle most people. You can handle those whose names are in your record book, and you can handle those whom you come across by accident. As soon as you come across someone, you will take the opportunity to witness to him, and you will be able to tell immediately the type of person he is. You will know in your heart what to do with this type of person and how to speak to him. He will most likely be saved. If you study your cases one by one, you will become a very skillful soul-winner after one or two years. You will realize that soul winning takes wisdom. By God's mercy, you may lead some to the Lord, maybe a few dozen, or even a few hundred. If you study all these cases carefully, you will become a very powerful soul-winner.

APPENDIX:
PASSING OUT TRACTS

A. No Time Limit

During the past two to three hundred years, the Lord has used tracts in a particular way to save many people. One thing special about winning people with tracts is that tracts are not limited by time. If you try to testify with your mouth, you are restricted by time and personnel. You cannot speak twenty-four hours a day, and your audience may not be available all the time. You may be preaching a wonderful message, but the audience may not be there. However, tracts are not limited by time. You can pass out tracts any time of the day, and men can receive and read your tracts any time of the day. Today many people do not have the time to come to our meeting. But tracts are not limited by time. We can give them out to people who are walking on the streets, who are cooking in their kitchens, or who are working in their offices. This is the first convenience that tracts afford.

B. Tracts Can Convey the Gospel in Full

Many people are very zealous in testifying for the Lord and leading men to Christ. However, their knowledge is limited and their words are lacking. They cannot convey the gospel message adequately and fully. In addition to leading men to Christ through other means, a new believer has to do his best to select some good tracts in his spare time and pass them out to others. This will enable him to do what he himself could not do otherwise.

C. Tracts Not Being Affected by Human Factors

There is another advantage to using tracts. In preaching the gospel, sometimes we feel too shy to use strong words in front of people. Tracts do not have this inconvenience. They can go to anyone and say anything they want. A living preacher is often restricted by circumstances. But the preaching of the tracts is not affected by any human factors. New believers should learn to sow seeds with the tracts.

D. Passing Out Tracts Being a Way of Sowing

Another advantage of passing out tracts is that one can sow anywhere. The Old Testament says that we should sow our seed in many waters (Num. 24:7). It takes a considerable effort to speak to three, five, or ten persons together. But there is no difficulty in passing out a thousand, two thousand, or three thousand tracts a day. If one person can be saved out of the thousand tracts we pass out, this is wonderful enough. New believers should learn to pass out tracts in large quantities.

E. God Saving Men through Tracts

God has indeed used tracts to save people. I know of some people who slip tracts under doors. Others drop them into mailboxes. I remember an incident in which a person received a tract and then threw it away on the street. Another person, who had a nail stuck in his shoe, was looking for something to cushion his foot. He picked up the tract and stuffed it in his shoe. He returned home and began to mend his shoe. Then he saw the tract and was saved. There are numerous similar cases of people being saved by tracts. Some of these cases are actually quite marvelous.

F. Much Prayer and Dedication of Heart

A newly saved brother always should have tracts ready in his pockets, and he should pass them out when he is free. Like the work of leading men to Christ, we should do this with much prayer and dedication of heart. While we are passing out tracts, we can speak a word or two to others or we can remain silent. Either way is good. If a new believer practices this, he will receive great benefit from it.

CHAPTER TWENTY

HOUSEHOLD SALVATION

I. GOD'S PROMISE OF SALVATION BEING TO THE HOUSEHOLD

Now we come to the subject of the unit of salvation. Everything is measured by units. The unit of salvation is the household.

According to the Bible, in God's dealings and communications with man, He has given man many promises. If we know these promises, we will reap great benefit for ourselves. If we do not know them, we will suffer great loss.

God's promise of salvation takes the household as a unit, not the individual as a unit. If a newly saved person sees this from the very beginning, he will be spared many headaches, and he will gain much benefit for himself. When God saves man, He takes the whole family, rather than an individual, as a unit.

Concerning eternal life, the Bible takes an individual, not a household, as the unit. However, concerning salvation, it shows that men are saved household by household. The unit of salvation is the household. We want to spend a little time to consider several portions of the Word. This will show us clearly that salvation is for the whole household. We can inquire of God according to these words. We can deal with Him not only for ourselves individually but also for our whole family.

We hope that all the children who are born among us will not need our extra effort in the future to bring them to salvation and to rescue them out of the world. Some have already been born into our fleshly family. We should make sure that they are born into our spiritual family also. We cannot afford to lose them year by year and then fight to rescue them back year by year. We cannot just beget them into the world; we still must bring them to the Lord.

If all the brothers and sisters agree that this is the way we should take, we will have at least as many saved ones as the number of children in our midst. The Lord has placed them in our hands. We should not let them go; we must make sure that they are saved. Otherwise, it will take considerable effort to bring them back from the world. All the little fishes born of our big fishes should be on our side; we should not let them go back into the sea and then struggle to catch them again. Whether or not the church will continue with its second generation depends on whether our children belong to the Lord.

I hope that the brothers and sisters will see the importance of this matter. Whether or not the church will go on in the next generation, whether or not those after us will go on, depends on whether we can bring our own children to the Lord. If we lose as many as are born to us, our second generation will be gone. If generation after generation all those who are born into our midst stand fast and if we also have some increase from the outside, the church will be strong and its number will increase. We must never give birth to a child only to lose it later. Instead, those who are born to us must be regenerated.

II. EXAMPLES FROM THE BIBLE

The Bible reveals the basic principle that God saves men household by household. How can we prove this? Let us examine various portions of the Word.

A. In the Old Testament

1. The Whole House Entering the Ark

Genesis 7:1 says, "And the Lord said unto Noah, Come thou and all thy house into the ark," and 1 Peter 3:20 says, "A few, that is, eight souls, were brought safely through by water."

The ark was not for an individual; it was for the whole house. In Genesis 6 we see a man who was righteous before

God—Noah. The Bible does not say that the sons and daughters-in-law of Noah were righteous. The Bible only says that Noah was a righteous man before God. However, when God prepared a way of salvation for Noah, He commanded Noah's whole house to enter the ark. Therefore, the household, not an individual, entered the ark.

A new believer should bring every member of his household into the ark. You can say to the Lord, "I have believed in You. You have said that my whole household can enter into the ark. Lord, please bring my whole household into the ark now." God will honor your faith.

2. The Whole House Being Circumcised

Genesis 17:12-13 says, "Every man child in your generations, he that is born in the house, or bought with money of any stranger, which is not of thy seed. He that is born in thy house, and he that is bought with thy money, must needs be circumcised: and my covenant shall be in your flesh for an everlasting covenant."

God called Abraham and made a covenant with him, saying, "I will establish my covenant between me and thee and thy seed after thee" (v. 7). The sign of the covenant between God and Abraham was circumcision. All who were circumcised belonged to God, and all who were not circumcised were not of God. God also told Abraham that his whole household needed to be circumcised, including those who were born in his house and those who were bought with his money. Therefore, the promise of circumcision was not given to Abraham alone but to his whole household. Circumcision takes the household as a unit. God's promise came to Abraham's house, not to him alone.

3. A Passover Lamb for Each Household

Exodus 12:3-7 says, "Speak ye unto all the congregation of Israel, saying, In the tenth day of this month they shall take to them every man a lamb, according to the house of their fathers, a lamb for a house...and they shall take of the blood, and strike it on the two side posts and on the upper doorpost of the houses, wherein they shall eat it."

The Passover lamb was clearly given to a household, not to an individual. Again we see the importance of a household before God. The Passover lamb had to do with a household; it was not an individual matter. A lamb was not prepared for each person, but for each household. The blood struck on the doorpost and side posts was to protect the whole household. The angel of destruction would pass over a whole household.

It is marvelous to see that the salvation prepared by the Lord Jesus Christ is not for an individual alone but for the whole household, just like the Passover lamb. If one man eats the lamb, it means that only he is being saved. But if the whole household eats the lamb, it means that the whole household is being saved. Salvation is for the whole household. The whole household eats the lamb, and similarly the whole household strikes the blood. The whole household enjoys these things together. May God open our eyes to see that salvation is a matter of the whole household, not individuals.

4. The Priesthood Being for the Household

God's promise of the priesthood was also for a whole house. It was not for one or two individuals. Numbers 18:1 says, "And Jehovah said to Aaron, You and your sons and your father's house with you shall bear the iniquity of the sanctuary."

Verse 11 says, "This also is yours, the heave offering of their gift, all the wave offerings of the sons of Israel; I have given them to you, and to your sons and daughters with you, as a perpetual due; every one who is clean in your house may eat of it." God gave all the sacrifices and offerings to the house of Aaron. The sacrifices were for the house of Aaron, not for Aaron alone. This is because God accepts the house as a whole. Please remember that the priesthood was for Aaron's house, not for Aaron alone. The priesthood took the household as a unit.

5. Household Salvation

Joshua 2:19 says, "Anyone who goes forth from the doors of your house into the street, his blood will be upon his own head, and we will be innocent. And whoever is with you in the house, his blood will be upon our heads if a hand should come upon him." Joshua 6:17 says, "And the city shall be devoted to Jehovah for destruction, it and all that is in it. Only Rahab the harlot shall live, she and all who are with her in her house, because she hid the messengers we sent."

Here we see Rahab the harlot and her household being saved. What did she do? She received the spies. When she received the spies, God gave her a sign. She was to tie a line of scarlet thread in the window. All who were in the house which had the scarlet thread were spared, while the rest of the inhabitants of Jericho were killed. The scarlet thread signifies salvation. The scarlet-thread salvation saved Rahab's household; it did not save just her.

We need to be very clear about the scope of salvation. Chapter two of Joshua gives the promise, and chapter six gives the actual execution. Both the promise in chapter two and the execution in chapter six show us that Rahab's whole household was saved. All who were in the house which had the scarlet thread were saved. God's salvation is for the whole household, not for individuals.

6. The Household Being Blessed

Second Samuel 6:11 says, "And the ark of Jehovah remained in the house of Obed-edom the Gittite three months; and Jehovah blessed Obed-edom and all his household."

Jehovah's blessing in the Old Testament was to the household. While the ark remained in the house of Obed-edom, Jehovah blessed the whole household. The unit of the blessing is the household, not the individual.

Earlier we spoke of the matter of salvation. We will see that this principle is not just confined to salvation. It governs many matters in both the Old Testament and the New Testament. The house is considered one unit. God's children, especially those who are the head of their house, should realize that God deals with man according to households. If you are ignorant of this fact, you will miss much. If you are the head of a family, you need to lay hold of this fact. You need to say, "Lord, You have told me that You are dealing with my household, not with just myself alone. Therefore, I ask You to save my whole household."

Not only does the head of a household need to lay hold of this fact, but other members of the household also need to inquire of the Lord concerning their father's house. Rahab was not the head of her house; she had a father. But Rahab held to God, and her household was blessed and saved. It is very good if you are the head of your household because you can speak for your household. But even if you are not the head of your household, you can still speak in faith as Rahab, saying, "Lord, turn my household to You to receive Your grace and blessing."

7. Rejoicing with the Household

Deuteronomy 12:7 says, "There you shall eat before Jehovah your God, and you and your households shall rejoice in all your undertakings, in which Jehovah your God has blessed you." You and your household receive the blessing of God and rejoice therein.

Deuteronomy 14:26 says, "You shall exchange the money for anything that your soul desires, for oxen, for sheep, for wine, for strong drink, or for anything that your soul would like; and you and your household shall eat there before Jehovah your God and rejoice."

Have you seen this? God promised the Israelites that they would eat, drink, and rejoice before God on that day household by household. In other words, blessing is for the household, not for the individual.

B. In the New Testament

What about the New Testament? In the Old Testament, God gained men household by household, and the same is true in the New Testament.

1. The House of Zaccheus

Luke 19:9 says, "Jesus said to him, Today salvation has come to this house." This is wonderful. The New Testament declares the same principle. I am afraid that many people have been preaching for over twenty years about personal salvation only. However, the Lord tells us that "salvation has come to this *house.*"

When you preach the gospel, you must pay attention to household salvation. You must not look merely for individual salvation. If you truly believe and expect this, your work will undergo a great change. This depends entirely on your faith and expectation. If you expect others to come to the Lord one by one, they will come one by one. If you believe that they will come household by household, they will come household by household. The scope of God's salvation is the household. You must not make this scope smaller than it should be.

2. The Household of a Nobleman

John 4:53 says, "Then the father knew that it was in that hour in which Jesus said to him, Your son lives; and he believed, he and his whole house." Here only one person was healed—the son. However, the Bible says that "he believed, *he and his whole household.*" You can lay hold of this fact before the Lord. Although the son was the one who directly received His grace, the whole household turned and believed. Our hope and expectation is that we would bear fruit in such a prevailing way.

3. The Household of Cornelius

Acts 10:2 says that Cornelius was "devout and one who feared God with all his household, giving many alms to the people and beseeching God continually," and 11:14 says, "...who will speak words to you by which you shall be saved, you and all your house."

Cornelius's entire household was saved; it was not just one person who was saved. Cornelius invited his relatives and close friends to hear the words of Peter. While Peter was speaking, the Holy Spirit fell upon all those who were in Cornelius's house, and all of them received salvation.

4. The Household of Lydia

Acts 16:15 says, "She was baptized, as well as her household." The apostle preached the gospel to Lydia's household, and the whole household believed and was baptized.

5. The Household of the Jailer

Acts 16:31 says, "Believe on the Lord Jesus, and you shall be saved, you and your household." This is one of the most outstanding verses in Christianity. Believe on the Lord Jesus, and you shall be saved, you and your household. God's Word does not say that if you believe on the Lord Jesus, you and your household shall receive eternal life. It says that if you believe on the Lord Jesus, you and your household will be saved.

Throughout the entire Old Testament, God dealt with man by households. Likewise in the New Testament, He deals with man by households. This is the smallest unit; one cannot reduce it to a smaller one. If anyone believes in the Lord Jesus, his whole household shall be saved. This is indeed a wonderful thing. I do not know why this is so, but the Lord's Word says it is so. The Old Testament and the New Testament are consistent; both recognize the same unit.

The church in Philippi started with a jailer. Paul said, "Believe on the Lord Jesus, and you shall be saved, you and your household." Verse 34 says, "And he brought them up into his house and set a table before them; and he exulted because he had believed in God with all his household." Here we see a wonderful picture. In the beginning the promise was given to the jailer; no one else heard it. "Believe on the Lord Jesus, and you shall be saved, you and your household." Later, the jailer brought his household to Paul. After Paul spoke to them, they were baptized. Then the jailer brought them into his house and set a table before them; and he exulted, having believed in God. "Believe on the Lord Jesus, and you shall be saved, you and your household"—this is not something difficult to achieve. The apostle gave the jailer a promise, and his whole household was saved. Everyone listened, everyone was baptized, and everyone exulted.

Suppose the apostle told the jailer, "Believe on the Lord Jesus, and you shall be saved." If this was the case, we would have to wait a few days after a person was saved, teach him something, and hope that he would understand. Then he might gradually testify to his family, and his family might eventually believe and be saved. If this had been the case, how long would it have taken for the jailer's household to be saved? The apostle did not preach the gospel this way. He did not deal with individuals one by one; instead, he addressed the whole household. He said, "You and your household" shall be saved. You need to see this: The salvation of a household is no different and certainly no more difficult than the salvation of one person. You should never forfeit the privilege of saving the whole household. If you bring the whole household along, the whole household will be saved.

I hope that when the church preaches the gospel five or ten years from now, household after household will be turning to the Lord. From now on, the goal of our workers in evangelism should be whole households. If our goal is a household, we will gain a household. If our goal is only an individual, we will gain only an individual. God does things according to our faith.

If we are clear about God's way with men, we will not suffer unnecessary loss. God takes a household as a unit. If God gains a person, He should gain his whole family as well, regardless of how many persons there are in that family. I hope you will tell the brothers to rise up household by household. Those who are the head of a family have the ground to bring their whole household to the Lord, and they should help their families be saved.

Household salvation means household rejoicing. This is a great matter! If we see that God's dealing with man is by households, we will experience much blessing. We must learn to lay hold of this promise of God.

6. The Household of Crispus

Acts 18:8 says, "Crispus, the ruler of the synagogue, believed in the Lord with his whole household...and were baptized."

In the Bible there are individuals who believed in the Lord and there are households which believed in the Lord. Notice how easy it is for God's grace to come to a household. The whole household of Crispus believed and was baptized.

7. The Promise of Pentecost
Being Given to You and Your Children

Let us consider the condition at Pentecost. Acts 2:39 says, "For to you is the promise and to your children, and to all who are far off, as many as the Lord our God calls to Himself."

The promise of Pentecost includes the forgiveness of sins and the receiving of the Holy Spirit. It was given "to you" *and* "to your children"; it was not merely given "to you." Those who are heads of the family in particular should lay hold of this promise and say, "Lord, Your promise is for me and also for my children. It cannot be mine without my children also being included. I want it for myself, and I want it also for my children."

8. Peace to a House

Luke 10:5-6 says, "Into whatever house you enter, first say, Peace to this house. And if a son of peace is there, your peace shall rest upon it; but if not, it shall return upon you."

The Lord says that when a person sets out to preach the gospel, he should say as he enters into a house, "Peace to this *house.*" This shows that God's peace comes to man by households. It is not just given to individuals, but to households. If anyone is worthy of peace in a house, peace will come to his entire household. This verse is clear enough. God deals with man by households. Thank God, peace comes to man household by household.

9. The Household of Stephanas

First Corinthians 1:16 says, "I did baptize the household of Stephanas also." Here Paul said that he baptized every member of the household of Stephanas. Like the jailer and the house of Lydia, Stephanas's whole household believed and was baptized.

10. The Household of Onesiphorus

Second Timothy 4:19 says, "Greet Prisca and Aquila and the house of Onesiphorus," and 1:16 says, "May the Lord grant mercy to the house of Onesiphorus, for he often refreshed me and was not ashamed of my chain." Here was a family that took care of Paul, a household that was not ashamed of his chain. Notice again that it was not an individual matter but something to do with a household.

These numerous cases provide ample proof in both the Old Testament and the New Testament that God deals with man by households. This is particularly true in the case of salvation; God takes the household as a unit.

III. THE HOUSEHOLD BEING ALSO THE UNIT OF GOD'S PUNISHMENT

We need to see some verses which show that the unit of God's punishment is also the household. When man rebelled against God, God was provoked and He judged man. In judging man He took the household as a unit. God's judgment comes through one man to the entire household, just as God's blessing comes through one man to the entire household. Once we see this, we will take a stand for our household and declare that our household is for the Lord.

A. Pharaoh and His House

Genesis 12:17 says, "The Lord plagued Pharaoh and his house with great plagues, because of Sarai, Abram's wife." The sin of Pharaoh brought God's plague to his whole household. God punished his whole household. If God's judgment comes to a household, we should expect that His blessing also will come to a household. We are not those under condemnation but those under His blessing.

B. The House of Abimelech

Genesis 20:18 says, "For the Lord had fast closed up all the wombs of the house of Abimelech, because of Sarah, Abraham's wife." God closed up all the wombs of the women of the house of Abimelech. His whole household was punished, not just one or two men.

C. The House of David

Second Samuel 12:10-11 says, "Now therefore the sword will not depart from your house forever because you have despised Me and have taken the wife of Uriah the Hittite to be your wife. Thus says Jehovah, I will now raise up trouble against you from within your house; and I will take your wives before your eyes and will give them to your companion, and he will lie with your wives in the sight of this sun."

After David sinned, God did not rebuke and punish him individually. He said, "Now therefore the sword will not depart from your house." This is very clear. David sinned individually, but the result was that his whole household was judged by God. In God's eyes the people of this world are divided into households, not individuals. We need to come to God household by household.

D. The House of Jeroboam

First Kings 13:34 says, "This matter became a sin to the house of Jeroboam, so as even to cut it off and destroy it from the face of the earth." Jeroboam was the one who set up the idols, but God judged his house and destroyed it from the face of the earth.

First Kings 14:14 says, "Jehovah will raise up for Himself a king over Israel who will cut off the house of Jeroboam this day and even now." Jeroboam worshipped idols, but God cut off his house. I do not know why God did this. I can only say that in God's eyes a household is a unit. This is too clear. Unless we purposely ignore this fact, we have no choice but to acknowledge it.

E. The House of Baasha

First Kings 16:3 says, "I am now sweeping up after Baasha and after his house, and I will make your house like the house of Jeroboam the son of Nebat." Because of the sin of one man, Baasha, God took away the posterity of Baasha and his house, in the same way that he cut off the house of Jeroboam. God deals with man by households.

F. The House of Ahab

I think one of the most well-known houses in the book of 1 Kings is the house of Ahab. First Kings 21:22 says, "I will make your house like the house of Jeroboam the son of Nebat and like the house of Baasha the son of Ahijah because of the provocation by which you have provoked Me to anger and caused Israel to sin." Why did God deal with the house of Ahab? Because Ahab provoked God. Ahab was an evil king in the Old Testament. God said that He would deal with his house as He dealt with the house of Jeroboam and the house of Baasha. The entire house would be cut off. The unit of God's dealing is the household. This is more than clear and obvious.

G. The Households of Dathan and Abiram

We will consider one last portion which illustrates our point quite clearly. Deuteronomy 11:6 says, "And what He did to Dathan and Abiram, the sons of Eliab, the son of Reuben, when the earth opened its mouth and swallowed them up and their households and their tents and all their substance that went with them, from the midst of all Israel." When Dathan and Abiram sinned, God opened the earth and swallowed not only Dathan and Abiram, but also their households.

In the Bible, both on the positive side and on the negative side and both in the Old Testament and in the New Testament, all records show clearly that God deals with man by households. Brothers, we need to take care of how we live before God, because what we do individually can affect our whole household.

IV. THE NEED FOR THE HEAD OF THE HOUSEHOLD TO MAKE A DECLARATION

I would like to speak specifically to the heads of households. In the Bible most of those who bore some responsibility were the heads of households. The head of a family has the special responsibility before God for bringing his whole household to the Lord and to His service. You need to take your stand as the head of your family to declare that your household will believe in the Lord and that you will not tolerate anyone who will not believe. The head of the household can decide for his entire household. Even if the little children do not believe, you can still say that your household will believe in the Lord, because this household is yours and not your children's. You are responsible for your household, not your children. You can declare Joshua 24:15 before the Lord and before your whole family: "As for me and my house, we will serve Jehovah." You have to acknowledge that your family is a believer's family. You need to declare this by faith, and you need to put your wife and children on this ground. Always lay hold of this fact: I am the head of my family, and my family will believe in God. My household will not believe in the devil. I have decided that this family will be a family that worships God. I have decided that this family will be a family that believes in the Lord. If you declare this with faith, and if you exercise your authority to take the lead, your children will go along.

I believe the head of every household should make the declaration of Joshua 24:15. You should gather your children and dependents together and tell them, "As for me and my house, we will serve Jehovah." Then as long as you are in the household, your household will serve the Lord. The household is yours, and you have the power to decide whether this house will serve the Lord. When you take this stand, everyone who is under you will come to the Lord; they will have no other way to take. This is marvelous!

V. EXAMPLES IN ENGLAND

I read about this in the Bible in my earlier days, but I did not have much experience of it then. Thank the Lord, when I was in England, He provided me the opportunity to meet brothers who also believed in household salvation. I found dozens of families here and there where whole households were Christians. This gave me a very deep impression. God works according to the way man believes. Among them almost every household experienced household salvation. "Believe on the Lord Jesus, and you shall be saved, you and your household." There were very few exceptions among them. They were all saved by households—father, mother, wife, children, and all. I was very amazed as I spoke to them one by one.

Once I visited Mr. George Cutting, the author of the famous booklet "Safety, Certainty, and Enjoyment." The best-selling book in the world is the Bible. The second best-selling book is this booklet. Although it is small, it is one of the most widely circulated books in the world. When I met Mr. Cutting, he was over eighty years old. His hair and beard were all white. He was in bed all the time, and his mind was not very clear. When I met him, he said, "Brother Nee, I cannot live without Him, and He cannot live without me." He had such a deep fellowship with the Lord. Thank the Lord, there were over eighty members in his household. All of them were saved. Every one of his sons, daughters-in-law, grandsons, granddaughters, nephews, nieces, great-grandchildren, old or young, male or female, were saved. George Cutting himself believed in the word: "Believe on the Lord Jesus, and you shall be saved, you and your household." His whole household was saved.

George Cutting was very serious about this matter. He paid much attention to household salvation, not just individual salvation. He had at least eighty to ninety people in his household. All of them were saved. Thank the Lord, "Believe on the Lord Jesus, and you shall be saved, you and your household." Faithful is the word.

VI. THE NEED TO BRING
THE WHOLE HOUSEHOLD TO THE LORD

I hope that the newly saved brothers and sisters will pay attention to this matter. Once you are saved, you should gather your family members together and declare to them, "From this day forward, my household belongs to God." You need to declare this whether or not they belong to the Lord and whether or not they agree. You are the head of the house and you should do this. You should take the matter into your own hands. You should declare that your household will serve the Lord. When you exercise your faith to stand firm this way, you will prevail.

If those who are saved through us are saved household by household instead of one by one, what a difference it will make! Brothers and sisters, do not be too loose with your children at home. One of the greatest failures of the Protestants is that they are too loose with their next generation; they allow their next generation to have the freedom to choose their own faith. The Catholics do not have to preach the gospel. Their increase through natural birth alone is greater than the increase the Protestants have in a lifetime. Have you seen Catholics preaching the gospel on street corners like the Salvation Army? No. They just propagate through natural birth, generation after generation. Two become four, and four become eight. Every Roman Catholic child automatically becomes a Roman Catholic. The Catholics do not pay much attention to increase from the outside. As long as a person is born into Catholicism, he is dragged into the religion whether or not he eventually becomes a true believer. It is no wonder that the Catholic population exceeds the Protestant population by more than three times. Do not be nonchalant in this matter, and do not allow your own children to drift away.

Let me repeat: A new believer needs to declare right from the start that his household belongs to the Lord. Not only must he be the Lord's individually; he also must declare that his household is the Lord's. Take full control of this matter, and it will be done for you. You have to declare again and again at home, "As for me and my house, we will serve the Lord. All who live in this house should decide to serve the Lord." You should bring your family to the Lord. You should not make any excuse. Do not allow anyone to drift away.

Household salvation is one of the greatest principles in the Bible. Once you are saved, your whole household should be saved. As an individual you must first stand firm for the Lord, and then your household will change. I hope that you will pay attention to this matter. This is a great blessing. If you do this, you will bring more people to the Lord.

CHAPTER TWENTY-ONE

IF ANYONE SINS

Scripture Reading: John 5:14; 8:11; Rom. 6:1-2; Num. 19:1-10, 12-13, 17-19; 1 John 1:7—2:2

After we are saved, we should *sin no more*. John 5 records the incident of the Lord Jesus healing one who had been sick for thirty-eight years near the pool in Bethesda. After the man was healed the Lord met him in the temple and said to him, "Behold, you have become well; *sin no more* so that nothing worse happens to you" (v. 14). John 8 speaks of the Lord Jesus forgiving a woman who had committed adultery. He said to her then and there, "From now on *sin no more*" (v. 11). Once we are saved, we are charged by the Lord to *sin no more!* As saved ones, *we surely should not continue in sin.*

I. SINNING AFTER BEING SAVED

Since a Christian should not sin and should not continue in sins, is it then possible for a Christian not to sin? The answer is yes! It is possible for Christians not to sin because we have God's life within us. This life does not sin. It cannot tolerate any trace of sin. This life is as holy as God is holy. The life within us makes us very sensitive to sin. If we walk according to the sense of this life and if we live by this life, we will not sin.

However, it is possible for Christians to sin. We are still in the flesh. If we do not walk according to the Spirit and live in life, we can sin at any time. Galatians 6:1 says, "Brothers, even if a man is overtaken in some offense..." First John 2:1 says, "My little children...if anyone sins..." It is possible for Christians to be overtaken by sins. There is still the possibility of sinning. First John 1:8 says, "If we say that we do not have sin, we are deceiving ourselves." Verse 10 says, "If we say that we have not sinned, we make Him a liar." Hence, our experience shows us that it is possible for Christians to fall *accidentally* into sin.

Will a saved person who has fallen accidentally into sin still perish? No! The Lord said, "And I give to them eternal life, and they shall by no means perish forever, and no one shall snatch them out of My hand" (John 10:28). In other words, once a person is saved, he is saved forever. "They shall by no means perish forever." Nothing can be surer than this! First Corinthians 5 speaks of a brother who had committed fornication. Paul said, "To deliver such a one to Satan for the destruction of his flesh, that his spirit may be saved in the day of the Lord" (v. 5). Even though the flesh of a believer who sins may be destroyed, his spirit will still be saved.

Does this therefore mean that after a person is saved, it does not matter whether he sins? No! If a person sins after he is saved, there will be two terrible consequences. First, he will suffer in this life. If you sin after you are saved, you will suffer the consequence of your sin. The person in 1 Corinthians 5 was delivered to Satan. This is a great suffering. After a person has repented and confessed to the Lord, God will forgive him and the blood will cleanse him. With some sins, however, there are further consequences that one must face. Although Jehovah removed David's sin of taking Uriah's wife, the sword never departed from his house forever (2 Sam. 12:9-13). Brothers and sisters, sin is like a venomous serpent; it is not an amusing plaything. If you are bitten by it, you will suffer.

Second, if a man sins he will be punished in the coming age. If a Christian sins and does not deal with it properly in this age, he will have to deal with it in the coming age. When the Lord comes again, "He will repay each man according to his doings" (Matt. 16:27). Paul said, "For we must all be manifested before the judgment seat of Christ, that each one may receive the things done through the body according to what he has practiced, whether good or bad" (2 Cor. 5:10).

Besides these two terrible consequences, there is another immediate result of sin—the breaking down of fellowship with God. To a Christian, fellowship with God is a most glorious privilege. Such fellowship is the greatest blessing he can have. However, if he sins, he will immediately lose his fellowship with God. The Holy Spirit within him will grieve for him, and the life in him will feel uncomfortable about his sin. He will lose his joy as well as his fellowship with God. Formerly, when he saw God's children, he was warmly attracted to them, but now he no longer feels that warmth; there seems to be a barrier between him and them. Formerly, prayer and Bible reading were sweet. But now they have lost their sweetness; he can no longer touch God. Formerly, he treasured the church meetings very much; when he missed one meeting, he felt that he had suffered a great loss. But now the meetings are tasteless to him; it no longer makes a difference whether or not he goes. When he sees God's children, he wants to run away instead of meeting them. Everything has changed.

It is a serious thing for a person to sin after he is saved! We must never be loose in our conduct. We must never tolerate sin and must never give ground to it.

But what do we do "if anyone sins"? If a Christian becomes careless and sins by mistake, if he is overtaken by sins, what should he do? How can he come back to the Lord? How can he recover his fellowship with God? This is a very important subject, and we have to study it carefully.

II. THE LORD HAVING BORNE ALL OUR SINS

To take care of this matter, we must first realize that the Lord Jesus has borne all our sins on the cross. All the sins which we have committed, as well as those we are committing and will commit during our whole life, were borne by the Lord on the cross.

However, on the day we believed in the Lord, under God's light we only saw the sins that we had committed before we had believed. A man can only be conscious of the sins which God shines His light upon; he cannot feel the sins which he has not yet committed. Therefore, the actual sins the Lord Jesus bore on the cross are more than the sins that we see. The Lord Jesus bore all of our sins on the cross, but we see only the sins which we have committed.

You may have been saved at the age of sixteen, or you may

have been saved at the age of thirty-two. All the sins you committed before your salvation are absolutely and totally forgiven by the Lord. However, at the time of your forgiveness, the number of sins that you were conscious of was actually much less than the actual number of sins which the Lord bore for you. Your experience of the Lord's grace went only so far as your personal experience of your sin. But the Lord's work on our behalf was based on His knowledge of our sins. We must realize that even the sins that we are not conscious of are included in the Lord Jesus' redemption.

Perhaps you were saved at the age of sixteen. Suppose you had committed a thousand sins during the first sixteen years of your life. You might have said at the time you believed in the Lord, "I thank You. My sins have been forgiven because You have taken away all my sins." In saying that the Lord had taken your sins away, you meant that the Lord had dealt with your one thousand sins. What would have happened if you had been saved at the age of thirty-two instead? Proportionally, you probably would have committed two thousand sins by the age of thirty-two. You might have said the same thing: "O Lord, You have borne all my sins." If you were saved at sixty-four years of age, you would have said the same thing: "O Lord, You have borne all my sins." It is quite clear then that the Lord has dealt with the sins that were committed during the first sixteen years of your life as well as the sins that were committed from age sixteen to age sixty-four. The Lord dealt with all of your sins on the cross. The criminal on the cross did not believe in the Lord until just before he died, but the Lord took away all his sins (Luke 23:39-43). In other words, the Lord took away the sins of our whole life on the cross. Although, when we first believed in the Lord, we only felt the forgiveness of our past sins, in actuality, the Lord took away all our sins, even those we commit after we are saved. We must understand this fact before we can understand how to recover our fellowship with God.

III. THE TYPE OF THE ASHES OF THE RED HEIFER

We have a picture of the Lord's vicarious death for our sins in the type of the ashes of the red heifer.

Numbers 19 is a very special chapter in the Old Testament. A heifer was used, which speaks of something special. This heifer was used not to meet a need at that moment but to meet a need in the future. This, too, is very significant.

In verse 2 God told Moses and Aaron, "Tell the sons of Israel to bring you a red heifer without blemish, in which there is no defect, and upon which a yoke has never come." A heifer, not a bull, was offered here. In the Bible gender is very meaningful. Male signifies everything related to the testimony of the truth, while female signifies everything related to the experience of life. This is a principle we should be familiar with in reading our Bible. Abraham speaks of justification by faith, while Sarah speaks of obedience. Justification by faith is objective; it has to do with truth and testimony. Obedience is subjective; it has to do with life and experience. Throughout the Bible the church is symbolized by females, because the church is subjective, being related to the Lord's work in man. A heifer is used here instead of a bull because it represents another aspect of the Lord's work—His work toward man. The red heifer signifies a work that is subjective rather than objective.

What happened to the heifer? It was slaughtered, and its blood was taken and sprinkled seven times directly in front of the tent of meeting. In other words, the blood was offered to God because the work of the blood is always for God. The heifer's blood was sprinkled seven times in front of the tent of meeting, signifying that it was for God and for the redemption of sin.

After the red heifer was killed, it was burned. The skin, the flesh, the blood, and the dung were all burned. The whole red heifer was burned. As it was being burned, the priest cast cedar wood, hyssop, and scarlet into the midst of the fire. What do cedar wood and hyssop signify? First Kings 4:33 said that Solomon discoursed about trees, from the cedar to the hyssop. Cedar wood and hyssop therefore signify all the trees. In other words, they signify the whole world. What does scarlet signify? This word is also translated *scarlet* in Isaiah 1:18, which says, "Though your sins are like scarlet, / They will be as white as snow." Scarlet, therefore, signifies our sins. For the cedar wood, hyssop, and scarlet to be burned together means that the sins of the whole world were gathered together with the red heifer when it was offered up to God; they were all burned together. Here, we see a picture of the cross. The Lord Jesus offered Himself up to God. He embraced all our sins. The gross sins were there as well as the lesser sins. The sins of the past, the present, and the future were also there. The sins for which man feels the need of forgiveness, as well as the sins for which man does not feel the need of forgiveness, were there. All sins were upon the heifer, and they were all burned with it.

After they were burned, what was done next? Numbers 19:9 says, "A man who is clean shall gather up the ashes of the heifer, and place them outside the camp in a clean place; and they shall be kept for the assembly of the sons of Israel for the water for impurity; it is a purification of sin." What does this mean? This is what makes the red heifer so distinct. After the cedar wood, the hyssop, and the scarlet were burned with the heifer, the ashes were gathered up and kept in a clean place. Thereafter, if any of the Israelites touched something unclean and became unclean before God, another clean person could mix the water for impurity with the ashes and sprinkle it on the unclean person. This would remove the person's uncleanness. In other words, the ashes were used to remove uncleanness. They were prepared for the future. They would be used when uncleanness was detected at a later time.

In the Old Testament, sinners needed to offer up sacrifices to the Lord. If a person had offered up a sacrifice and then touched something unclean, he would become unclean again before God and could no longer fellowship with Him. What did he have to do? Another person would take some ashes of the red heifer on this person's behalf, put them in a vessel, pour in living water, mix it into the water for impurity, and sprinkle it on his body. The man's uncleanness would then be removed and his sin forgiven. When an Israelite brought a bull or a lamb to the Lord and offered it up as a sin offering, he did it because of some known sin. But the red heifer was related to another matter. The burning of the red heifer was not for known sins which had been committed in the past, but for future uncleanness. The burning of the red heifer was not for past sins but for future transgressions.

This shows us another aspect of the Lord Jesus' work. One aspect of the Lord's work is like that of the ashes of the red heifer. The efficacy of redemption is signified by the ashes. The sins of the whole world are in it, and the blood is also in it. Whenever a man becomes unclean or has touched some unclean things, he does not need to kill another red heifer and offer it to God. He only needs to take the ashes of the red heifer that was offered once and mix them with water and sprinkle them on the body. In other words, there is no need for the Lord to do anything a second time. His redemption accomplished everything. He made provision for all of our future uncleanness and future sins. Everything has been fully accomplished by His redemption.

What do the ashes signify? In the Bible, ashes signify something in its final form. Whether a bull or a lamb, its final form after being burned is ashes. Ashes are very stable; they do not corrupt into something else. We cannot corrupt or destroy ashes. Ashes signify something in its final form.

The ashes of the red heifer signify the eternal and unchanging efficacy of the Lord's redemption. The redemption which our Lord accomplished for us is most stable. Do not think that rocks on mountains are stable. Even rocks can be burned into ashes. Ashes are more stable than rocks. The ashes of the red heifer signify the Lord's redemption which He has prepared for us. It is forever unchanging and incorruptible. We may apply it any time. If a Christian touches something unclean by accident and there is uncleanness in him, he does not have to ask the Lord to die for him again. He only needs to trust in the eternal and incorruptible efficacy of the ashes and to sprinkle his body with the water of life, and he will be clean. In other words, the ashes of the red heifer tell us that the past work of the cross is applicable for our use today. We also can say that the effectiveness of the cross covers all the needs we will ever have in the future. These ashes are specifically for the future. Only one red heifer needs to be burned, and it only needs to be burned once. Its ashes are enough to cover one's whole life. Thank the Lord that His redemption is sufficient for our whole life. His death has taken away all our sins.

IV. THE NEED FOR CONFESSION

We have covered the side of the Lord's work, which is redemption and the removal of our sins. What should we do on our side?

First John 1:9 says, "If we confess our sins, He is faithful and righteous to forgive us our sins and cleanse us from all unrighteousness." In this verse the word *we* refers to believers, not to sinners. When a believer sins, he must confess his sins. Only after he has confessed his sins will he be forgiven. When a believer sins, he should not ignore it or cover it up. Proverbs 28:13 says, "He that covereth his sins shall not prosper: / but whoso confesseth and forsaketh them shall have mercy." When a believer sins, he must confess his sin. Do not give sin a nice name. Do not excuse yourself. Lying is a sin. When you lie, you should confess that you have sinned. You should not say, "I have said a little more (or less) than I should have." You should say, "I have sinned." You should not explain it away or cover it up. You should confess that you have committed the sin of lying. You must condemn lying as sin.

Confession means to stand on God's side and judge sin as sin. There are three things here: God, ourselves, and sins. God and sins are at the two ends, and we are in the middle. What does it mean to commit a sin? It means that we stand on the side of sin and that we are away from God. Once we sin, we are away from God. Once we join ourselves to sins, we cannot be together with God. As soon as Adam sinned, he hid from God and dared not meet Him (Gen. 3:8). Colossians 1:21 says, "And you, though once alienated and enemies in your mind because of your evil works." Sin alienates us from God. What does it mean to confess our sins? It means to come back to God's side and to acknowledge that what we have done is sin. We have come back to God. We are no longer with sin. We are standing opposite of sin and calling sin a sin. This is confession. Only those who walk in the light and who have deep feelings and a repulsion for sin can have genuine confession. Those who are callous to sin, who consider it natural to sin, are not making any confession when they merely acknowledge something with their lips in a heartless way.

Believers are the children of light (Eph. 5:8) and the children of God (1 John 3:1). They are no longer outsiders but members of God's family. In a family one should behave in a way that is worthy of the family. You are a child of God, and you should know sin. You should have the same attitude towards sin as your Father. The way the Father considers sin should be the way you consider sin. Confession in God's house comes when His children take the same attitude as their Father towards sin. They condemn sin in the same way that their Father condemns sin. They take the same attitude as their Father with regard to sin. When a child of God sins, he should condemn sin as sin just as the Father does.

If we confess our sins this way, God "is faithful and righteous to forgive us our sins and cleanse us from all unrighteousness." When we sin and when we know our sin and acknowledge it as sin, God will forgive us our sin and cleanse us from all unrighteousness. God is "faithful," which means that He must honor and fulfill His own words and promises. He is also "righteous," which means He must be satisfied with His Son's redemptive work on the cross and must recognize it. Based on His promise and based on His redemption, He has to forgive us. He is faithful, and He is righteous. He must forgive us our sins and cleanse us from all unrighteousness.

We have to pay attention to the words *every* and *all* in 1 John 1:7 and 9. "Every sin" and "all unrighteousness" are fully forgiven and cleansed. The Lord has done this. When the Lord says "all," He means all. We should never change it to something else. When He says every sin, He means every sin, not just every sin committed before we believed or every sin committed in the past. He has forgiven us of all sins.

V. AN ADVOCATE WITH THE FATHER

First John 2:1 says, "My little children, these things I write to you that you may not sin." *These things* refer to the forgiveness and cleansing from our sins through God's promise and work. John wrote these things to us so that *we may not sin*. It shows us that the Lord has forgiven our many sins and that, as a result, we do not sin. When we find out that we are forgiven, we do not become free to sin; rather, *we will not sin.*

Following this it says, "And if anyone sins, we have an Advocate with the Father, Jesus Christ the Righteous." "With the Father"—this is a family affair; it is something that happens after we are saved. We have already believed and have become one of God's many children. Now we have an Advocate with the Father, who is Jesus Christ the Righteous; "He Himself is the propitiation for our sins." Through the Lord Jesus' death and by His becoming the propitiation for our sins, He has become our Advocate with the Father. These words are spoken to Christians.

The propitiation spoken of here is the reality of the type of the ashes of the red heifer in Numbers 19. It speaks of God's forgiveness of our future sins according to the accomplished work of the cross. There is no need to have a new cross. We only need the work of the cross once and it is sufficient. With the eternal redemption of the cross, our sins are forgiven. That sacrifice was not an ordinary sacrifice. It was a sacrifice whose efficacy could be applied at all times. It was ashes; therefore, it was applicable all the time. Based on His blood, the Lord Jesus Christ has become our Advocate. He has accomplished redemption on the cross. Based on His accomplished work, we can be cleansed. If we sin by accident, we should not be disheartened by our sin; we should not wallow in it or remain in it. When we sin, the first thing we should do is confess our sin to the Lord. God says that it is a sin, and we should acknowledge it as a sin. God says that this is wrong, and we also should say that it is wrong. When we ask God to forgive our sin, He forgives our sin, and our fellowship with Him is restored immediately.

In the eyes of God, no brother or sister should sin. However, if anyone sins by accident, the first thing to do is deal with it immediately before God. He or she should take care of the problem of sin immediately. Never delay. Deal with it as soon as possible. You must confess immediately. Tell God, "I have sinned!" Our confession is our judgment of ourselves.

If we confess our sins, God is faithful and righteous to forgive us our sins and to cleanse us from all unrighteousness.

When a child of God sins and does not confess his sin but instead remains in his sin, he loses his fellowship with God. There will be no further fellowship between him and God. There is a leak in his conscience, and he will not be able to stand up before God. He may still have a little fellowship with God, but that fellowship will not be pleasant. Indeed, he will suffer. When a child who has done something wrong comes home, he will feel that something is not right because his father will not speak to him. He cannot have an intimate fellowship with his father. He knows that there is a barrier between him and his father. This is the pain that results from a loss of fellowship.

There is only one way to recovery—it is to go to God and confess our sins. We have to believe that the Lord Jesus Christ has become our Advocate and has borne all our sins. We have to confess our failures and shortcomings before God in a humble way. We have to look to Him so that we will no longer be proud or loose when we set out on our journey again. We have to realize that we are no better than anyone else, and that it is possible for us to fall at any time. We have to ask God for mercy and strength to go on step by step. Once we confess this way, we will immediately recover our fellowship with God, and the joy and peace that were lost will come back.

Finally, we should point out once more that Christians *should not sin*. Sin results in suffering and loss. May God have mercy upon us, keep us, preserve us, and lead us on in the way of unceasing fellowship with Him!

CHAPTER TWENTY-TWO

CONFESSION AND RECOMPENSE

Scripture Reading: Lev. 6:1-7; Matt. 5:23-26

I. A CONSCIENCE VOID OF OFFENSE

After we have believed in the Lord, we must build up a habit of confessing and recompensing. If we have offended anyone or have come short of anyone, we should learn to confess or to recompense. On the one hand, we have to confess to God, and on the other hand, we have to confess to and recompense man. If a man does not confess to God nor apologize or recompense man, his conscience will easily become hardened. Once the conscience becomes hardened, a serious and fundamental problem develops: It becomes difficult for God's light to shine into a man. A person must build up a habit of confessing and making recompense so that he can maintain a sensitive and keen conscience before the Lord.

There was once a worker of the Lord who used to ask others, "When was the last time you confessed to someone?" If it has been a long time since a person's last confession to another person, there has to be some problem with this person's conscience. We often offend others. If a person has offended someone yet has no feeling about it, his conscience must be sick or abnormal. The length of time since your last confession is an indication of whether or not there is a problem between you and God. If the period of time is long, it proves that there is a lack of light in your spirit. If the time is short, that is, if you recently have made a confession to others, it proves that the feeling of your conscience is still sensitive. In order to live under God's light, we need a sensitive conscience, and in order for our conscience to remain sensitive, we need to continually condemn sin as sin. We need to confess to God, and we also need to make confessions and recompenses to man.

If we have offended God and the offense has nothing to do with man, we do not need to confess to man. We should not overdo anything. If a brother or sister's sins are unrelated to man, having only offended God, he or she only needs to confess to God; there is absolutely no need to confess to man. I hope that we will pay attention to this principle.

What kind of sins offend man? How should a person apologize to another person or recompense another person when he offends him or comes short in his dealings with him? In order to be clear about this, we need to carefully study two portions of Scriptures.

II. THE TRESPASS OFFERING IN LEVITICUS 6

There are two sides to the trespass offering: One is revealed in Leviticus 5 and the other in Leviticus 6. Chapter five tells us that we should confess to God and offer up sacrifices for forgiveness of our miscellaneous sins. Chapter six tells us that it is not enough to offer up a sacrifice to God if we have offended a person materially; we should also restore something to the offended party. Chapter six says that if we have offended anyone in material things, we should take care of the matter with men. Of course, we also need to confess to God and ask for His forgiveness. But just dealing with God is not enough. We cannot ask God to forgive us on behalf of the ones whom we have offended.

How should we take care of the matter from man's side? Let us look at the trespass offering in Leviticus 6.

A. Some Sins That Are Trespasses against Man

Leviticus 6:2-7: "When a person sins and acts unfaithfully against Jehovah,"—All sins are ultimately trespasses against Jehovah—"and lies to his fellowman in regard to a deposit or a security, or through robbery, or if he has extorted from his fellowman, or has found what was lost and lied about it, and has sworn falsely—concerning any of the things a man may do to sin thereby—then it shall be, when he sins and is guilty, that he shall return what he took by robbery, or what he got by extortion, or the deposit which was deposited with him, or the lost thing which he found, or anything about which he swore falsely; he shall make restitution for it in full and add to it one-fifth more; he shall give it to whom it belongs on the day he is found guilty. Then he shall bring to the priest his trespass offering to Jehovah, a ram without blemish from the flock, according to the valuation, for a trespass offering. And the priest shall make propitiation for him before Jehovah, and he shall be forgiven for whatever he may have done by which he has become guilty." A person who has offended anyone or transgressed against anyone in material things has to settle it with men before he can be forgiven. If he does not settle it with men, he will not be forgiven.

There are six kinds of transgressions against man in these verses:

(1) Lying to one's fellowman in regard to a deposit: This means to be entrusted with something and then to purposely withhold the good and costly portions while surrendering the inferior portions. This is lying, and it is a sin before God. We should not lie to others in regard to their deposit but rather guard it faithfully. God's children should always guard faithfully the things that others have entrusted to them. If we cannot guard it, we should not accept such a deposit. Once we accept it, we should do our best to guard it. If anything happens to it through our unfaithfulness, we have trespassed against man.

(2) Lying to one's fellowman in regard to a security: This means to deal falsely or to lie in business transactions or to profit through improper means or to usurp something that is not yours in trade. This is to sin before the Lord, and it should be dealt with in a strict way.

(3) Robbing a fellowman: Although this may not happen among the saints, we still have to say something about it. No one may acquire anything by way of robbery. Anyone who tries to usurp the possessions of others by means of his status or power has committed a sin.

(4) Extorting from one's fellowman: It is a sin to take advantage of anyone through the influence of one's own

position and power. In God's eyes His children should never do such a thing. This kind of conduct must be dealt with.

(5) Finding what is lost and lying about it: New believers must pay special attention to this matter. Many people have lied about the things which others have lost. To turn something into nothing, to reduce much to little, or to exchange what is bad for what is good is the same as lying. Something is there, yet you say that nothing is there. There may be much, but you say that there is little. Something may be good, but you say that it is bad—all this is lying. Others have lost something, and you take advantage of them, extorting some gain and benefit out of them; this is sin. A Christian must not take possession of others' belongings and make them his own. If you have picked up something by accident, you have to guard it well and return it to the owner. Never claim lost items as your own. It is wrong to keep lost articles; it is more wrong to usurp the possessions of others by illegal means. To turn other's possessions into one's own by any unrighteous means is wrong. A believer should not do anything that profits himself at the expense of others.

(6) Swearing falsely: It is a sin to swear falsely concerning any material thing. You know something, yet you say that you do not know. You have seen something, yet you say that you have not seen it. Something is there, yet you say that nothing is there. Anyone who swears falsely has sinned.

"Concerning any of the things a man may do to sin thereby"—this refers to transgressions against men in terms of material things. God's children should learn and always remember this lesson—they should not make the possessions of others their own. The possessions of others belong to them. Do not make their possessions yours. Whoever swears falsely in any of the things mentioned above and transgresses against others has sinned.

Brothers and sisters, if there is any dishonesty in anything you do, if you have acquired anything at the expense of others, or if you have acquired anything by means of these six ways, you have sinned. You have to deal with these sins thoroughly.

B. How to Return

Our manner of life has to be righteous, and our conscience must be void of offense before God. God's Word says, "Then it shall be, when he sins and is guilty, that he shall return what he took by robbery" (v. 4). The word *return* is very important. There are two aspects to the trespass offering. On the one hand, there is the need of propitiation before God. On the other hand, there is the need to "return" to man that which has been taken. Do not think that propitiation before God is sufficient. You must also return to man that which has been taken. If you do not return it, something is lacking. The trespass offering in Leviticus 5 deals with sins that do not involve material transgressions against people. Of course, there is no need to return anything in that case. But the sins spoken of in chapter six involve material loss, in which case one must return something. Propitiation through sacrifice was not enough. One still had to "return" that which was taken. This is why verse 4 says, "Then it shall be, when he sins and is guilty, that he shall return what he took by robbery." Everything acquired through sinful means must be returned. One must return what was taken by robbery, what was gained through extortion, what was deposited with him, whatever has been found, and whatever has been falsely sworn. All of these things must be returned.

How does a person return these things? "He shall make restitution for it in full and add to it one-fifth more; he shall give it to whom it belongs on the day he is found guilty" (v. 5). Here are three things that we need to take note of.

First, we have to make restitution in full. We are wrong if we do not make any restitution. We are equally wrong if our restitution is not made in full. No one should consider an apology as being sufficient. If the object in question remains in our house, it proves that we are still wrong; we have to return it in full.

Second, God wants us to not only return in full, but also to add one-fifth more when we make a recompense. Why must we add one-fifth? According to this principle, we have to return abundantly. If we have taken money or things from others, God wants us to add one-fifth to the full amount when we return it. God does not want His children to return the bare minimum. In printing books one has to leave margins at the top, bottom, left, and right of a page. Similarly, we should not be stingy in apologizing to people and returning what has been taken from them. We must be generous and liberal.

Some people do not add one-fifth to their recompense. In fact, they return much less than one-fifth of what was owed. They apologize by saying, "Although I offended you in this matter, I was not wrong in other matters. In other matters I did not offend you; rather, you offended me." This is a settling of accounts, not a confession. If you want to confess, do not be that stingy. It is all right to apologize more than you need to, but do not apologize less. Why did you sin in the first place? Since you have to recompense now, be more generous. Do not take things away from others and then return only that much to them. You have to return generously.

God's children should behave in a way that is worthy of their dignity. Even in the matter of confession, we should do it in a way that is worthy of our dignity. An apology that is in the way of settling accounts is not the kind of confession that God's children should have. God's children should confess their transgressions thoroughly and add one-fifth to the recompense. No one should be calculating and unwilling to make the smallest of sacrifices when confessing. If you are concerned about how much each party owes the other when you apologize, you are not behaving like a Christian. Some people say, "I was not angry at first, but your words made me angry. Since I have confessed my wrong already, it is your turn to confess your wrong." This is altogether a matter of settling accounts; this is not a confession. If you are making a confession, you should go an extra mile. Be more generous in the matter of confession. Do not withhold anything in your confession; instead, try to be liberal in it.

Adding one-fifth to our confession or recompense reminds us that offending others is a losing proposition and that we should never do it again. When a new believer offends others, he should realize that he will suffer loss eventually, even though he may gain something temporarily. He took five-fifths, but he has to return six-fifths. It is easy to take something from someone. But when you return it, you have to not only return it in full but also add one-fifth.

Third, we should make our confession and recompense as soon as possible. Verse 5 says, "He shall give it to whom it belongs on the day he is found guilty." If it is within our ability to return the object, or if the object in question is still in our hand, we should return it on the day we learn of this sin. It is easy for people to delay in this matter. But the more God's children put off confession and recompense, the more their feeling will become dull. As soon as we receive the light, we have to act upon it. We have to return it that very day. Hopefully, our brothers and sisters will take a straight path from the day they become a Christian. We should never take advantage of others and never be unrighteous. The basic principle of the Christian life on earth is not to take advantage of others. Taking advantage of others in any way is wrong. We must not take advantage of others. Instead, we must be righteous from the very beginning.

We have to give back to others. But this is not all. We should not think that everything is settled after we have made our apology and recompense. The matter is not settled. "Then he shall bring to the priest his trespass offering to Jehovah, a ram without blemish from the flock, according to the valuation, for a trespass offering" (v. 6). After we have confessed to and recompensed others, we still have to go to God for forgiveness. The trespass offering in chapter five deals with just God because no material loss is involved. But chapter six speaks of transgression against man. Therefore, one must deal with man first, before going to God to ask for forgiveness. Before a matter has been settled with man, one cannot go to God to ask for forgiveness. What happens once one has settled the matter with man and has asked for forgiveness before God? "The priest shall make propitiation for him before Jehovah, and he shall be forgiven for whatever he may have done by which he has become guilty" (v. 7). This is what the Lord wants. Whoever has transgressed materially against man should try his best to make recompense. Then he can come before God and ask for forgiveness through the Lord's blood.

We should not consider this as a trivial matter. Once we are careless, we take advantage of others and transgress against them. God's children should remember this point and pay attention to it all their lives. In whatever matter they have transgressed against others, they should return these things to them and ask God for forgiveness.

III. THE TEACHING OF MATTHEW 5

Now let us turn to another portion—Matthew 5. This chapter is different from Leviticus 6, which speaks of transgressions against man just in terms of material things. Matthew 5 deals with more than just transgressions in material things.

Matthew 5:23-26 says, "Therefore if you are offering your gift at the altar and there you remember that your brother has something against you, leave your gift there before the altar, and first go and be reconciled to your brother, and then come and offer your gift. Be well disposed quickly toward your opponent at law, while you are with him on the way, lest the opponent deliver you to the judge, and the judge to the officer, and you be thrown into prison. Truly I say to you, You shall by no means come out from there until you pay the last quadrans." The quadrans spoken of here do not refer to just physical quadrans. They refer to the principle of coming up short in something.

The Lord says, "Therefore, if you are offering your gift at the altar and there you remember that your brother has something against you." This specifically refers to disputes among God's children and among the brothers. If you are offering a gift at the altar, that is, if you are offering something to God, and suddenly remember that your brother has something against you, this *remembering* is God's leading. The Holy Spirit often gives you a necessary thought and reminds you of necessary things. When you remember something or are reminded of something, do not put the thought aside and think that it is merely a thought. As soon as you remember something, you should carefully deal with it.

If you remember that your brother has something against

you, this means you have transgressed against him. Your transgression may or may not be in material things. Perhaps you have offended him by acting unrighteously towards him. The emphasis is not on material things but on that which sets others against you. A new believer should realize that if he offends a person and does not apologize and ask for forgiveness, he is finished as soon as the offended party mentions his name and sighs before God. Whatever he offers to God will not be accepted. Whatever he prays will be turned down. We should not allow any brother or sister to sigh before God because of us. Once he or she sighs, we are finished before God. If we have done something wrong or if we have offended or hurt someone, the offended party need not accuse us before God. All he has to say before God is, "Oh! So-and-so..." or, for that matter, he just needs to utter an "Oh" and whatever we offer to God will be rejected. All he has to do is sigh a little because of us before God. We must not give any brother or sister the reason or the ground to sigh before God because of us. If we give him or her a reason to sigh, we will lose all our spiritual prospects and all our gifts to God will be annulled.

If you are offering a gift at the altar and remember that your brother has anything against you or has any reason to sigh because of you, do not offer up your gift. If you want to offer to God, "First go and be reconciled to your brother, and then come and offer your gift." God wants the gift, but you must first be reconciled to others. Those who are not reconciled to men will not be able to offer a gift to God. You must "leave your gift there before the altar, and first go and be reconciled to your brother, and then come and offer your gift." Do you see the proper way? You must first go and be reconciled to your brother. What does it mean to be reconciled to one's brother? It means to remove the brother's wrath. You may need to either apologize or recompense. However, the point is to satisfy your brother. It is not a matter of adding one-fifth or one-tenth; it is a matter of reconciliation. Reconciliation means satisfying the other's demand.

When you have offended and transgressed against your brother, when he is disturbed and feels that you are unrighteous, and when you have caused him to sigh before God, your spiritual fellowship with God is interrupted; your spiritual prospects are gone. You may not have the slightest feeling that you are in darkness, and you may feel that you are all right, but the gift you offer at the altar has become void. You cannot ask anything of God. You cannot even give anything to God. You cannot offer anything to God, much less receive any answer from Him. You may have offered up everything on the altar, but God is not pleased with any of it. Therefore, when you come to God's altar, you must first be reconciled to your brother. Whatever demands he has, you must try your best to satisfy him. Learn to satisfy the righteous requirement of God as well as the righteous requirement of your brother. You can offer your gift to God only after you have done this. This is quite serious.

We should not offend others easily. In particular, we must not offend a brother or a sister lightly. If we offend a brother or a sister, we immediately fall under God's judgment, and it is not easy to be recovered. In verse 25 the Lord emphasized, "Be well disposed quickly toward your opponent at law, while you are with him on the way." Here is a brother who has suffered injustice at our hand; he is not at peace before God. The Lord's words to us are in human terms. Our brother is like a plaintiff in a court of law. The expression *while you are with him on the way* is wonderful. Today we are all still *on the way*. Our brother has not died and neither have we. He is here, and we are here. He is on the way, and we are also on the way. We have to be well disposed quickly with him. It is very easy for us to not be here someday; it is very easy for us to not be *on the way*. It is also very easy for our brother to not be here and to not be on the way. No one knows who will go first. By then it will be too late to do anything. While he and we are still on the way, that is, while both parties are still here, there is the opportunity to speak to one another and apologize. We should be reconciled to each other quickly. The door of salvation will not be open forever. The same is true with the door of mutual confession among the brothers. Brothers have often regretted that they lost their opportunity to confess to each other; the offended party is no longer on the way. If we have any offense toward men, we should seize whatever opportunity we have to be reconciled to them quickly while we are both still on the way. We do not know whether or not others will be here tomorrow. We also do not know whether or not we ourselves will be here tomorrow. Therefore, we have to be well disposed with the brothers while we are still on the way. Once one party is no longer on the way, it is impossible to settle the matter.

We have to realize how serious this matter is! You cannot be nonchalant or careless about it. While there is still today, be well disposed with your brother quickly! If you know that a brother has a complaint against you, you have to deal with it. You must try your best to apologize lest there be no opportunity to reconcile later.

Following this, the Lord speaks again in human terms, saying, "Lest the opponent deliver you to the judge, and the judge to the officer, and you be thrown into prison. Truly I say to you, You shall by no means come out from there until you pay the last quadrans." We will not go into biblical interpretation concerning the paying of the last quadrans. We are only pointing out the practice of paying the last quadrans. We have to see that this matter must be resolved properly. If we do not resolve it properly, the case will not be settled. The Lord is not speaking of a future judgment or of being thrown into and being released from an actual prison. The Lord's emphasis is not on these things. His concern is that we would be reconciled today, that we would pay every quadrans today, not putting the matter off until later. We must do this while we are still on the way. We must not put off the matter today and hope that it will be resolved later. This is unwise, and it does not pay to leave the matter to the future.

God's children should learn this lesson well. We must make recompense when recompense is due and confession when confession is due. We should make recompense again and again and apologize again and again. We should not allow a brother or sister to harbor any complaint against us. If our conscience is pure, and the wrong is clearly not on our side, we can be at peace. Otherwise, if there is any wrongdoing on our part, we must confess. We must be above reproach in our conduct. We should not always think that others are wrong and we are right. It is certainly wrong to ignore the complaints of others and to instead insist that we are right.

IV. A FEW PRACTICAL CONSIDERATIONS

First, the scope of your confession should be as wide as the scope of your offense. You should do everything according to God's Word and should not take the extreme way. Do not overdo anything. Once you overdo, you will come under Satan's attack. If you offend many people, you must confess to many people. If you offend only one individual, you should confess only to that individual. To confess to an individual when you have offended many people is to under-confess. To confess to many people when you have offended only one individual is to overdo. The scope of confession depends on the scope of offense. The scope of testifying is another matter. Sometimes you have offended one individual, but because you want to testify to the brothers and sisters, you tell them about it. That is another matter altogether. As far as apology and confession is concerned, it should only be according to the scope of the offense. We should not go beyond that scope. We have to pay particular attention to this point.

Second, our confession must be thorough. We must not hide anything to save our "face" or our interest. There are, of course, times when we have to exercise due care in the way we confess; we have to take care of the interest and benefit of others. Perhaps we only should confess that we have offended others in a general way without going into detail. If we have difficulties in making decisions in complicated situations, it is best for us to fellowship with some experienced brothers and sisters so that they can help us do the right thing.

Third, there may be times when you are unable to make the necessary recompense. However, the ability to recompense and the desire to recompense are two different things. Some may not be able to recompense, but at least they should have the desire to recompense. If one is unable to make recompense immediately, he should tell the offended one, "I want to recompense you, but I cannot do it today. Please bear with me; I will do it as soon as possible."

Fourth, the law in the Old Testament states that if the

rightful recipient of one's recompense has passed away and has left no relatives to accept the recompense, it should go to the priests who serve Jehovah (Num. 5:8). According to this principle, if the recipient of your recompense is no longer available, the recompense should go to his relatives. If he has no relatives, you should give it to the church. If you can make recompense to someone, you should give it to him or to his relatives. You cannot give it to the church for the sake of convenience. However, if someone wants to make confession but the offended party has passed away and there seems to be no opportunity to confess, he can confess the matter to the church according to this principle.

Fifth, after making confession you need to make sure that you are not condemned in your conscience. It is possible for one's conscience to suffer repeated condemnation even after he has confessed. We must be clear that the Lord's blood has cleansed our conscience. His death has given us a conscience that is void of offense before God and has enabled us to draw near to God. All these are facts. However, we must see that in order to be clean before man, we need to deal with many sins. We need to settle all offenses in material things as well as in other matters. But we should not allow Satan to condemn us excessively.

Sixth, confession is related to physical healing. James 5:16 says, "Therefore confess your sins to one another and pray for one another that you may be healed." The result of confession is often God's healing. Sickness often comes in when there are hindrances among God's children. If we confess our sins one to another, our sickness will be healed.

Hopefully, the brothers and sisters will be thorough in the matter of confession and recompense. This is the way to maintain their purity. If anyone has transgressed against man, he should confess his sins to God on the one hand, and he must deal with the matter seriously with man on the other hand. Only then will his conscience remain bold. When the conscience is bold, a person can make considerable progress in his spiritual pursuit.

CHAPTER TWENTY-THREE

FORGIVENESS AND RESTORATION

Scripture Reading: Matt. 18:21-35, 15-20; Luke 17:3-5

What should we do if a brother offends us? We all have to deal with this question. What should we do when it is not we who have offended others but others who have offended us? When we examine the above three portions of the Lord's Word, we find that we should not only forgive a brother who has offended us but we should also restore him. Let us first consider the matter of forgiveness.

I. FORGIVING ONE'S BROTHER

A. Being Required to Forgive

Matthew 18:21-22 says, "Then Peter came and said to Him, Lord, how often shall my brother sin against me and I forgive him? Up to seven times? Jesus said to him, I do not say to you, Up to seven times, but, Up to seventy times seven."

Luke 17:3-4 says, "Take heed to yourselves. If your brother sins, rebuke him; and if he repents, forgive him. And if he sins against you seven times in a day and turns again to you seven times, saying, I repent, you shall forgive him."

The verses in Matthew say that we should forgive a brother seventy times seven times, not just seven times. The verses in Luke say that we have to forgive a brother who sins against us seven times a day, repents, and turns to us seven times. Whether or not his repentance is genuine, we must forgive him as long as he repents. Whether or not he is genuine is not our responsibility. We have to forgive him.

Seven times is not too much, but seven times within one day is not that infrequent. Suppose the same person does the same thing to you seven times a day, and suppose he says that he has sinned against you seven times a day. Would you still believe that his confession is genuine? I am afraid that you would think that he was only confessing with his lips. This is why Luke 17:5 says, "The apostles said to the Lord, Increase our faith." They felt that this was a problem to them. It was unthinkable to them that a brother could offend someone seven times in a day and then turn around to repent seven times. They could not believe it, and they said, "Lord, increase our faith." But God's children should forgive even if they are called upon to do so seven times a day. When a brother sins against you, you should not hold it against him.

B. God's Measure

The Lord continues with a parable in Matthew 18:23-27: "For this reason the kingdom of the heavens has become like a king who desired to settle accounts with his slaves. And when he began to settle them, one who owed him ten thousand talents was brought to him. But since he did not have the means to repay, the master commanded him to be sold, as well as his wife and children and all that he had, and repayment to be made. Then the slave fell down and worshipped him, saying, Be patient with me and I will repay you all. And the master of that slave was moved with compassion and released him and forgave him the loan."

The slave owed ten thousand talents, which was a very large amount of money. He had no ability to repay because "he did not have the means to repay." We can never repay all that we owe God. It is far more than what men owe us. Once a child of God arrives at a proper evaluation of his debt to God, he will generously forgive what his brother owes him. When we forget the immensity of the grace we have received from God, we become merciless toward others. We need to see how much we owe God before we can see how little others owe us.

The slave did not have the means to repay, and the master ordered him "to be sold, as well as his wife and children and all that he had, and repayment to be made." Actually, even if he sold all that he had, he still could not have repaid everything. "Then the slave fell down and worshipped him, saying, Be patient with me and I will repay you all."

It is difficult for man to understand clearly what grace is and what the gospel is. Man often thinks that he may not be able to repay today, but that he will be able to repay someday. He may not make it today, but he will make it someday. In these verses, however, we see a slave who, even if he were to sell all that he had, would not have had enough to repay. He said, "Be patient with me and I will repay you all." His intention was good. He was not trying to avoid his debt. He was only asking the Lord for more time. He intended to repay all. Such a thought can only come from those who have no knowledge of grace.

"And the master of that slave was moved with compassion and released him and forgave him the loan." This is the gospel. The gospel is not God working for you according to your idea. You may say, "Lord, be patient with me, and I will repay You all," but the Lord does not respond by saying, "Pay what you have and repay the rest later." The Lord forgave all of your debt. Man's prayers and requests do not even come close to the grace of the Lord. Our Lord works for us and answers our prayer according to what He has. The master of the slave released him and forgave the debt. This is God's grace; this is His measure. Anyone who asks for grace will receive grace from God, even though his knowledge of grace is very limited. We should be clear about this principle: The Lord loves to bestow grace on men. As long as we have a little desire for grace, the Lord will pour it out on us. He is afraid that we will not ask. As soon as a man hopes a little and opens his mouth to say, "Lord, be gracious to me," the Lord pours out His grace to him. Moreover, this grace from the Lord is given to His own satisfaction. We may think that one dollar is enough, but He will give ten million dollars, not just one dollar. He acts for His own satisfaction. His acts are compatible with Himself. We would settle for one dollar, but God cannot give anyone such a small sum. Either He does not give at all, or He gives according to His own measure.

We need to realize that salvation is accomplished in man according to God's measure. Salvation is not carried out according to man's thought. It is accomplished in man according to God's thought and plan.

The criminal on the cross pleaded with the Lord, saying, "Remember me when You come into Your kingdom." The Lord heard his prayer, yet He did not answer him according to his prayer. Instead He said, "Today you shall be with Me in Paradise" (Luke 23:42-43). Salvation is God saving man according to His own will, not according to the sinner's will. Salvation is not according to the thoughts of a sinner's limited mentality about God's work for him. Rather, salvation is God's work upon sinners according to His own thought. The Lord did not wait until He came into His kingdom to remember the criminal. He promised the criminal that he would be with Him in Paradise that very day.

The tax collector prayed in the temple and beat his breast, saying, "God, be propitiated to me, the sinner!" At the most, he was asking God to be propitiated to him. But God did not answer him according to his prayer. The Lord Jesus said, "This man went down to his house justified rather than that one" (Luke 18:9-14). In other words, that sinner went back justified. This was much more than what was in the mind of the sinner. The sinner had no thought of justification; he asked only for pity. But God said that he was justified. This means that God did not consider him a sinner but a justified person. Not only were his sins forgiven; he was justified by God. This shows us that God does not accomplish His salvation according to man's thought but according to His own thought.

The same thing is seen in the return of the prodigal son (15:11-32). When he was a long way off from home and before he met his father, he was prepared to go back home to serve as a servant. But when he reached his home, his father did not ask him to be a servant. Instead, he asked his slaves to bring out the best robe and to put it on him. He put a ring on his hand and sandals on his feet and slaughtered the fattened calf. They ate and were merry because the son who was dead had come to life again; he was lost but had been found. From these verses we see again that God does not accomplish His salvation according to a sinner's thought but according to His own thought.

Mark 2 speaks of four men who took a paralytic to the Lord Jesus. When they were unable to bring him to the Lord because of the crowd, they removed the roof where the Lord was and lowered the bed on which the paralytic was lying, hoping that the Lord Jesus would heal the paralytic and make him rise and walk. But the Lord Jesus said, "Child, your sins are forgiven" (v. 5). The Lord Jesus not only healed him but also forgave him of his sins. This also tells us that God works to His own satisfaction. All we have to do is go to God and ask. It does not matter whether we have asked enough. God always works to His own satisfaction, not to the sinner's satisfaction. Therefore, we should not consider salvation from our point of view but from God's point of view.

C. God's Expectation

God expects to see one thing from us: Whoever wants to receive grace must first learn to dispense grace. Whoever receives grace must first learn to share grace. If a man receives grace, God expects him to share this grace with others.

Matthew 18:28-29 says, "But that slave went out and found one of his fellow slaves who owed him a hundred denarii, and he took hold of him and began to choke him, saying, Repay me what you owe. Then his fellow slave fell down and begged him, saying, Be patient with me and I will repay you." Here the Lord shows us that we owe Him ten thousand talents, while others only owe us only a hundred denarii. When we say to the Lord, "Be patient with me and I will repay you all," He not only releases us but also forgives our debt. Our fellow slave, our brother, owes us a hundred denarii at the most. When he says, "Be patient with me and I will repay you," he has our same hope and request. How can we not be patient with him? But the slave "would not; instead, he went away and threw him into prison until he would repay what was owed" (v. 30).

The Lord spoke such a parable to expose the unreasonableness of those who do not forgive others. If you do not forgive your brother, you are the very slave spoken of in these verses. When we read this parable, we are indignant at this slave. The master had forgiven his debt of ten thousand talents, but he would not forgive his fellow slave's debt of a hundred denarii. He put his fellow slave into prison and kept him there until the latter would pay what he owed. He acted according to his standard of "righteousness"! A believer should treat himself according to righteousness but should treat others according to grace. Your brother may owe you something, and the Lord knows clearly that your brother owes you something. But He also clearly shows us that if a believer does not forgive his brother, he is not dealing with others according to grace. Such a one is short of grace in God's eyes.

Verses 31-33 say, "His fellow slaves, seeing what had taken place, were greatly grieved and came and explained fully to their master all that had taken place. Then his master called him to him and said to him, Evil slave, all that debt I forgave you, because you begged me. Should you not also have had mercy on your fellow slave even as I had mercy on you?" The Lord expects us to do to others as He has done to us. He has not made demands on us according to righteousness. In the same way He expects us to not make demands on others according to righteousness. The Lord has forgiven our debts according to mercy, and He expects us to forgive others' debts according to mercy as well. With what measure the Lord measures to us, He expects us to measure the same measure to others. The Lord dispenses grace to us according to a good measure, pressed down, shaken together, and running over. He expects us to do the same thing to others according to a good measure, pressed down, shaken together, and running over. The Lord expects us to do to our brother as He has done to us.

The ugliest thing in the eyes of God is for a forgiven person to refuse to forgive others. Nothing is uglier than refusing to forgive when one has been forgiven or refusing to be merciful when one has obtained mercy. A person should not receive grace for himself on the one hand and refuse to share grace with others on the other hand. A person must realize before the Lord that he should treat others the same way that the Lord has treated him. It is very ugly for a man to

receive grace while refusing to share grace. Being forgiven yet
refusing to forgive others is a most uncomely sight. God condemns a debt-ridden person's attempt to demand payment
from another debt-ridden person. He has no pleasure in those
who remember others' shortcomings when they themselves
have come short.

The master asked the slave, "Should you not also have had
mercy on your fellow slave even as I had mercy on you?" God
wants us to have mercy on others as He has had mercy on us.
We need to learn to have mercy on others and to forgive them.
A man who has experienced grace and who is forgiven by God
should learn to forgive others' debts. He should learn to forgive others, to have mercy on them, and to be gracious to
them. We need to lift up our eyes and say to the Lord, "Lord,
You have forgiven my debt of ten thousand talents. I am willing to forgive those who have offended me today. I am also
willing to forgive those who will offend me in the future. You
have forgiven me of my great sins. I also will learn to be like
You in a small way by forgiving others."

D. God's Discipline

Verse 34 continues, "His master became angry and delivered him to the torturers until he would repay all that was
owed." This is a man who has come under God's discipline.
God delivers him to the torturers until he should repay all
that he owes.

Verse 35 says, "So also shall My heavenly Father do to you
if each of you does not forgive his brother from your hearts."
This is a serious matter. We hope that no one would fall into
God's hand. We must forgive our brother from the heart, as
God has forgiven us from His heart. We hope all the brothers
and sisters will learn to forgive all offenses. Do not try to
remember the sins of your brother. We should not ask our
brother to repay us. God's children should be like God in this
matter. Since God treats us generously, He expects us to treat
our brothers generously as well.

II. RESTORING THE BROTHER

It is not sufficient for us to just forgive our brother. This only takes care of the negative side. We still need to restore him. This is the charge in Matthew 18:15-20.

A. Telling the Person

Matthew 18:15 says, "If your brother sins against you, go, reprove him between you and him alone. If he hears you, you have gained your brother." Offenses occur all the time among God's children. If a brother offends you, what should you do? The Lord says, "Go, reprove him between you and him alone." If a brother offends you, the first thing you should do is not to tell others. Do not tell the brothers and sisters or the elders of the church about it or make it the subject of your conversation. This is not the Lord's charge. If a brother offends you, the first thing you should do is go to him and tell him.

A problem often arises when a brother offends another brother and then the offended brother goes around publicizing it. He continually talks about it until the whole church knows about it. However, the brother who supposedly offended him remains unaware of the offense. Such tale-telling is typical of the conduct of a weak person; only a weak one would be so timid as to not talk directly with the offending brother. He would only dare to speak about the matter behind his back; he would dare not speak about it face-to-face. It is an unclean thing for anyone to speak of matters behind others' backs and to spread gossip. We do have to deal with our brother's fault, but the Lord does not want us to tell others first. The first one who needs to be told is the person who is directly involved, not others. If we learn this basic lesson well, the church will be spared many problems.

How do we tell others? Should we write a letter to them? The Lord did not tell us to do this. The Lord did not say that we should deal with it in writing, but rather by going to our brother and speaking to him face-to-face. However, just as it is wrong to speak about a matter behind someone's back, it is equally wrong to speak about it in front of many people. The matter should be communicated "between you and him alone." Many children of God fail in this matter. They publicize things before many people. But the Lord charges us to speak only when the involved parties are together. In other words, individual sins should be dealt with by the individuals alone; no third party should be involved at all.

We need to learn this lesson before God. We should never say anything behind the back of the brother who has offended us, and we should not speak to him in front of many people. We must point out his fault only when we are alone together. We do not have to talk about other things or bring up other problems; we simply need to point out the fault. This requires grace from God. It is one lesson God's children must learn.

Some brothers and sisters may think that this is too troublesome. While this is, in fact, quite troublesome, you cannot be afraid of trouble if you want to walk according to God's Word. If you feel that your brother's offense against you is too small to be bothered with, you may feel no need to speak to him. If this is the case, there is also no need to tell others about it. If you feel that a matter is insignificant, simple, trivial, and unworthy of bringing to his attention, you should not tell others about it either. You should not think that he does not need to be informed but that others do need to be informed. If you want to speak of it, speak to him alone. If there is no need to speak of it, simply keep silent. It is wrong for others to know about something when the offending brother is ignorant of it.

B. The Reason for Telling

The second half of verse 15 says, "If he hears you, you have gained your brother." This is the reason for telling. The reason for telling your brother is not to receive any compensation. There is only one reason for telling: "If he hears you, you have gained your brother."

Therefore, the issue is not how much loss you have sustained. If your brother has offended you, and the matter is not cleared up, he will not be able to get through to God; there will be obstacles in his fellowship and prayer. This is why you have to admonish him. It is not a matter of venting your hurt feelings, but a matter of your responsibility. It is a very small matter if it is simply a matter of hurt feelings. If it is just a matter of hurt feelings, if the issue does not pose a problem to you, and if you think you can get over it, you do not need to speak to your brother or anyone else. No one knows better than you do how serious the matter is to you. The responsibility of making the decision to go or not to go rests with you. Such responsibility rests with the party who is clearest about the matter. There are many things that can be let go of, but there are also many things that must be dealt with. If some offenses will indeed stumble your brother, you must point out his fault to him while he and you are alone together. Anything that should be dealt with must be dealt with carefully. You may let the matter go easily, but the other party may not be able to get through like you. He has committed an offense before God, and God has not yet forgiven him. If a brother has committed a mistake that will jeopardize his relationship with God, this is not a small matter, and you should go and clearly tell him about it. You must find an opportunity while he and you are alone together and say, "Brother, it was not right for you to offend me in such a way. Your offense will ruin your future before God. You will create obstacles and bring loss to yourself before God." If he listens to you, "You have gained your brother." In this way you restore your brother.

Today many of God's children do not obey the teaching of this portion of the Word. Some people always speak of others' wrongdoings, continually publicizing them. Some do not tell others, yet they never forgive and always harbor grudges in their hearts. Some forgive but do not try to restore. But this is not what the Lord wants us to do. It is wrong to speak of others' faults; it is wrong to keep silent yet be unforgiving in the heart; and it is equally wrong to forgive but not to exhort.

The Lord did not say that it is good enough for us to forgive the brother who has offended us. The Lord also showed us that the offended one has the responsibility to restore the offending one. Since it is not a small thing to offend someone, we have the responsibility to tell the one who has offended us for his sake. We must think of some way to restore our brother and gain him back. When we speak to him, we must be proper in our attitude and pure in our intention. Our purpose is to restore our brother. If our intention is to gain him, we will know how to point out his fault. If our intention is not to restore him, it will only worsen the relationship. The purpose of exhortation is not to ask for recompense or to justify our own feelings; it is for the purpose of restoring our brother.

C. The Proper Attitude in Telling Others

If our intention is pure, we will know how to do this step by step. First, we must have the right spirit. Next, the words we speak, the way we speak them, including our attitude, countenance, voice, and tone, must all be right. Our purpose is to gain him, not just to inform him of his fault.

If we are simply trying to rebuke him, our rebuking may be right, and the strong words we use may be justified, but our attitude, tone, and countenance may never achieve the goal of gaining him.

It is easy for us to say good things about a brother; it is easy to praise a person. It is also very easy to lose our temper with a person. We only need to let go of our emotions and we will lose our temper. But pointing out a person's fault and, at the same time, restoring and gaining him is something that can be done only by those who are full of grace. One must forget about himself completely before he can be humble, meek, free from pride, and willing to help those who are at fault. In the first place one must be right himself.

You should realize that the Lord allows a brother to offend you because He has shown favor to you and has chosen you. He has put a great responsibility upon you. You are His chosen vessel, and God is using you to restore your brother.

If a brother offends you in a small matter and you forgive him, the matter is settled; there is no need to do anything further. But if a brother offends you to such an extent that it becomes an issue, you cannot close your eyes and say that there is no problem. The problem is there, and you cannot ignore it. If the problem is not solved, it becomes a burden to the church. The church is often weakened because of these burdens. The life of the Body is drained through these burdens, and the work of the ministers is wasted through these burdens. Before God we need to learn to deal with every problem when it arises. If a person offends us, we should not close our eyes and try to ignore it. We must deal with it properly.

However, our spirit, attitude, word, countenance, and tone must all be proper. This is the only way to gain our brother.

D. Telling Others

Verse 16 says, "But if he does not hear you, take with you one or two more, that by the mouth of two or three witnesses every word may be established." If you go to him by yourself and speak to him with a proper motive, a good attitude, and gentle words, and he still does not hear you, then go and tell others about it. However, you must tell someone else only after he has rejected your words. You must not tell others loosely.

If a problem arises between two of God's children and if both of them go to the Lord and deal with it, everything will be solved easily. But suppose one is not careful with his words and the problem spreads to the ear of a third person. The problem will be compounded, and it will be hard to solve. If there is no contamination of a wound, the healing process is relatively simple. If dirt gets into a wound, not only does the level of pain increase, but the dirt makes it harder for the wound to heal. Unnecessarily spreading a problem to a third person is like adding dirt to a wound. Any problems between the brothers and sisters should be dealt with directly by the involved persons. The only time we should tell another person or persons is when one party will not receive the admonition. The purpose of telling others is not to multiply the gossip but to invite others to exhort, help, and fellowship together.

The "one or two more" here should be experienced persons in the Lord; they should be those who are weighty in their spiritual measure. You should present the case before them and ask for their opinions. They should check whether the fault lies with the offending one. The mature ones should pray and consider the matter before the Lord and then arbitrate according to their spiritual discernment. If they feel that the fault lies with the offending brother, they should go to that brother and say, "You are wrong in this matter. By doing this you have cut yourself off from the Lord. You must repent and confess."

"That by the mouth of two or three witnesses every word

may be established." The "one or two more" must not have a loose tongue. Do not invite talkative persons to such a meeting. Talkative ones can never convince people; instead, invite those who are trustworthy, honest, spiritual, and experienced before the Lord. In this way every word will be established by the mouth of two or three witnesses.

E. Finally Telling the Church

Verse 17 says, "If he refuses to hear them, tell it to the church." If we cannot deal with the problem by ourselves, we should bring one or two with us to deal with it. If the other person still refuses to hear them, we have to tell it to the church. Telling the church does not mean that we publicize the matter when the whole church is gathered together. It means telling the responsible elders in the church. If the conscience of the church also feels that this brother is wrong, he must be wrong. If the offending brother is one who walks before God, he should lay aside his own view and accept the witness of two or three. If he does not accept the witness of two or three, he should at least accept the verdict of the church. The unanimous view and judgment of the church reflect the heart of the Lord. The brother should realize that it is wrong to ignore the church. He should be meek and not trust in his own feelings or his own judgment. Rather, he should accept the feeling of the church.

What if he still refuses to hear? Verse 17 continues, "If he refuses to hear the church also, let him be to you just like the Gentile and the tax collector." This is a serious word. In other words, if he refuses to hear the church, all the brothers and sisters in the church should no longer communicate with him. Since he does not want to face his problem, the church should consider him as a Gentile and a tax collector and should have no fellowship with him. Though he is not excommunicated, all the brothers should consider him as a Gentile and tax collector, and no one should pay any attention to him. If he speaks, no one should listen. If he comes to break bread, everyone should ignore him. If he prays, no one should say "amen." If he wants to come, he can come. If he wants to go, he can go. But everyone should consider him as an outsider. If God's children will hold such an attitude in one accord, it will be easy to restore a brother. The purpose for dealing with him in this way is still to restore him.

Verse 18, which says, "Truly I say to you, Whatever you bind on the earth shall have been bound in heaven, and whatever you loose on the earth shall have been loosed in heaven," is related to the previous verses. The Lord in heaven acknowledges what the church does on earth. If the church considers a person who refuses to hear the church as being wrong, the church will look upon him as a Gentile and a tax collector, and our Lord in heaven will acknowledge the same thing.

Verses 19 and 20 are also based on the preceding portion. "Again, truly I say to you that if two of you are in harmony on earth concerning any matter for which they ask, it will be done for them from My Father who is in the heavens. For where there are two or three gathered into My name, there am I in their midst." Why does the previous verse say "that by the mouth of two or three witnesses every word may be established"? Here we see that the principle of two or three is the principle of the church. If two or three act upon a matter in one accord, and if these two or three deliberate something before God in one accord, God will acknowledge the decision. Matthew 18:18-20 is spoken in the context of our dealing with the brothers. When a matter is brought up to two or three people and then to the whole church, the Father in heaven will acknowledge such a decision.

Here we want to mention something in passing. How does the church make important decisions? Acts 15 shows us that when brothers come together, everyone can speak and debate. Even those who are for the law can stand up and speak their mind, even though their opinion is altogether wrong. In other words, all the brothers have equal opportunity to speak. But not all the brothers can arbitrate matters. All the brothers can express how they feel before the Lord. After the elders have listened to all of them, they should speak their feelings before God and make a final judgment on the matter. The responsible brothers may have the same feeling before the Lord. This feeling is the feeling of the church; it is also the conscience of the church. After they have spoken, everyone should submit and go along with them in one accord. This is the way of the church. The church does not muzzle people's mouths or forbid anyone to speak. But no one should speak carelessly. When the time comes for a decision, the elders should speak under the guidance of the Holy Spirit, and all the brothers and sisters should listen to the elders. If the Holy Spirit's authority is present in the church, such matters can be resolved easily. If the Holy Spirit has no authority in the church and there are many opinions of the flesh, the church will not be able to arbitrate anything at all. We must learn to submit to the authority of the Holy Spirit and to listen to the church.

May God be gracious to us. May we be like our Master who is so full of grace. If a brother offends us, we should forgive him from the heart. Moreover, we should bear the responsibility of restoring him according to the Lord's Word. May the Lord lead us to live such a life in the church.

CHAPTER TWENTY-FOUR

BELIEVERS' REACTIONS

Scripture Reading: Matt. 5:38-48

More than half of our life is spent in reactions. When we feel happy about what others are saying, we are reacting. When we feel angry about what others are saying, we are reacting as well. Whether we feel good or bad about a certain thing, we are reacting. We react when we are agitated, and we react when we resent mistreatment. When others accuse us unjustly, we try to defend ourselves. This is one reaction. When others persecute us, we try to endure it. This is another reaction. When we analyze human living carefully, we find that we live in our reactions more than half the time.

I. CHRISTIAN REACTIONS
BEING DIFFERENT FROM THOSE OF UNBELIEVERS

As Christians we also react. However, believers have one kind of reaction, while unbelievers have another kind of reaction. We can know a person by the way he reacts. No Christian should ever react as a unbeliever, and no unbeliever can react as a Christian. If you want to know a person, just observe the way he reacts.

Believers should have their own way of reacting. The Lord has commanded us to react according to specific ways. The Lord does not want us to react in any way we want. The Christian life is made up of a series of reactions. You are a good Christian if you react properly, and you are a poor Christian if you react improperly.

We have believed in the Lord and we are now Christians. When we encounter events, trials, persecution, opposition, or are challenged by any situation, we should know the Lord's commandment concerning how to react. A Christian should be disciplined by God not only in his walk but also in his reactions. All our reactions should be strictly directed by the Lord and governed by His discipline. We should react only as God has directed us. This is the kind of life that the Lord has given us.

II. THE LORD'S TEACHING ON THE MOUNT

Let us read Matthew 5:38-48. This section of the Word deals with reactions. "You have heard that it was said, 'An eye for an eye, and a tooth for a tooth'" (v. 38). "An eye for an eye, and a tooth for a tooth" means that if anyone hurts my eye, I will also hurt his eye. If anyone breaks my tooth, I will also break his tooth. I will do to others as they have done to me. This is one kind of reaction. Men in the Old Testament age reacted this way under the law.

However, the Lord said, "But I tell you not to resist him who is evil" (v. 39). The Lord said that our reaction should be different. We should be different in the way we react. We should not resist those who are evil. Then the Lord spoke of three more things. These three things have become the most famous words in the Bible. Many people are familiar with these words. "Whoever slaps you on your right cheek, turn to him the other also. And to him who wishes to sue you and take your tunic, yield to him your cloak also; and whoever compels you to go one mile, go with him two" (vv. 39-41). Do you realize that the left cheek, the cloak, and the second mile are all Christian reactions? The right cheek, the tunic, and the first mile are man's demand. Man's demand is the right cheek, but our reaction is to give the left cheek as well. Man's demand is the tunic, but our reaction is an additional cloak. Man's demand is one mile, but the Christian reaction is two miles. The whole of Matthew 5 reminds us of one thing—our reactions have to be different. The Christian life is expressed through a totally different set of reactions.

I would like to show you what Christian reactions are. It is wrong to go on living as a Christian for eight to ten years without knowing what Christian reactions are. A person should know what reactions are demanded by the Lord from the first days of his Christian life. We can never be proper Christians if our reactions are not proper. If our reactions are not proper, we are not acting according to God's nature or life within us, and we are not meeting God's standard. We must react in a Christian way in our living. It is wrong for us to claim to be Christians yet react the same as worldly people.

"To him who asks of you, give; and from him who wants to borrow from you, do not turn away" (v. 42). These are reactions. When others ask of you, you should give to them. When others want to borrow from you, you should not reject them. You cannot refuse anyone unless you do not have the means yourself.

"You have heard that it was said, 'You shall love your neighbor and hate your enemy'" (v. 43). This is how men under the law react. If one is a neighbor, they react with love. If one is an enemy, they react with hate.

"But I say to you, Love your enemies" (v. 44). The Christian reaction is different. Even if a person is your enemy, you still need to love him. "And pray for those who persecute you." They may persecute you, but your reaction must be to pray for them.

"So that you may become sons of your Father who is in the heavens, because He causes His sun to rise on the evil and the good and sends rain on the just and the unjust" (v. 45). This is God's reaction. God sends rain on the just as well as on the unjust. The sun shines on the good ones and on the evil ones. God does not react in an evil way toward men.

Following this it says, "For if you love those who love you, what reward do you have?" (v. 46). If others love you, your natural reaction is to love them. But what reward do you receive? "Do not even the tax collectors do the same?" If this is all that a Christian can do, he is the same as the tax collectors. Such a reaction is too cheap and easy.

"If you greet only your brothers, what better thing are you doing?" (v. 47). If someone is your brother, you greet him. If he is not your brother, you do not greet him. Or you may greet a person when you have nothing against him but turn away from him when there is something against him. If you do this, how are you different from the Gentiles? Such conduct is too low.

"You therefore shall be perfect as your heavenly Father is perfect" (v. 48). This means that we should react as God reacts.

III. IT BEING IMPERATIVE
TO DEAL WITH OUR REACTIONS

The above portions of the Word all speak of one thing—Christian reactions. Once we settle the matter of reactions, we have dealt with at least half the problems of our Christian life. We react when others behave in a certain way. We react when others say certain things. We adopt a certain attitude when others adopt certain attitudes. We are filled with reactions. This is why I say that more than half of our Christian life is occupied with reactions. If more than half our life is occupied with reactions and if our reactions are Christian-like, we can expect God to be pleased with us. But if our reactions are improper, we can never expect to be proper Christians.

Perhaps some may wonder why we need to emphasize this matter. Let me be quite frank with you. Do not think that we are touching something that is unimportant. I have had this deep sense within me for the last twenty or more years. Many people have been Christians for eight, ten, even twenty years. They have read the sermon on the mount dozens of times. Yet they still do not know how the Lord wants them to react. They have been Christians for years, yet they are still fundamentally wrong in their reactions. They argue about everything, and they talk about the law, about their rights, and about what others should or should not do. They have not seen what Christian reactions are.

Such ones have righteous reactions, legal reactions, Gentile reactions, and tax collector reactions. But they certainly do not have Christian reactions. They say, "Am I not right?" They feel that they have all the reasons on their side. But they have forgotten that a Christian's reaction should not be based on reason. They are totally unfamiliar with what Christian reactions should be. This is a big problem. Because they do not know how a Christian should react, they also do not know how other people should react. When a brother is silent about an unjust thing, these ones may think that he is admitting his guilt. Recently, I heard someone say, "So-and-so was silenced by the rebukes of others." He thought that speaking up was right and keeping silent was wrong. But this person does not know the meaning of the cross. He does not know what the Christian life is. In fact, he does not know what a Christian is.

A newly saved brother should know the Christian way to react from the very beginning. Once he becomes clear about this, he will know how he should live before God. Christians have their own kind of reactions. If you are not reacting in this way, you are just like a tax collector and a Gentile. Let me repeat that half of our human life involves reactions. We act a certain way because others act a certain way. We feel a certain way because others feel a certain way. We are reacting every day. If our reactions are wrong, I am afraid that our daily walk will amount to very little before God. This is why we need to deal with reactions.

IV. THREE DIFFERENT KINDS OF REACTIONS

Now let us consider the principles of reactions from this portion of Matthew. Man's reactions to ordinary matters can be classified according to three levels. The first is on the level of reasoning. The second is on the level of good behavior. The third has to do with God's holy life. If you are on the level of reasoning, your reaction will be temper and wrath. If you are on the level of good behavior, your reaction will be to endure. But if you are on the level of God's holy life, you will transcend everything. These are the three possible reactions.

If someone strikes your right cheek today and you are full of reasonings, you may say, "How could he have done that? Why did he hit me?" When others strike your cheek, you may fly into a rage and reason about it. This means that you are on the level of reasoning. Perhaps you have the knowledge that Christians should have proper behavior and that temper is wrong. When others ask for your tunic, you may endure silently and allow them to take it away. This kind of reaction is much better than losing one's temper. But the Lord tells us that there is another kind of reaction; it is the kind that He requires.

When others strike our cheek, the Lord does not want us to react with wrath. Neither does He want us to endure passively when others take our tunic. The Lord tells us to turn our left cheek when others strike our right cheek and to give others our cloak when they want our tunic. When others want us to walk one mile, we should walk two. This is not endurance but transcendence. This kind of reaction goes beyond man's demand. Man demands only so much, but we can do more before the Lord than just meet man's demand. We can exceed man's demand, not just meet it.

Brothers and sisters, the Lord tells us that Christians should have only one kind of reaction. We should react by transcending, not reasoning or enduring. Please remember that those who do not transcend are not acting like Christians. The Lord does not tell us to return an eye for an eye, to hurt the other person's eye when they hurt our eye. Neither does He say that we should passively endure when others hurt our eye. He says that we should add an eye to an eye. In other words, when one strikes my eye, I should let him strike my other eye.

Please remember that turning from an eye for an eye to an eye plus an eye involves at least two steps forward. Turning from a cheek for a cheek to a cheek plus a cheek, from a tunic for a tunic to a tunic plus a cloak, and from a mile for a mile to a mile plus a mile involves at least two steps forward. An eye for an eye is a reaction. Anger is a reaction. Endurance is a reaction. An eye plus an eye is another kind of reaction. Of these reactions, all but the last should be rejected.

V. A CHRISTIAN BEING DELIVERED
FROM HUMILIATION, POSSESSIONS, AND THE WILL

Let me briefly go over these three things again. Striking the cheek has to do with humiliation. The Chinese understand this; so did the Jews and the Romans at that time. There are many records which show that many of the Roman slaves would rather have been killed by their masters than struck on the cheek. Killing was bearable, but striking the cheek was unbearable. Hence, striking the cheek signifies extreme humiliation; it signifies the greatest shame at that time.

Tunics and cloaks are what man rightfully owns. Among man's possessions, there is hardly anything more rightfully his than his clothes. Even the poorest person wears a tunic and a cloak. No matter how insistent a man is in rejecting material enjoyment, he still has to wear a tunic and a cloak. This is a very legitimate demand. Here is a person who is not asking for your property or your farm but your tunic. Moreover, if he wants to take your tunic, you must take off your cloak first. Therefore, this matter touches one's possessions in the deepest way. If striking the cheek has to do with humiliation, taking away the tunic has to do with one's most essential possessions.

Compelling others to walk is particularly related to the will. I may not intend to take a certain way or go to a certain place, but others compel me to do so. This means I must deny myself to take their way. This is to bend the will.

I would like my brothers and sisters to see that Christian reactions have to do with the left cheek, the cloak, and the second mile. When others strike my right cheek, I turn my left cheek to them as well. When others want my tunic, I give my cloak as well. When others compel me to walk one mile, I walk two miles. This means that the right cheek has not touched me, the tunic has not touched me, and the one-mile journey has not touched me. This is why I call this a transcendent reaction. If my right cheek is struck and I have some feeling about it, I will not turn my left cheek. If after walking for one mile I have reached my limit, I cannot walk the second mile. The issue is the kind of reaction we have under such circumstances.

Christians are those who have been delivered from any feeling of glory and humiliation. They are those who have been delivered from the bondage of material possessions and their own will. When we are delivered from humiliation, possessions, and the will, these things will never touch us again.

VI. THE PRIMARY LESSON OF THE CROSS
BEING TO STOP ALL REASONINGS

We must learn never to reason before God. The first lesson of the cross is to not reason. No one among us should be so low or so fallen as to become a revenger. Hence, there is no need to talk about the option of taking an eye for an eye or a tooth for a tooth. However, I am afraid that many people reason and insist on their rights, saying, "You should not have struck me." Whenever a person reasons with others, it means that he is touched by the things that happen to him. The Lord shows us that the proper response to unreasonable evil is unreasonable good. Others can be unreasonably evil to us, but we return unreasonable good to them. The first mile is unreasonable enough, but the second mile is even more unreasonable. Actually, both are unreasonable. Striking the right cheek is unreasonable, but so is turning the left cheek. Taking away one's tunic is absolutely unreasonable, but so is giving away the cloak. Christians are those who do not reason. They return unreasonable goodness for unreasonable evil.

You should not be trapped in your own reasoning. You should not say whether something is reasonable or unreasonable. You may say that the first mile is unreasonable. But I say that the second mile is even more unreasonable. If the first mile is unreasonable, the second mile is even more unreasonable. If you cannot take the first mile, how can you take the second mile? But thank God! His children do not react by reasoning. None of God's children should lose their temper. They are not in the realm of arguing between right and wrong. Reasoning is something outside of a believer's realm. If you fall into reasoning, you have already lost your Christian standing; you are no longer standing on Christian ground.

VII. CHRISTIANS NOT BEING THOSE
WHO DO RIGHT OR GOOD THINGS,
BUT THOSE WHO ARE TRANSCENDENT

May we all see something here. If someone wants my tunic, it is perfectly all right if I do not give it to him. It is good if I give it to him. But it is Christian if I give him my cloak as well. I think this is clear. When someone wants my tunic, why should I give it to him? I am right even if I do not give it to him. If I give it to him, that is good. I am a good man; therefore, I give it to him. However, doing the right thing is not being Christian. Being a good man does not mean that one is therefore a Christian. A Christian gives away not merely the tunic but also the cloak. A Christian is a person who gives away the second garment.

What is the Christian reaction? The Christian reaction is not doing the right things or the good things, but doing the transcendent things. The more God's children are persecuted, cornered, and shut out, the higher they should climb. It is a pity that some stumble when they are cornered. It is unfortunate that they lose their temper and reason. It is especially unfortunate that they try to endure. A Christian is one who soars when persecution comes, when all escapes have been blocked and there is only a wall before him.

I remember a comment made about a brother who passed away many years ago: "Anyone who never made himself an enemy of this man does not know how great the love of this man was." This is a wonderful comment. The more you persecuted him, the stronger he became. The more you mistreated him, the higher he climbed. The more you were fierce towards him, the more generous he was towards you. When he died, many brothers commented, "In order to know the strength of his love, one needed to be his greatest enemy. We did not do him enough evil. The more evil you did to him, the greater was his love for you." This is the Christian reaction. The more you persecute a Christian and shut him up, the broader is the way before him.

Do not think that this is a very profound lesson. Matthew 5—7 contains the first sermon of the Lord Jesus. The teachings on the mountain were the first teachings the disciples heard. That is why this should be told to new believers. We should practice this from the very beginning. As long as we are Christians, we have to practice this. If we do not practice this, we will not have peace within. A Christian who reasons with people will not have peace. We may be upset and fretful when others take away our things, but we will have no peace. However, when others want our tunic and we give them our cloak also, we will shout "hallelujah" all the way home. We will feel happy. When others want to borrow some of our money, we may spare our money if we turn them down, but we will also spare our joy. If others ask us for money, we should give it to them. This is the way to live a happy Christian life.

Many Christians have sad faces all day long because they are not willing to walk the second mile. If you walk the second mile, you will be able to sing within your being.

VIII. PROBLEMS WITH BELIEVERS' REACTIONS

Many brothers and sisters have problems with their reactions because they do not know the Lord. They cannot bear turning the left cheek, giving away the cloak, or walking the second mile. They keep saying, "How unreasonable are these people!" I have a frank word for these ones: This is what the Lord demands of us. A person may strike your right cheek and be satisfied. But the Lord tells you to turn your left cheek to him as well. Another may receive your tunic and be satisfied. But the Lord tells you to give him your cloak as well. Someone may compel you to walk only one mile and be satisfied. But the Lord compels you to walk the second mile. We have to realize that the left cheek, the cloak, and second mile are the Lord's demand, not man's demand. All those who have trouble with the second cheek, the second garment, and the second mile do not have any trouble with men, but with the Lord, for it is He who makes these demands.

You may say that man is unreasonable. But remember, it is actually the Lord who is unreasonable. If no one should strike your first cheek, then even more no one should strike your second cheek. If the demand for the first garment is unreasonable, the demand for the second garment is even more unreasonable. If the first mile is unreasonable, the second mile is even more unreasonable. But the Lord demands the second. This is the Lord's commandment. We can say that the Lord's commandment is more severe than that of an unreasonable man. No unreasonable man can be stricter than the Lord in His commandment.

Why is the Lord so severe? Because He knows that the life He has given us is a transcendent life. Unless this life transcends, there is no peace. This life is happy only when it transcends. The more you try to embarrass, disgrace, or hurt this life, the more its power is manifested.

This is what it means to be a Christian. It is not merely a matter of not being angry and of forbearing and enduring, but of transcending all things. Others may compel us to walk a mile, but we will walk two miles. Others may want to take one of our garments, but we will give them two. Others may want to strike our right cheek, but we will give them our left cheek also. Brothers, this life is transcendent; it soars. This is how believers react. Unless we act this way, we are not behaving like Christians.

IX. GRACE IN GOD'S CHILDREN

Some who are ignorant of the Bible think that the teachings on the mountain in Matthew 5—7 have to do with the law. Is this law? No! This is grace. The law is an eye for an eye and a tooth for a tooth. What is grace? Grace is to give to others what they do not deserve. In fact, the first cheek, the first garment, and the first mile are grace. All these are what others do not deserve. But because the life in us transcends all things, none of these things can touch us. This is why we allow others to strike our right cheek and then turn the left cheek to them. This is why we can give to others not just the tunic, but the cloak as well. This is why we can walk not just one mile, but two. This is grace upon grace. But this is not God's grace; this is the grace of God's children. This is what God's children do when they act according to the God of grace. God gives men what they do not deserve. We also can give men what they do not deserve, even more than what they do not deserve.

X. BEING ENLARGED THROUGH OUR REACTIONS

Why do we have to do this? Let me tell you: The teaching on the mountain was given to enlarge our capacity. God increases our measure through our reactions. Many things are too dear to us. As soon as we live out the teaching on the mountain, God strips these things from us. The tunic and the cloak are taken away again and again. But this enlarges us again and again. We will be enlarged many times more than our capacity for the cloak or the tunic.

Many Christians are the same size as the garments they wear; they are very small. They can be affected by one little garment. One garment alone is worth their wrath and the sacrifice of their Christian propriety. Everywhere we go, we find these "small" people.

Christians can be large. But, even more, they can be enlarged, because God has given them a large life. If you can let go of one garment, you can let go of one hundred garments. If you can yield to someone's demand for one mile, you can yield to his demand for two miles. If you do this, you will be enlarged by God.

It is a big thing to save one's face. Many people cannot bear humiliation and disgrace. They can give away all their garments, but they cannot be struck or disgraced. It is hard for them to take insulting words from others. But here is one who is struck in the face. He not only endures but also takes it willingly, gladly, and happily. As soon as we turn our left cheek to others, we are enlarged. We are enlarged through all of our unreasonable experiences.

Suppose you have a strong will. If you are oppressed and persecuted and you accept oppression and persecution willingly, even walking the second mile, you will be enlarged as time goes on.

In the past years, I have met many "small" people in this world. I have not met too many "big" people in the church either. I hope that the new believers will take this way from the very beginning. Take God's life and react in a transcendent way. This is the basic condition for maturity. If you continually react according to God's transcendent life, you will be enlarged more and more. No material thing will bind you. No despising or disgrace will limit you. Even your own strong will will not hold you down. You will grow continuously.

If we do not practice this, the church will be filled with "small" people.

XI. CHRISTIAN VICTORY
BEING A TRANSCENDENT VICTORY

I am not saying that walking the second mile is enough. Walking the second mile is a principle. That principle involves being transcendent. The left cheek is also a principle that involves being transcendent.

What does it mean to be transcendent? To transcend means to be on top. Suppose someone strikes your right cheek. If you try to remember Matthew 5 and say, "I am determined to let him strike. If he wants my tunic, I will give him my tunic reluctantly. If he forces me to walk one mile, I will force myself to accompany him two miles." This kind of behavior is useless. This is not transcending. You have not climbed high enough. Who can give their other cheek? It is those who, when insulted, realize that they have received a rich life from the Lord. This is why they can turn their left cheek to others when they are struck on the right cheek. Others may force them to walk a mile. But the life they have received from the Lord is so abundant that they can go a second mile. Christians are never reluctant people, and the Christian reaction never just meets the minimum requirement.

A sister once said, "I almost lost my temper!" She sounded very victorious when she said this. But this is not a Christian reaction. A Christian reaction does much more than what is needed; it stands the challenges well. This is the meaning of the second mile. Have you seen this? Some people are extremely unkind to you; that is the "right cheek." If you can return kindness to them and still be victorious before God, that is the "left cheek." The "left cheek" speaks of abundance. It denotes surplus. The Christian victory is not a meager victory. The Christian victory is an overflowing victory. Christians should always have a surplus; they should always transcend their experience. Christian victory never comes by force; it is never achieved by gritting one's teeth or arguing. Christian victory is always easy to come by. May the Lord enlarge us again and

again, and may we express the grace of God's children again
and again.

XII. OUR REACTION BEING
FOR THE INCREASE OF THE LORD'S WORK

Why do we have to turn our left cheek when others strike
our right cheek? When the Lord grants us sufferings through
man's hand, we should rather enhance His work than annul
His work. This is why we turn our left cheek. The Lord is
using man's hand to enlarge our capacity and to help us grow.
The hand stops at the right cheek. But we can add our left
cheek. This means that we do not react by frustrating the
Lord's work through man's hand. On the contrary, we further
this work. The Lord is striking us, and we also strike ourselves. The Lord is dealing with us, and we also deal with
ourselves. When others strike our right cheek, we join in to
strike ourselves. We do not stand with ourselves to oppose our
attacker. On the contrary, we stand with our attacker. One
strike is not enough; we need more striking. The Lord is dealing with us, and we are also dealing with ourselves.

The Lord's hand is on me, and my prayer is for His hand to
remain there. If I lose everything, I have nothing more to lose.
If I die completely, I cannot die any further. If I can still die, it
means I have not died enough. If I can still lose, it means I
have not lost enough. I want the Lord's hand to be heavier on
me. I do not want to reduce the weight of His hand upon me.

If you can stand on the Lord's side and deal with yourself
this way, you will have no grudge against anyone. Man's
demand can never be higher than the Lord's. Man's demand
is, at most, one mile. The Lord's demand is the second mile.
The most that man can do is force you to go a mile. But you
can give him more; you can add something to it. You can do
your best to enhance what the Lord has already done.

XIII. STANDING FAST ON OUR CHRISTIAN STANDING

Let me ask you another question: Is it better to be the one
who strikes or the one who is struck? Do you envy others?
Others are striking. Are you going to do the same? Those who
strike are not acting like Christians, and those who endure

others' striking are not acting like Christians either. Only those who take the striking willingly and who turn their left cheek to their strikers, saying, "Please do more," are acting like Christians.

Today if a brother strikes you, do you know what he has given you? He has given you the greatest opportunity to be a good Christian. He honors you by striking you, having offered you the opportunity to be a proper Christian.

Please remember that a Christian who strikes others has lost his Christian dignity. We should not envy those who have lost their Christian standing. Every time you are mistreated or are threatened, you are given the opportunity to live the Christian life. In fact, those who treat you this way are saying, "So-and-so, I no longer want to be a Christian. I will let you be a Christian in my place!" Their actions are equivalent to this.

If a brother takes you to court or demands money or clothing from you, he is, in effect, saying, "Today I do not want to be a Christian. I will let you be one in my place!" He has resigned from the position of a Christian and put you in his position instead. Should you not thank God for this? You need to say, "O God! I thank You and praise You. You have put me in the position of a Christian. This is truly Your grace." Brothers and sisters, we should learn to strive for our Christian standing.

Once, I had some business dealings with a brother. By common understanding, I did not owe him any money, but he demanded perhaps sixty-eight thousand dollars from me. My first reaction was to be angry. I felt that he did not have the slightest ground to ask for it. How could this man be a Christian? He was too much. If he had any sense of righteousness, how could he want this money? But my next reaction was that of joy. Although he was wrong, I still enjoyed giving it to him. I asked him, "Brother, do you really want it?" He said, "Yes." At that moment, the Lord put this word in me: "This man is giving you the opportunity to be a Christian." This was the first time the Lord spoke such a word to me. I said, "That is right," and went away to prepare the money for him.

From that day on, I learned this lesson. When a person

behaves the way this man did, he is giving up his position as a Christian. When a person does this to us, what a shame and pity it is if we also resign from our Christian standing. We should learn to say, "The Lord has put me here, and He is giving me the opportunity to live as a Christian." We should say, "Lord, I want to be a Christian." No loss is greater than the loss of our Christian standing. To be struck is a great loss; to lose our possessions is also a great loss; and to be put to shame and deprived of freedom are even greater losses, but the Lord has entrusted us with the responsibility of expressing His grace and forbearance. If we fail in this, we have suffered the greatest loss.

Some may think that the strong ones are those who can strike others. But I say that the ones who are really strong are those who can afford to be struck and not strike back. A person who cannot control his own temper is a weak person. A strong person is one who can control his own temper. We need to know how to evaluate things spiritually before God. We should not evaluate things according to the worldly way. We should not hold to worldly views. We need to have a spiritual view.

I hope that new believers will see what our Christian reactions should be from the very beginning. We should set this course right from the start. Do not allow three, five, eight, or ten years to go by before taking this way. Do not think that the teaching on the mount is that profound. No Christian should wait a long time before picking up the teaching on the mount. The teaching on the mount should be the first teaching. It should be something one finds at the main entrance, not something he sees after years of advancement. The teaching on the mount is the fundamental Christian response to everything. It is the reaction that issues from our Christian nature. When a person believes in the Lord Jesus, he spontaneously reacts this way and behaves this way. Walking the second mile results in joy in the heart. A person cannot have real peace and joy until he practices this. This life calls for persecution, disgrace, and mistreatment. The more severe the persecution, the stronger the manifestation of the power of God's life.

XIV. TWO THINGS CONCERNING THIS LIFE'S REACTION

Finally, we need to pay attention to two things concerning this life's reaction. First, we have to pray every day. We have to ask the Lord to deliver us from temptations and from the evil one. We have to pray every day to be delivered from temptations. Humanly speaking, it is impossible to live on earth according to the principles spoken of above. The reactions required by the Lord are impossible to find on earth. You will exhaust all you have after trying to live this way a few times. This is why the Lord inserts a prayer in the teachings on the mount. It is a prayer that prays for deliverance from temptations and from the evil one. We can live in this world only with the Lord's protection. Without His protection, we cannot go on even for a single day. This prayer is indispensable. If we have no intention to live this kind of life or have this kind of reaction, nothing more needs to be said. But as soon as we want to live by God's life, we have to pray this prayer. We even have to pray this prayer every day.

Do not share this principle of the Christian life with the unbelievers. Do not share this principle of the Christian life with nominal Christians. This is what Matthew 7 tells us. Do not give spiritual things to dogs, and do not throw pearls before swine. Dogs and swine are unclean. Dogs signify everything evil and unclean, and swine signify nominal Christians who are void of life. Outwardly, they have split hooves, but inwardly they do not chew the cud. Outwardly, they are Christians, but inwardly they are not. Do not tell them these words. If you do, you are asking for trouble. If you say this, they may say, "Turn your cheek. Let me try this on you." Telling them such things is to ask for trouble for yourself. Pay attention to this. You should pray so that you can be spared such trouble.

Second, we have to maintain our Christian standing. We should not seek trouble for ourselves. However, with God's permission and under His sovereignty and the Holy Spirit's administration, we may face such situations, either at the hand of believers or unbelievers. At such times we should have the proper reactions and not retreat.

The Christian life is a wonderful life. The more you are

persecuted, embarrassed, and unreasonably treated, the happier you are before God. This is the only way to happiness. If I hit a brother today, and he immediately turned his right cheek, I would be uncomfortable for a whole month; that would be the most unhappy thing for me.

For as long as a Christian lives on earth, he cannot take advantage of anyone. If you take advantage of something or someone once, you will not be able to lift up your head for a whole month before the Lord. Any gain on earth is loss in reality. It is better to let others strike you. When others strike you, you can go home and sleep well, eat well, and sing well. You can climb up the hill, and the moon will shine brighter upon your face. Do not think that you have gained something by taking advantage. The only way to take the right course is to react the right way, and the only way to live according to proper principles is to have the right reactions.

CHAPTER TWENTY-FIVE

DELIVERANCE

Scripture Reading: Rom. 7:15—8:2

It is possible for a person to be free from sin immediately after he has believed in the Lord. However, this may not be the common experience of all believers. After believing in the Lord, many people fall back into sin instead of being freed from sin. It is true that they are saved. They belong to the Lord and possess eternal life. However, they are still troubled by sin and are unable to serve the Lord as they wish.

It is a very painful experience for a person to be continually troubled by sin after he has believed in the Lord. A person who has been enlightened by God has a sensitive conscience. He is sensitive toward sin and has a life that condemns sin. However, he may still be bothered by sin. This results in much frustration and even discouragement. It is indeed a very painful experience.

Many Christians try to overcome sin. Some think that if they try hard enough to renounce sin, they will eventually be free from sin. As a result, they try their best to reject the temptations of sin. Some realize that sin should be overcome, and they continually wrestle with sin in the hope of overcoming it. Others think that sin has made them a captive and that they must strive hard to free themselves from its bondage. However, all these are man's thoughts; they are not God's word or teaching. None of these methods lead to victory. God's Word does not tell us to struggle with sin by our own efforts. It says that we should be delivered from sin, that is, be released or freed from sin. Sin is a power which enslaves man. The way to deal with this power is not by destroying it ourselves but by allowing the Lord to free us from it. We have sin, and there is no way to separate ourselves from it. The Lord's way is not to vanquish sin. He is saving us from sin's power by moving us away from it. New believers should know from the start the right way to be delivered from sin. There is no need to travel a long and tortuous path to find deliverance from sin. We can take the way of freedom as soon as we believe. Now let us try to deal with this matter according to Romans 7 and 8.

I. SIN BEING A LAW

Romans 7:15-25 says, "For what I work out, I do not acknowledge; for what I will, this I do not practice; but what I hate, this I do....For to will is present with me, but to work out the good is not. For I do not do the good which I will; but the evil which I do not will, this I practice. But if what I do not will, this I do, it is no longer I that work it out....I find then the law with me who wills to do the good, that is, the evil is present with me. For I delight in the law of God according to the inner man, but I see a different law in my members, warring against the law of my mind and making me a captive to the law of sin which is in my members....So then with the mind I myself serve the law of God, but with the flesh, the law of sin."

In verses 15 through 20, Paul repeatedly uses the word *will* and the phrase *do not will*. The emphasis is on willing or not willing, resolving or not resolving. In verses 21 to 25, there is another emphasis on the law. These two things are the keys to this passage of the Word.

First, we need to understand the term *law*. The common understanding of a law is that it is something that remains the same all the time, something that allows no exceptions. Moreover, there is power in a law. This power is a natural power, not an artificial power. All laws have power. For example, gravity is a law. If you throw something up, it will eventually fall back to the ground. You do not have to pull the object down with your hands; the earth has a force that pulls it down for you. If you throw a stone up, it will fall. If you throw an iron up, it also will fall. If you throw something up in China, it will fall. If you throw the same thing up in other countries, it will fall. An object in the air will fall the same today and tomorrow. Any object in the air, as long as nothing is holding it, will fall regardless of time and space. A law remains the same all the time and allows no exceptions. It is a natural force which requires no human effort for its perpetuation.

Romans 7 shows us that Paul was trying to be victorious. He was trying to free himself from sin. He wanted to please God. He did not want to sin or to fail. However, he eventually admitted that his resolutions were all futile. He said, "To will is present with me, but to work out the good is not." He did not want to sin, yet he sinned. He wanted to do good and walk according to God's law, yet he could not do it. In other words, what he willed he could not do, and what he resolved to do, he was unable to accomplish. Paul willed again and again, but the result was only repeated failure. This shows us that the way to victory lies not in the human will or human resolution. Paul willed and resolved again and again, but he still failed and sinned. Obviously, to will is present, but to work out the good is not. The best that a man can do is make resolutions.

The willing is present but not the good, because sin is a law. Following verse 21 Paul showed us that he remained defeated even after he made numerous resolutions. This is because sin is a law. This law of sin was present with him every time he resolved to do good. He was subject to the law of God in his heart, but his flesh yielded to the law of sin. Whenever he willed to obey God's law, a different law rose up in his members, subjecting him to the law of sin.

Paul was the first person in the Bible to point out that sin is a law. This was a very important discovery! It is a pity that many who have been Christians for years still do not realize that sin is a law. Many people know that gravity is a law and thermal expansion of objects is another law. But they do not know that sin is a law. Paul did not know this at first. After sinning repeatedly, not voluntarily but involuntarily by a potent force in his body, Paul discovered that sin is a law.

Our history of failure tells us that whenever temptations come, we try to resist them. But we are never successful in this resistance. When temptations come again, we again try to resist them, only to end up in another defeat. This experience repeats itself ten times, a hundred times, or a thousand times, and we still find ourselves defeated. This is the story of our failure. We fail again and again. This is not something that happens by chance; it is a law. If a person committed only one sin in a lifetime, he could consider sin as something incidental. However, those who have sinned a hundred or a thousand times will say that sin is a law; it is something that continually drives them on.

II. MAN'S WILL BEING UNABLE
TO OVERCOME THE LAW OF SIN

Paul failed because he exercised his will to make resolutions. After verse 21, Paul's eyes were opened. He saw that the enemy he was dealing with—sin—was nothing less than a law. When he saw that sin was a law, he could only sigh and say, "Wretched man that I am! Who will deliver me from the body of this death?" He realized that it was impossible for him to prevail over sin by his will.

What is the will? The will is man's own volition. It is what man wants, determines, and decides to do. It is man's opinions and judgments. Once a man's will resolves to do something, he begins to carry it out. Man's will can produce some power. Therefore, there is power in the will.

But herein lies the problem. When the will comes in conflict with the law of sin, which one prevails? The will usually prevails at the beginning, but ultimately sin prevails. Suppose you hold up a book that weighs one catty [a Chinese measure of weight] with your hand. Gravity is pulling it down while you are trying your best to hold it up. But the unceasing operation of the law of gravity will eventually prevail, and the book will fall to the floor. You may try to hold it up with your hand. You may prevail for an hour, but after two hours you will feel tired, and after another hour your hand will no longer obey you. Eventually, you will let go of it. Gravity never tires out, but your hand does. The law of gravity is pulling the book down continuously, every hour, every minute, and even every second. Your hand cannot fight against the law of gravity forever. The longer you hold the book, the heavier it feels.

The book has not become heavier, but the law of gravity has triumphed over the power of your hand, and you feel as if the book has become heavier and heavier. The same principle applies when you try to overcome sin with your will. The will can stand against sin for a while. But the power of sin far exceeds the power of the will. Sin is a law; it is not destroyed by the resistance of man's will. Whenever the power of the will slackens, the law of sin surfaces. The human will cannot persist forever, but the law of sin is always active. The will may prevail for a little while, but in the end it will always be overcome by the law of sin.

Before we see that sin is a law, we keep trying to overcome it by our own will. When temptation comes, we hold our breath and try to overcome, only to find that it has overcome us instead. When temptation comes again, we make a stronger resolution because we think that our last failure was caused by a faulty resolution. We tell ourselves that we will not sin this time and that we will overcome. But the result is the same—we fail again. We do not know why our resolution cannot bring us victory over sin. We do not realize that overcoming sin by the will never works.

It is easy to see that temper is a sin. When someone says something unkind, you feel hurt and upset. If he continues to speak unpleasant words, you may hit your desk, blow up, exchange words, or do anything. Afterwards, you may feel that as a Christian you should not have lost your temper, and you may resolve to control your temper the next time. You pray and believe that God has forgiven you. You confess your sin to others, and your heart is once again filled with joy. You think that you will never lose your temper again. But a little later, you hear more unkind words and become upset once again. When these words come to you the second time, you begin to murmur within. By the third time, your temper explodes. Afterwards, you realize that you were wrong again, and you ask the Lord for forgiveness, promising Him that you will never lose your temper again. But the same thing happens the next time you hear unkind words; after a while, your temper flares up again. You exercise your will again and again, only to find that you fail again and again. This proves that sin is not an accidental mistake; it is not something that happens only once. It is something that happens repeatedly, something that haunts you all your life. Those who lie continue to lie, and those who lose their temper continue to lose their temper. This is a law; no human power can overcome it. Paul did not learn this lesson at first, so he exercised his will repeatedly to no avail. It is impossible for man to try to overcome the law of sin by his will.

Once the Lord grants you mercy and shows you that sin is a law, you will not be far from victory. If you continue to think that sin is an occasional act and that victory can be secured through additional prayers and struggles against temptations, you are far from victory. Paul's story shows us that sin is a law. The power of sin is strong; our own power is weak. The power of sin always prevails, while our own power always fails. As soon as Paul realized that sin is a law, he knew that none of his methods would work. His determination was useless; he would never overcome the law of sin by his will. This was a great discovery, a great revelation to him.

Paul saw that a man cannot experience deliverance by the exercise of the will. As long as a man trusts in the power of his own will, he will not turn to God's way of deliverance. The day will come when you will prostrate yourself before God and acknowledge that you can do nothing and henceforth will do nothing. That will be the day you find deliverance. Only then will you understand Romans 8. Brothers and sisters, please do not belittle Romans 7. We must first have the knowledge of chapter seven before we can have the experience of chapter eight. The problem is not whether you understand the doctrine in Romans 8 but whether or not you have emerged from Romans 7. Many have buried themselves in Romans 7; they are still trying to deal with sin by their will. The result is nothing but failure. If you have not seen that sin is a law and that your will can never overcome this law, you are trapped in Romans 7; you will never arrive at Romans 8. Our newly saved brothers and sisters must accept God's Word as it is written. If you try to find your own way out, you will end up with nothing but sin. You will sin again and again, and your eyes will continue to be veiled. You will remain in your blindness. Your eyes need to be opened to see that all your willing and struggling is in vain.

Since sin is a law and the will cannot overcome this law, what is the way of victory?

III. THE LAW OF THE SPIRIT OF LIFE
FREEING US FROM THE LAW OF SIN

Romans 8:1-2 says, "There is now then no condemnation to those who are in Christ Jesus. For the law of the Spirit of life has freed me in Christ Jesus from the law of sin and of death." The way to victory is to be freed from the law of sin and of death. This verse does not say, "The Spirit of life has freed me in Christ Jesus from sin and death." (I am afraid that many Christians think this way.) Rather, it says, "The law of the Spirit of life has freed me in Christ Jesus from the law of sin and of death." Many Christians see the Spirit of life setting them free from only sin and death. They do not see the law of the Spirit of life freeing them from the *law* of sin and of death. It takes many years for some Christians to realize that sin and death are a law in them and that the Holy Spirit is another law in them. When the Lord opens their eyes, they will see that sin and death are a law and that the Holy Spirit is a law as well. The realization of the Holy Spirit as a law is a great discovery. When we realize that the life-giving Spirit is a law, we will jump up and exclaim, "Thank God, Hallelujah!" Man's will cannot overcome the law of sin, but the law of the Spirit of life has freed us from the law of sin and of death. Only the law of the Spirit of life can free man from the law of sin.

Once we realize that sin is a law, we will no longer try to do anything by our will. When God grants us mercy to see that the Holy Spirit is a law, we will experience a great change. Many people only see the Spirit of life giving us life. They do not see that the Holy Spirit is another law in us, and that we can be freed spontaneously from the law of sin and of death when we trust in this law. There is no effort involved for this law to deliver us from the other law. We do not need to will, to do anything, or to hold on to the Holy Spirit. We do not need to be that busy when the Lord's Spirit is in us. If we fear that the Lord's Spirit will not work in us unless we rush in to help Him in times of temptation, we have not seen the Spirit as a law within us yet. May we see that the Holy Spirit is a spontaneous law within us. The way of deliverance from sin is not through the exercise of the will. If we exercise our will, we will end up in failure. God has given us another law which spontaneously frees us from the law of sin and of death. The problem of one law can only be resolved by another law.

There is no effort involved when we try to overcome one law with another law. We have mentioned before that gravity is a law. It pulls every object down to the ground. But helium is a gas which is lighter than air. If we seal it in a tight balloon, the balloon will rise up. It will rise spontaneously; there is no need to fan it or support it by any force. As soon as we let go, the balloon will rise. The rising is a law, and we do not need to do anything about it. In the same way, no effort is involved when we deal with the law of sin and of death by the law of the Spirit of life.

Suppose someone scolds you or strikes you without cause. It is possible for you to overcome the situation even without realizing what has happened. After the whole thing is over, you may wonder how you did not get angry when you were scolded. You should have been very angry at the other person's word. But surprisingly you overcame the situation without even realizing it! Indeed, all victories are unconscious victories because the law of the Holy Spirit is operating and upholding us, not our own will. This kind of spontaneous victory is genuine victory. Once you experience this, you will realize that only the indwelling Spirit can keep you from sin; you do not have to will not to sin. It is also the indwelling Holy Spirit who is enabling you to overcome; you do not have to will to overcome. Since this law dwells in you, you are delivered from the law of sin and of death. You are in Christ Jesus, and the law of the Spirit of life is in you. Spontaneously, you are free. As long as you do not rely on your own will and effort, the Holy Spirit will bring you into victory.

Hence, victory over sin has nothing to do with our effort. We did not exert any effort when the law of sin directed us to sin. Similarly, we do not need to exert any effort in order for the law of the Holy Spirit to free us from sin. Genuine victory is one that requires no effort on our part. There is nothing for us to do. We can lift up our eyes and say to the Lord, "All is well." Our past failures were the result of a law and today's victories are also a result of a law. The former law is powerful, but the present law is more powerful. The former law is indeed potent in bringing us to sin, but the present law is more absolute in saving us from condemnation. When the law of the Spirit of life is expressed through us, its power is far greater than that of the law of sin and of death.

If we see this, we will truly be freed from sin. The Bible does not say that we can overcome sin with our will. It speaks only of freedom from sin: "The law of the Spirit of life has freed me in Christ Jesus from the law of sin and of death." The law of the life-giving Spirit has pulled us out of the realm of the law of sin and of death. The law of sin and of death is still present, but the one on whom it worked is no longer there.

Every saved person should be clear about the way to deliverance. First, we must see that sin is a law in us. If we do not see this, we cannot go on. Second, we need to see that the will cannot overcome the law of sin. Third, we need to see that the Holy Spirit is a law, and this law frees us from the law of sin.

The sooner a new believer realizes this way of deliverance, the better it is. In fact, no one needs to wait for many years before seeing the way of deliverance. You do not need to suffer many hardships before experiencing freedom. Many brothers and sisters have wasted their time unnecessarily; they have shed many tears of defeat. If you want to experience less pain and tears, you should realize from the start that the way to deliverance lies in these words: "The law of the Spirit of life has freed me in Christ Jesus." This law is so perfect and powerful that it will save you to the uttermost; there is no need to do anything to help it. This law frees you from sin completely, sanctifies you wholly, and fills you with life spontaneously.

Brothers and sisters, do not think that the Holy Spirit within us only expresses His life through us occasionally. If we think this way, it proves that we only know the Spirit; we do not know the *law* of the Spirit. The law of the Spirit expresses His life continuously. It remains the same at all times and in all places. We do not have to tell this law to behave in a certain way; it behaves the way it does without our guidance. Once the Lord opens our eyes, we will see that the treasure within is not just the Holy Spirit or a life, but a law as well. Then we will be released, and the problem of sin will be over.

May God open our eyes to see this way of deliverance. May He open our eyes to see this secret to victory, and may we have a good start on this straight path.

CHAPTER TWENTY-SIX

OUR LIFE

Scripture Reading: Col. 3:4; Phil. 1:21; Gal. 2:20

I. CHRIST OUR LIFE

Many Christians have a wrong concept about the Lord Jesus. They think that the Lord set up a good pattern for us while He was on earth and that we should imitate this pattern. It is true that the Bible charges us to imitate the Lord (Rom. 15:5; 1 Cor. 11:1; etc.). But the Bible does not tell us to do this by ourselves. There is something we must see before we can imitate Him. Many people want to imitate the Lord, but they repeatedly fail. They regard the Lord like they regard good Chinese calligraphy, something to be copied stroke by stroke. They do not realize how frail man is and that no fleshly energy could give man enough strength to imitate Him.

Some Christians think that they can ask the Lord to empower them simply because the Bible says, "I am able to do all things in Him who empowers me" (Phil. 4:13). They feel that there are many things that need to be done, many biblical precepts that need to be obeyed, and many examples of the Lord that need to be imitated. They also feel that none of this can be done unless they have more power. Therefore, they ask the Lord for power. They think that if the Lord would only give them the power, they would be able to do all things. Many people just wait and hope daily for the Lord to give them the power to conduct their activities.

It is true that we need to look to the Lord for power. But in addition to asking for power, we need to see something further. Without seeing this one thing, we will not always have the power, even though we may be looking to the Lord. We can pray to the Lord every day for power. But sometimes the Lord answers such prayer, and sometimes He does not. To some people this means that they can do all things when He empowers them and that they can do nothing when He does not empower them. This is precisely the reason so many Christians fail again and again. We have to ask the Lord to empower us. But if we take this as an isolated commandment or as the only way, we will fail.

The fundamental relationship between Christ and us is conveyed in the words *Christ our life*. We can imitate the Lord only because He has become our life. We can ask Him for strength only because He has become our life. There is no way to imitate Him or be empowered by Him unless we understand the meaning of *Christ our life*. Hence we must first understand, see, and grasp the secret of *Christ our life* before we can imitate Him or ask Him for strength.

Colossians 3:4 says, "Christ our life." Philippians 1:21 says, "For to me, to live is Christ." This shows us that the way to victory is for Christ to be our life. Victory is, "For to me, to live is Christ." If a Christian does not know what is meant by *Christ our life,* and what is meant by *for to me, to live is Christ,* he will not experience the Lord's life on earth; he will not be able to follow the Lord, to experience victory in Him, or to proceed on the course before him.

II. FOR TO ME, TO LIVE IS CHRIST

There are many Christians who have greatly misunderstood Philippians 1:21. When Paul said, "For to me, to live is Christ," he was stating a fact. They think *for to me, to live is Christ* is a goal or a hope. But Paul did not say that his goal was to live Christ. Paul was saying, "I live because I have Christ; I cannot live without Him." This was a fact in him, not a goal he was seeking. It was the secret to his living, not the hope he was cherishing. His living was Christ. For him to live was for Christ to live.

Galatians 2:20 is a very familiar verse to many Christians. But many misunderstand it more than they misunderstand Philippians 1:21. They have made Galatians 2:20 their goal, praying with aspiration and hoping they will reach the state when "it is no longer I who live, but it is Christ who lives in me." Each time this verse is read, they are full of aspiration. Many people pray, fast, and hope that one day they will be crucified with Christ and reach the state when "it is no longer I who live, but it is Christ who lives in me." Galatians 2:20 has become their goal and their hope.

According to our experience, no one with such a hope ever reaches his goal. If you make it your goal and hope to attain such a state, if you aspire to be crucified, that is, to no longer be the one who lives but instead to have Christ living in you, you will wait forever before seeing your aspiration fulfilled, because you are hoping for something that is impossible to achieve.

God has given us a wonderful gift of grace. There is a way. Those who fail can overcome; those who are unclean can be clean; those who are worldly can be holy; those who are earthly can be heavenly; and those who are carnal can be spiritual. This is not a goal, but a way. This way lies in the life of substitution. Just as we found a vicarious death in the Lord's grace, we also can find a vicarious living in Him. On the cross the Lord bore our sins. Through His death we were spared death. Our sins were forgiven, and we were spared judgment. Similarly, Paul tells us that we are spared of our living through the Lord living in us. The implication is simple: Since He lives in us, we no longer need to live. Just as He died once for us on the cross, today He is living for us and in us. Paul did not say, "I hope that I will not live. I hope that I will allow Him to live." Instead, he was saying, "I no longer live anymore. He is the One who is living." "It is no longer I who live, but it is Christ who lives in me." This is the secret to victory. This is the way to be victorious.

The day we heard that we did not need to die, we embraced that word as the gospel. Similarly, it should also be a day of the gospel to us when we hear that we do not need to live. I hope that the new believers will pray much for God's enlightenment and will see that Christ lives in us and that we no longer need to live by ourselves.

Unless we see this, maintaining a testimony or living the Christian life is a great burden. It is a great burden to fight temptation, to bear the cross, or to obey God's will. Many believers feel that it is very hard to maintain the Christian life. Daily they try, yet daily they sigh. Daily they struggle, yet daily they fail. Every day they try to maintain their testimony, yet every day they bring shame to the Lord. Many people do not have the strength to reject sin, yet they feel guilty when they do not reject it. They feel condemned when they lose their temper, yet they cannot be patient. They feel sorry for hating others, yet they have no strength to love. Many people are exhausted from trying to live the Christian life. They feel that the Christian life is like climbing a hill with a heavy burden on their back; they can never reach the top. Before they were saved, they had the burden of sin on their back. Now that they have believed in the Lord, they have the burden of holiness on their back. They exchange one burden for another, and the new one is just as tiresome and burdensome as the old one.

This experience clearly shows that they are practicing the Christian life in a wrong way. Paul said, "It is no longer I who live, but it is Christ who lives in me." This is the secret of Christian living. It is the Lord in you who is living the Christian life, not you living it by yourself. If you live the Christian life by yourself, endurance will be a suffering to you, as will love, humility, and bearing the cross. But if Christ lives in you, endurance will be a joy; so will love, humility, and bearing the cross.

Brothers and sisters, you may be tired of trying to live the Christian life. You may feel that the Christian life is consuming you and binding you. But if you see that you no longer need to live, you will agree that this is a great gospel to you. Every Christian can be spared such a wearisome living. This is a great gospel! You no longer have to exert so much effort trying to be a Christian. You no longer have to bear such a heavy burden for your Christian life! You can say, "In the past I heard the gospel which told me that I could be spared death. Thank God, I no longer need to die. Today I am tired and weary of living. God says that I can be spared living. Thank God, I no longer need to struggle to live."

It is, of course, a suffering for us to die. But it is equally a suffering for us to live before God. We have no idea what God's holiness is all about. We do not know what love is and what the cross is. For men like us to try to live unto God is indeed an unbearable burden. The more we try to live, the more we sigh and suffer. It is a big struggle to labor and strive to live the Christian life. In fact, it is altogether impossible for us to do it. We could never satisfy God's demands. Some people always have a bad temper. Others can never be humble; they are always proud. For a proud person to try to live in God's presence and act humbly every day is a very wearisome and tiring task. Paul was a weary and worn-out Christian in Romans 7. He said, "For to will is present with me, but to work out the good is not" (v. 18). Every day he willed, but every day he failed. This is why he could only sigh, "Wretched man that I am!" (v. 24). Actually, being a Christian is not an exercise akin to putting a carnal man in heaven and subjecting him to slavery there. Fortunately, no carnal man can enter heaven. Otherwise, as soon as he entered it, he would run away quickly; he would not be able to stand even one day there. His temperament would be too different from God's temperament, and his thought too far from God's thought. His ways would be too different from God's ways, and his views too different from God's view. How would he ever be able to meet God's demands? There would be nothing he could do before God except run away.

But this is a gospel for you. God does not want you to do good. He does not want you to make up your mind to do good. God only wants Christ to live in you. God does not care about good or bad; He cares about who is doing the good. God is not satisfied with good alone; He wants to know who is doing the good.

Hence, God's way is not for us to imitate Christ or to walk like Christ. Neither is it to plead on our knees for strength to walk like Christ. God's way is for us to experience that it is "no longer I who live, but it is Christ who lives in me." Do we see the difference here? This is not a matter of imitating

Christ's life, nor of being empowered to live this life, but a matter of no longer being the ones living at all. God does not allow us to live according to ourselves. We do not come to God by ourselves; we come to God through Christ living in us. It is not a matter of imitating Christ or of receiving some power from Christ, but of Christ living in us.

This is the living of a believer. The living of a believer is one in which it is no longer him who lives, but it is Christ living in him. In the past I was the one who lived, not Christ. But today, it is not I who live, but Christ. Another One has come to live in my place. If a person cannot say, "It is no longer I who live, but it is Christ who lives in me," this person does not know what Christianity is; he does not know the life of Christ, nor the life of a believer. He is merely aspiring to be "not I but Christ." But Paul did not say that he was striving to be this way. He told us that this was how he lived. His way was to stop living by himself and to let Christ live instead.

III. I HAVE BEEN CRUCIFIED WITH CHRIST

Perhaps some will ask, "How can we experience *it is no longer I who live*? How can 'I' be eliminated?" The answer to this question lies in the first part of Galatians 2:20: "I am crucified with Christ." If I am not crucified with Christ, I cannot be eliminated. If I am not crucified with Christ, I am still I. How can I say, "It is no longer I"? Only those who are "crucified with Christ" can say, "It is no longer I."

In order for our crucifixion with Christ to become experiential, there is the need of cooperation from two sides. It is impossible to experience this crucifixion if there is cooperation on only one side; cooperation on both sides is essential.

Our inner eyes have to be opened. When Christ was crucified on the cross, God put our sins on Christ and crucified them on the cross. This is God's side of the work. Christ died for us and took our sins away. This occurred more than nineteen hundred years ago, and we believe it. Similarly, when Christ was crucified, God put *us* into Christ. Just as our sins were settled more than nineteen hundred years ago, our person was also dealt with at the same time. When God laid our sins on Christ, He also put our person in Christ. On the cross our sins were removed. On the cross our person was also dealt with. We must remember Romans 6:6: "Knowing this, that our old man has been crucified with Him." We do not have to hope to be crucified with Christ. We have been crucified with Him, forever and unchangeably crucified with Him. God has put us into Christ. When Christ died on the cross, we died on the cross as well.

If you take a piece of paper, write a few letters on it, and then tear the paper apart, you tear the letters apart as well. You are tearing the paper, but as the paper is torn, the letters are torn. The Bible tells us that the veil of the temple was embroidered with cherubim (Exo. 26:1). When the Lord died, the veil was split (Matt. 27:51), and therefore the cherubim were split as well. The veil refers to the body of Christ (Heb. 10:20). The cherubim had the face of a man, the face of a lion, the face of an ox, and the face of an eagle (Ezek. 1:10; 10:20). This signifies all created beings. When the body of the Lord Jesus was split, all the creation in Him was split as well. He died that He might "taste death on behalf of everything" (Heb. 2:9). The whole old creation passed away with Him. You have been trying in vain to do good and to be a successful Christian for years. Now God has crucified you with Christ. When Christ was crucified, the whole old creation was split, and you were split as well.

You have to believe in this truth. Your eyes need to be open to see that your sins were upon Christ and your person was also upon Christ. Your sins were on the cross, and your person was also on the cross. Your sins were taken away, and your person was also crucified. All this has been accomplished by Christ. Many people fail because they keep looking at themselves. Those who have faith should look at the cross and see what Christ has accomplished. God placed me in Christ. When Christ died, I also died!

But why is this "person" still living today? Since you have been crucified, why are you still living? To solve this problem you must believe and exercise your will to identify yourself with God. If you are looking at your own "self" every day, hoping that it will improve, this self will become more alive; it will not die by itself. What is death? When a person is so weak that he cannot be weakened any further, he has died. Many people do not admit their own weakness. They are still demanding so much from themselves. This means that they are not yet dead.

Romans 6 says that God has crucified us with Christ. But Romans 7 tells us of one person who is still trying to will. Even though God has crucified him, he still wills to do good. He cannot die, yet he cannot do good either. If he would say, "Lord, I cannot make it, and I do not believe I will make it. I cannot do good, and I will not will to do good," everything would be fine. But Romans 7 tells us that man is not willing to die. God has already crucified our old man, but we are unwilling to die; we still exercise our will to do good. Today many Christians are still trying when they know very well that they cannot make it. Nothing can be done about these Christians. Suppose there is a person who cannot be patient. What can he do? He may try his best to be patient by himself. Whenever he prays he asks for patience. Even while he is working he thinks about patience. But the more he tries to be patient, the less patient he becomes. Instead of trying to be patient, he should say, "Lord, You have already crucified this impatient person. I am impatient. I do not want to be patient and do not intend to be patient." This is the way to victory.

The Lord has crucified you. You should say simply, "Amen." He has crucified you, and it is futile for you to try to be patient by yourself. God knows you cannot make it. This is why He crucified you. Even though you still try to be patient, God considers you hopeless. He has even crucified you. It is a great mistake to think you can make it. It is also a great mistake to try to live the Christian life. God already knows that you cannot make it; the only way He has for you is crucifixion. Even though you think that you can make it, God says that you cannot make it and that you should die. How foolish it is to still make resolutions and to struggle! God knows that you cannot make it, and it would be well with you if you agreed with Him. God knows that you deserve to die. If you would say, "Amen, I will die," everything would be well. The cross is God's assessment of us. In God's view we cannot make

it. If we could make it, God would not have crucified us.
He knows that the only way for us is death. This is why He
crucified us. If we saw things the same way God sees them,
everything would be settled. Brothers and sisters, God must
bring us to the point where we accept His verdict.

Here we see two aspects: First, Christ died, and we were
crucified. This is something God has done. Second, we have to
acknowledge this fact; we need to say, "Amen." These two
sides must work together before God's work can take effect on
us. If we constantly frustrate Him by trying to do good and be
patient and humble, the work of Christ will have no effect on
us. Our resolution to be humble or to be patient only makes
things worse. Instead, we should bow down our head and say,
"Lord, You have said that I am crucified, and I will say the
same thing; You have said that I am useless, and I will say
the same thing; You have said that I cannot be patient, and
I will no longer try to be patient; You have said that I cannot
be humble, and I will no longer try to be humble. This is what
I am. It is useless for me to try to make any further resolutions. I am only fit to remain on the cross." If we did this,
Christ would live Himself out of us!

We should not think that this is a difficult thing to do.
Every brother and sister should learn this lesson after he or
she is saved. From the beginning we must learn not to live.
Instead, we should let the Lord live. The basic problem is that
many Christians have not given up on themselves. They still
try to solve their problems themselves. The Lord Jesus has
already given up on them, but they are still struggling and
trying to come up with ways to live. They stumble again and
again, only to rise up to try again and again. They sin again
and again, only to make more and more resolutions. They
have not given up on themselves. The day will come when God
grants mercy to them and opens their eyes. On that day they
will see that as God considered them hopeless, they should
consider themselves hopeless as well. Since God has pronounced
death to be the only way, they also should pronounce death as
the only way. Only then will they come to God and confess,
"You have crucified me, and I do not want to live anymore.

I have been crucified with Christ. From now on, it is no longer I who live, but it is Christ who lives in me."

For years we have been so wrong. We have committed so many sins and have been bound by so much weakness, pride, and temper. It is about time that we give up on ourselves. We should come to the Lord and say, "I have done enough; nothing has worked. I give up. You take over! I have been crucified on the cross. From now on live in my place!" This is the meaning of "it is no longer I who live, but it is Christ who lives in me."

IV. LIVING BY THE FAITH OF THE SON OF GOD

The other part of Galatians 2:20 is also very important: "And the life which I now live in the flesh I live in faith, the faith in the Son of God." Christ lives in us. From this point forward, we live by faith in the Son of God. We believe daily that the Son of God lives in us. We say to the Lord, "I believe that You are living for me. You are my life; I believe that You are living in me." When we believe this way, we live this way. No matter what happens, we will no longer make any move. The fundamental lesson of Romans 7 is that we should not make any resolutions. The basic teaching is that it is better that we not will to do anything, because such a willing is useless. Since it is useless to do anything by ourselves, we should simply stop all our moves.

The purpose of Satan's temptation is not only for us to sin but also for the old man within us to move. When temptation comes, we must learn to refuse to move and to say to the Lord, "This is not my business. This is Your business. I look to You to live in my place." Always learn to look to Him. Never try to move on your own. We are saved through faith, not through works. In the same way our life is based on faith, not on works. We were saved through looking to the Lord alone. Today we live through looking to Him as well. Just as salvation is accomplished by the Lord, without the involvement of any of our work, so also our living on earth today is a living of the Lord Himself, without the need for any involvement of ourselves. We must look up to the Lord who saves us and say, "It is You alone, not I."

After we say this, if we still move on our own, we are
saying this in vain. We must stop our own activity before
these words can be meaningful in any way. Brothers and sisters, we must remember that failure comes not because we do
too little, but because we do too much. As long as man keeps
on working, God's grace will not operate and man's sins will
not be forgiven. In the same way, as long as man is occupied
with his own work, trying to do everything by himself,
Christ's life will not be manifested. This is a rule. The cross
will not produce any effect on those who trust in their own
work. When we insist on our own goodness, we will not be
saved. But when we turn away from ourselves to the Lord, we
will be saved. The same is true today. If we are working and
operating, instead of the cross working in us and the life of
Christ operating in us, this speaking will be in vain. We must
learn to condemn ourselves. We must confess that we will
never overcome by ourselves. Do not will and do not try to do
anything. Simply look to the Lord and say, "I look to You as
the One who is living in me! Live on my behalf. I look to You
for victory! I look to You to express Your life through me." If
we say this, the Lord will accomplish it for us. But if we frustrate our faith by our own work, the Lord can do nothing. We
have to settle this question once and for all. We have to
believe daily and speak to the Lord daily in a definite way:
"Lord, I am useless! I take Your cross. Lord, keep me from
moving. Lord, be my Master and live out of me." If we can
believe, hope, and trust in this way, we will be able to testify
daily, "It is no longer I who live, but it is Christ who lives."

CHAPTER TWENTY-SEVEN

SEEKING GOD'S WILL

Scripture Reading: John 7:17; Matt. 10:29-31; 18:15-20; Rom. 8:14; Psa. 119:105; 1 John 2:27

I. THE NEED TO OBEY GOD'S WILL

Before we were saved, we did everything according to our own will. At that time we served ourselves and did everything to please ourselves. We would do anything as long as it pleased us or made us happy. However, now we have believed in the Lord and have accepted Christ Jesus as our Savior. We have acknowledged Him as our Master, the One whom we serve. We have acknowledged that He has redeemed us. We belong to Him and are of Him, and we are here to serve Him. For this reason, we need a fundamental change. We no longer should walk according to our preference; we must walk according to God's will. After we believe in the Lord, the focus of our living changes. The focus is no longer ourselves, but the Lord. The first thing we should do after we are saved is ask, "What shall I do, Lord?" Paul asked this question in Acts 22:10, and we should ask the same question. Whenever we come across a situation, we should say, "Lord, not as I will, but as You will." In making decisions or in choosing our paths, we should always say to the Lord, "Not as I will, but as You will."

The life we possess has one basic demand—to walk according to God's will. The more we obey God's will, the happier we become within. The more we deny our own will, the straighter our pathway will be before God. If we walk according to our own will as we once did, we will not feel happy. Instead, we will suffer. After we are saved, the more we walk according to our own will, the more suffering and the less joy we will have.

But the more we walk according to the new life and the more we obey God's will, the more peace and joy we will have. This is a wonderful change. We should not think that we will be happy if we walk according to our own will. After becoming Christians, we will find our path filled with peace and joy if we do not walk according to our own will but learn to submit to and obey God's will. Christian joy has to do with obeying God's will, not with walking according to our own will.

Once we become Christians, we have to learn to accept God's will and be governed by it. If a person can submit humbly to God's will, he will spare himself many needless detours. Many fail and stop growing in life because they walk according to their own will. The result of walking according to our own will is nothing but sorrow and poverty. In the end we still have to walk according to God's will. God always subdues us through things, circumstances, and the environment. If we have not been chosen by God, He will let us walk as we wish. But since we have been chosen by God, He will lead us to the way of obedience according to His way. Disobedience will only cost us unnecessary detours. In the end we will still have to obey.

II. HOW TO KNOW GOD'S WILL

Our question now is how do we know God's will. We often think that mortals like us could never understand God's will. However, we should have the assurance that not only do we want to obey God's will, but God Himself also wants us to obey His will. Not only do we seek to know His will, but God Himself also wants us to know His will. If God wants us to obey His will, He must first enable us to know His will. Therefore, it is God's business to reveal His will to us. None of God's children need to worry and say, "Since I cannot know God's will, how can I obey it?" This concern is unnecessary because God always has a way to show us His will (Heb. 13:21). We have to believe that God will always show us His will through the proper means. It is God's responsibility to tell us His will. If we are submissive in our attitude and intention, we will surely know His will. All of us must learn to believe that God is eager to reveal His will to man.

What are the ways to know God's will? A Christian must pay attention to three things in order to know God's will. If these three things are in agreement with one another, we can be quite sure that it is God's will. These three things are: (1) arrangements in the environment, (2) the leading of the Holy Spirit, and (3) the teachings of the Scripture. These three things are not mentioned according to the order of their importance. They do not necessarily have to be in sequential order. We are simply stating that these three things help us know God's will. When the testimonies of these three things are in agreement with one another, we can be assured that we know God's will. If one of these three things is not in agreement with the other two, we still need to wait. We must wait until all three agree with one another before we go ahead.

A. Arrangements in the Environment

Luke 12:6 says, "Are not five sparrows sold for two assaria?" Matthew 10:29 says, "Are not two sparrows sold for an assarion?" If one assarion could buy two sparrows, then by right two assaria should only buy four sparrows. But the Lord said two assaria could buy five sparrows. One assarion buys two, and two assaria buy four plus an additional one. This shows us the cheapness of a sparrow. However, even a cheap thing such as a sparrow is not allowed to fall to the earth if God forbids it. Although the fifth sparrow is an extra one that is given for free, no sparrow is forgotten by God. If our God does not allow it, no sparrow can fall to the earth. This clearly shows us that everything happens under God's permission. If our heavenly Father forbids it, even a sparrow will not fall to the earth.

It is difficult to number a person's hairs. However, the Lord said, "Even the hairs of your head are all numbered" (Matt. 10:30). No one knows how many hairs he has, and no one can count his own hairs, but God has counted and numbered our hairs. Our God is so fine and so exact!

If God takes care of a seemingly worthless creature such as a sparrow, how much more will He take care of His children! If God takes care of something as minute as a hair, how much more will He take care of other things! Once we believe in the Lord, we need to learn to know His will through the environment. Nothing that happens to us is a coincidence. Everything is measured by the Lord. Our career, spouse, parents, children, relatives, friends, and everything have been ordained by God. Behind everything that happens to us each day is God's sovereign arrangement. Therefore, we have to learn to read God's will in the environment. A new believer may not be that experienced in the leading of the Spirit, and he may not know that much of the teaching of the Scripture. But at least he can see God's hand in the environment. This is a believer's most basic lesson.

Psalm 32:9 says, "Do not be like a horse or like a mule, without understanding; / Whose trappings consist of bit and bridle to constrain them, / Else they do not come near you." Many times we are just like a horse or a mule, without understanding, and must be harnessed with outward bit and bridle by God before we can avoid mistakes. Have you ever seen a duck farmer? He has a long stick in his hand. When the ducks wander to the left or to the right, he herds them back with his stick. The ducks have no choice but to take the right path. In the same way, we can commit ourselves to the Lord and tell Him, "Lord, I am truly like a horse or a mule that has no understanding. But I do not want to make mistakes. I want to know Your will. Please harness me with Your bit and pull me with Your bridle. Once You let go of me, I will take the wrong way. Please guard me with Your will and direct me into Your will. If I wander away, I want You to stop me. I do not know many things, but I know what pain feels like. When I reject Your will, please come in and stop me!" Brothers and sisters, we must never belittle God's arrangement in the environment. Even though we may have fallen into shame and may have become like a horse or a mule, we often can still count on God's mercy to bridle us in time. God uses the environment to stop us from making mistakes. He forces us to have no alternative but to follow Him.

B. The Leading of the Holy Spirit

God's hand is seen through the environment. But He is not happy to always guide us like senseless horses or mules. He wants to guide us from within. Romans 8:14 says, "For as many as are led by the Spirit of God, these are sons of God." We are God's children and God's life is within us. God not only guides us through the environment but also speaks to us and guides us from within through His Spirit. The Spirit dwells within us, and God's will is revealed to us through our innermost being.

The book of Ezekiel tells us that God will "put a new spirit within you" (11:19). Again it says, "A new spirit will I put within you....I will put my Spirit within you" (36:26-27). We must distinguish between "a new spirit" and "my Spirit." "My Spirit" refers to the Spirit of God, whereas "a new spirit" refers to our spirit at the time of our regeneration. This new spirit is like a temple, a home where the Spirit of God dwells. If we did not have a new spirit within us, God would not have given us His Spirit, and the Holy Spirit could not have dwelt within us. Throughout the ages God has been trying to give man His Spirit. However, man's spirit was defiled, sin-ridden, dead, and fallen in the old creation. It was impossible for the Spirit of God to dwell in man even though this was His desire. Man has to receive a new spirit through regeneration before he can be in the position to receive God's Spirit and before God can dwell in him.

Once a new believer has a new spirit, the Spirit of God dwells in him. The Spirit of God spontaneously communicates to him His will; he spontaneously has an inner sense. Not only is he able to discern God's provision in the environment, but he also now possesses an inward knowledge and inward assurance. We should learn to trust not only in God's sovereignty in the environment but also in the leading of the Holy Spirit within. At the right time and when the need arises, the Spirit of God will enlighten us within. He will give us a sense and show us what is of God and what is not of God.

One brother loved to drink before he became a believer. Every winter, he would drink much wine. He even made his own wine. Later, both he and his wife were saved. He was not very literate and could not read the Bible very well. One day he prepared some food and wine and was going to drink as before. After thanking the Lord for the food, he asked his wife, "Can a Christian drink wine?" His wife said, "I do not know." He said, "Too bad no one is here to tell us." His wife said, "The wine and the food are ready. Let us go ahead today and ask others afterward." He gave thanks again but felt that something was not right. He thought that, as a Christian, he should find out whether Christians can take wine. He asked his wife to take out the Bible, but he did not know where to turn. He was stuck. Later, he met someone and told him about this incident. His friend asked whether or not he drank the wine that day. He answered, "In the end I did not drink it, because the *householder within* would not allow me. I did not drink the wine."

If a man has the desire to obey God's will, he will find out what this will is. Only those who are callous about their inner sense will remain in darkness. As long as one has the intention to obey God's will, the "householder within" will guide him. The householder that our brother spoke of is actually the Holy Spirit. When a person believes in the Lord, the Holy Spirit dwells within him. He guides the believer and becomes his Master. God reveals His will not only through the environment but also through the "householder within."

There are two kinds of leading of the Holy Spirit. The first is an inner urging, as in Acts 8:29 when "the Spirit said to Philip, Approach and join this chariot" and in Acts 10:19-20 when the Holy Spirit said to Peter, "Rise up, go down and go with them." These are inner urgings. The second kind of leading is an inner forbidding, as mentioned in Acts 16:6-7: "Having been forbidden by the Holy Spirit to speak the word in Asia. And when they had come to Mysia, they tried to go into Bithynia, yet the Spirit of Jesus did not allow them." This is the inner forbidding. The story of the "householder within" is a case of inner forbidding.

In order to know God's will, a new believer should be somewhat familiar with the inner sense. The Spirit of God dwells in the innermost part of man. Hence, the feeling of the Spirit is not something shallow or outward; it issues from the deepest part of man's being. It is a voice that is not quite a voice, a feeling that is not quite a feeling. The Spirit of God within shows us whether something is according to His will. Provided we have the divine life within, we will feel right when we act according to this life, and we will feel terrible and uneasy within if we disobey and deviate slightly from this life. A believer should live a life that yields to this life. We must not do things that will take away our inner peace. Whenever we sense any unrest, we should realize that the Holy Spirit within is displeased with what we are doing; He is grieved. If we do something that is contrary to the Lord, we will surely have no peace within. The more we go ahead with it, the less peace and joy we will have. If something is of the Lord, spontaneously we will have peace and joy.

However, do not overanalyze your inward feelings. If you keep analyzing whether or not something is right, you will be totally confused. Some people continue to ask what the feeling of the Holy Spirit is and what the feeling of the soul is. They are always analyzing whether something is right or wrong. This is very unhealthy; it is actually a spiritual sickness. It is very difficult to bring a self-analyzing person back to the proper path. I hope that you can avoid such a trap. Actually, a person analyzes only because he does not have enough light. If he has enough light, everything will be clear to him spontaneously, and he will not need to waste his energy on such analysis. If a person is sincere in trying to obey the Lord, it will be very easy for him to sense the inner leading.

C. The Teachings of the Scripture

God's will is not only revealed through the environment and made known through the indwelling Spirit; it is also revealed to us through the Bible.

God's will never changes. His will is revealed through the various experiences of men of the past, and all these things were recorded in the Bible. God's will is revealed in the form of principles and examples in the Bible. To know God's will, one must study the Bible carefully. The Bible is not a book of simple records, but a book rich in content. God's will is fully unveiled through the Scripture. One needs only to find what God has said in the past, and he will know what God's will is today. God's will never wavers. In Christ there is only one yes (2 Cor. 1:19). God's will for us never contradicts the teachings of the Bible. The Holy Spirit will never lead us to do something today that He has already condemned in the Bible.

God's word is a lamp to our feet and a light to our path (Psa. 119:105). If we want to understand God's will and His leading for us, we must study the Bible carefully and seriously.

God speaks to us through the Bible in two ways: One is through the teaching of biblical principles, and the other is through the promises in the Bible. We need the Spirit's enlightenment to understand biblical principles, and we need the Spirit's leading to receive biblical promises. For example, the Spirit may speak to us through the Lord's commandment in Matthew 28:19-20 that all Christians should preach the gospel. This teaching is a biblical principle. However, whether or not it is God's will for you to go to a certain place to preach the gospel depends on the leading of the Spirit. You still have to pray much and ask God for a specific word. When the Holy Spirit puts a certain phrase or verse within you in a powerful, fresh, and living way, you have a promise from the Spirit. This is how you identify God's will.

Some believers use superstitious ways to seek God's will. They open the Bible before them and pray, "O God, please move my finger to the verse which reveals Your will." After they pray with their eyes closed, they open their Bible and point their finger to any passage. Then they open their eyes and take the verse before them as God's will. Some childish believers try to know God this way. Because they are desperate, God will sometimes accommodate their ignorance and show them the way. However, this is definitely not the proper way. It will not work with most people, and it will not work most of the time. It is dangerous, and there is a great possibility for mistakes with this way. Brothers and sisters, please remember that we have the divine life and that God's Spirit is dwelling in us. We should ask God to reveal His word to us through the Holy Spirit. We should study the Bible conscientiously and consistently and memorize the Scripture well. When needs arise, the Holy Spirit will use the passages we have read to speak to us and to guide us.

Let us now combine the three things spoken of above. There is no fixed order for these three things. Sometimes, the arrangement of the environment comes first, followed by the leading of the Spirit and the teachings of the Bible. Sometimes, the Spirit's leading and the teachings of the Bible come first, and afterward, the confirmation in the environment. The environment is related especially to God's timing. In seeking after God's will, Brother George Müller always asked three questions: (1) Is it God's work? (2) Am I the person to do this work? (3) Is this God's time for such a work to be done? The first and second questions can be resolved by the teaching of the Bible and the leading of the Spirit. The third question is settled by provisions in the environment.

If we want to be sure that our inward feeling is the leading of the Spirit, we should also ask two questions: (1) Does this leading match the teaching of the Bible? (2) Does the environment confirm this leading? If such a leading does not match the teaching of the Bible, it cannot be God's will. If the environment does not give any confirmation, we should wait. Our feeling may be wrong, or it may not be the Lord's timing.

In seeking God's will, we should cultivate a healthy fear of making mistakes. We should not be subjective. We can ask God to block the ways that are not according to His will.

Suppose someone has invited you to work, and you have the intention to do a certain thing, or someone has advised you to reconsider your future, etc. How can you know whether these things are according to God's will? First, you should look at the teaching of the Bible. You should find out what God has actually said about such matters in His Word. After this, you should check with your inner feeling. The Bible may teach this, but do you feel right within? If your inward feeling is different from the testimony of the Bible, it proves that your inward feeling is not reliable. You should continue to wait and seek the Lord. If your inward leading agrees with the testimony of the Bible, you should lift up your head and say, "O Lord, You have always revealed Your will through the environment. It is impossible for my inward feeling and the teaching of the Bible to both point to one direction, and yet have the environment point to a contrary direction. Lord! Please work in the environment and line it up with the Scripture's teaching and the Spirit's leading." You will see that God always reveals His will through the environment. Not one sparrow will fall to the earth if it is not God's will. If it is God's will, what you see outwardly will surely line up with what you see inwardly and what you see from the Bible. If your inward sense, the teaching of the Bible, and the environment are all clear, then God's will for you will also be clear.

III. THE CONFIRMATION OF THE CHURCH AND OTHER FACTORS

God's will is revealed through His Word, man's spirit, and the environment. God's will is also revealed through the church. In seeking God's will concerning a certain matter, you should be clear about the Spirit's leading, the Scripture's teaching, and the environment's provision. As much as it is possible, you should also fellowship with those who know God in the church to see whether they will say amen to your guidance. This will give you additional confirmation concerning God's will. These ones know God's Word more, their flesh has been dealt with somewhat, and they are under the direction of the Spirit. Their spiritual condition allows God to speak His heart more freely through them. They will consider your condition in the church, and they will sense whether or not they can say amen to what you have seen. If they can say amen, you can be sure that what you have is God's will. If they cannot say amen to it, it is better for you to wait and seek more guidance. As individuals, we are limited. An individual's personal feeling, understanding of the Scripture, and knowledge of the environment may be wrong; they may not be that accurate. The church is much more reliable in this respect. If the other members of the church think that the "guidance" you have is not reliable, you should not insist on your opinion. Do not think that your "guidance" is always reliable. In such cases we should learn to be humble.

Matthew 18 speaks of the principle of the church. If a brother sins against another brother, the offended one should speak to the offending one while they are alone with each other. If the offending party does not want to listen, the offended party should take with him one or two more. By the mouth of two or three witnesses, every word may be established. If the offending party still refuses to listen, the matter should be told to the church. In the end the offending one has to hear the church. We have to accept the feeling of the church. The Lord Jesus says, "Whatever you bind on the earth shall have been bound in heaven, and whatever you loose on the earth shall have been loosed in heaven" (v. 18). Because the church is God's habitation and the beacon of God's light, we need to believe that God's will is revealed in the church. We should humble ourselves and should be afraid of our own judgment. This is why we need to fellowship with the church and receive the supply of the Body.

The church has a heavy responsibility before God. It has to act as God's light. If the church is careless or if it does things loosely according to the flesh, it will be impossible to have such a thing as the confirmation of the church. The church can render an accurate and divine confirmation because it has become the mouthpiece of the Holy Spirit. The church must be spiritual, and it must allow the Spirit to preside over it before it can be used by the Spirit to be God's mouthpiece. The confirmation of the church does not mean a discussion among all the brothers and sisters in the church together. It means the speaking of a group of people who know God and who are being led by the Spirit. For this reason, the elders taking responsibility in the church, as well as those given to the Lord's work, must have a certain amount of knowledge of spiritual things. Their flesh must be dealt with to a certain extent. They must be watchful at all times and have unceasing fellowship with the Lord. They must be full of God's presence and must live under the direction of the Holy Spirit. Only then can there be accurate judgment, and only then will the Spirit give accurate confirmation through them.

Some people may quote Galatians 1:16-17, which says that when Paul received a revelation, he did not confer with flesh and blood, neither did he go up to Jerusalem to see those who were apostles before him. They think that it is sufficient for them to be clear by themselves and that there is no need to fellowship with the church. No doubt a person with a clear revelation like Paul can be truly confident of what he sees. But have you received the revelation the way Paul received his? Even Paul received the Lord's help and supply through other brothers. He saw the great light on the way to Damascus, fell to the ground, and heard what the Lord said to him alone: "Rise up and enter into the city, and *it will be told to you what you must do.*" He received the laying on of hands from an obscure brother named Ananias, and he also received the laying on of hands and the commissioning from co-workers in the church in Antioch (Acts 9:3-6, 12; 13:1-3). The words he spoke in Galatians 1 were to prove that the gospel announced by him was not according to man, but that he had "received it through a revelation by Jesus Christ" (vv. 11-12). There is no flavor of self-exaltation in such words. We should be humble and not intractable. We must not think highly of ourselves. The fact is that we are too far behind Paul to compare ourselves to him! Because we are the party involved, we are clouded by our own interests and subjectivity when we seek God's will. It is difficult for us to see things clearly. This is where the church comes in; it can supply us and render us much help. This is why we should seek confirmation from the church when we are in need.

However, we should avoid another extreme. Some Christians are too passive. They ask the church about everything, and they want others to make decisions for them. This is against the principle of the New Testament. We cannot treat a group of spiritual people in the church as if they were the prophets in the Old Testament, asking them for advice in everything. First John 2:27 says, "And as for you, the anointing which you have received from Him abides in you, and you have no need that anyone teach you; but as His anointing teaches you concerning all things..." This anointing is the indwelling Holy Spirit. We can never replace the teaching of the anointing with the confirmation of the church. The confirmation of the church should not be regarded in the same way as one regards the words of the prophets. Its purpose is to confirm what we see so that we can be more assured of God's will. It is a protection rather than a replacement of an individual's pursuit of God's will.

We should note one other point: This way of seeking God's will should be applied only to important matters. As to the trivial affairs of daily life, we do not need to resort to such a method. We can make judgments according to our common sense. Our God has not eradicated our common sense. God wants us to make our own judgments concerning things that we can manage with our common sense. We need to employ this method only in seeking God's will concerning the more important matters of our life.

In seeking God's will, we must not fall into an abnormal state where the mind is blank and the will is passive. Hebrews 5:14 speaks of those "who because of practice have their faculties exercised for discriminating between both good and evil." We need to exercise our mind and will. We have to put our will on God's side and co-labor with God. It is true that we should put aside our own will. But it is wrong to annul the function of the mind and the will, allowing them to be passive and void of function. Many people trust only in their intellect and not in God. This is a big mistake. But many people think that relying on God means that one does not need to use his mind. This is also a big mistake. When Luke wrote his gospel, it was "carefully investigated" (1:3). In Romans 12:2 Paul told us to "be transformed by the renewing of the mind that you may prove what the will of God is." In seeking God's will, we need to use our mind and our will. Of course, this mind and will have to be transformed and renewed by the Holy Spirit.

We need to briefly touch on the matter of visions and dreams as well. In the Old Testament God revealed His will to man through visions and dreams. In the New Testament there are also visions and dreams, but God does not use them as an essential means of guidance. In the New Testament the Spirit of God dwells in us and speaks to us directly from within. The chief and common means of guidance are the inward leading. God will lead us by dreams and visions only when He has something very important to say and it would not be easy for us to accept this leading under normal circumstances. In the New Testament visions and dreams are not the usual means of God's leading. Therefore, even when we have visions and dreams, we should still safeguard ourselves by seeking the inward confirmation and the confirmation in the environment. For example, Acts 10 shows us that God wanted Peter to preach the gospel to the Gentiles. Peter, being a Jew, would never go to the Gentiles according to his tradition. In order to turn him from this prejudice, God had to show him a vision. After Peter saw the vision, Cornelius sent three men to him. This was the confirmation in the environment. At the same time there was also the speaking of the Holy Spirit. These internal and environmental confirmations assured him that he was acting according to God's will.

Of course, there are cases when one has little time to consider or wait. At such times one can prove God's will immediately if the vision or dream is clear and obvious and the feeling within approves it; there is no need to wait for the confirmation in the environment. For example, Paul was in a trance when he was praying in the temple. He saw the Lord speaking to him and charging him to leave Jerusalem without delay. At first he reasoned with the Lord and tried to refuse. But the Lord said to him again, "Go, for I will send you forth far away to the Gentiles" (Acts 22:17-21). Later, Paul met a heavy storm at sea, and all hope of salvation was gone. God sent His angel to stand beside him and speak to him, telling him not to fear (27:23-24). These were all clear visions. But they do not occur frequently in the New Testament. God revealed things to His children in visions and dreams only when there was a special need. Some Christians have so many so-called dreams and visions that these are like everyday meals to them. This is a kind of spiritual sickness. It may come from some kind of nervous disorder, attack from Satan, or deception from evil spirits. Whatever the cause, this situation is abnormal.

In conclusion, God leads men by many ways. Everyone is different in his spiritual condition and needs. This is why God leads us in different ways. However, His main means are the arrangement in the environment, the inward leading, and the teachings in the Bible. We need to point out once again that when these three things are in line with one another, we can have the confidence that we have God's will.

IV. THOSE WHO ARE QUALIFIED TO KNOW GOD'S WILL

Finally, even if we have all the right methods, not everyone

knows God's will. A right method is useful only when the
person is also right. When the person is not right, even the
right methods become useless. It is futile for a rebellious man
to seek to know God's will. If a man wants to know God's will,
he must have an inward yearning to do His will.

Deuteronomy 15:17 records the case of a slave who had his
ear run through with an awl into the door. This shows that
our ears have to listen to God's word all the time if we are to
serve Him. We should come to the Lord and say, "I am willing
to thrust my ear to the door. I will incline my ears to Your
word. I want to serve You and do Your will. I beseech You from
my heart. I will serve You. You are my Master. I have an earnest
yearning within my heart to be Your slave. Let me hear Your
word. Let me know Your will." We need to come before the
Lord and plead for His word. We have to incline our ears and
thrust them to the door. We have to wait for His commission
and listen to His command.

Many times my heart aches over the fact that many people
are looking for methods to know God's will, but they have no
desire to obey God's will. They merely study such methods for
the sake of knowledge. They have their own desires. They
merely take God as their counselor and His will as their ref-
erence point. Brothers and sisters, God's will is made known
only to those who are determined to obey His will! "If anyone
resolves to do His will, he will know" (John 7:17). In order to
know God's will, one must resolve to do His will. If you have
an intense and absolute desire to do God's will, God will make
known His will to you even when you know nothing about the
methods. There is a word in the Bible: "For the eyes of the
Lord run to and fro throughout the whole earth, to show Himself strong in the behalf of them whose heart is perfect toward
Him" (2 Chron. 16:9). The literal translation of this verse is,
"For the eyes of the Lord run to and fro throughout the whole
earth, to show Himself strong on behalf of those whose heart
is completely inclined towards Him." His eyes are running to
and fro, from here to there. His eyes do not run through just
once. Rather, they run continually to and fro to see whether
anyone's heart is after His will. He will appear to those whose
heart is completely inclined toward Him. If your heart is

completely inclined toward the Lord and you say, "Lord, I want Your will; I really want it," God will show you His will. He will not refrain from revealing Himself to you; He has to reveal Himself to you. We should not think that only those who have believed in the Lord for a long time can understand His will. We hope that every believer will offer up everything he has from the day that he is saved. This will pave the way for him to understand God's will.

We should never think that it is a trivial thing to know God's will. We are little worms in God's eyes. It is a tremendous thing for a tiny person like us to understand God's will! May we see that it is a glorious thing to understand God's will. Since God has humbled Himself to make His will known to man, we must seek to know His will, and we must worship, treasure, and do His will.

CHAPTER TWENTY-EIGHT

MANAGING ONE'S FINANCES

Scripture Reading: Luke 6:38; 1 Tim. 6:7-10, 17-19; 2 Cor. 9:6;
Mal. 3:10; Prov. 11:24; Phil. 4:15-19

I. MANAGING ACCORDING TO GOD'S PRINCIPLES

In this chapter we will cover monetary offering and giving.
After a person has sold everything, he will still receive
income; money will still find its way back to his hand. How
should he manage his money? Even after a person has offered
up all of his money, we should not think that money will no
longer have an influence on him. Some people can give away
their money all at once, but money can gradually regain its
power over them. Eventually, they will consider their money
to be their own once again. Therefore, a believer must learn to
continually let go of his money.

The Christian way of managing wealth is completely
different from that of an unbeliever. The Christian way of
financial management is the way of giving. The unbeliever's
way is the way of accumulating. Today we are concerned with
how a Christian should live in order to be free from want. God
has promised us that we will have no lack on earth. The birds
of the air have no lack of food, and the flowers of the field
have no lack of clothing. Even so God's children should have
no lack of clothing and food. If they have any lack, there must
be a reason or cause for it. If a brother is financially hard-
pressed, he is not managing his wealth according to God's
principle.

After you have forsaken all of your possessions to follow
the Lord, you should walk according to God's principle. If you
do not follow God's principle, you will eventually end up in

poverty. There is a great need for many of God's children to learn to manage their wealth. If they do not learn to manage their wealth, they should expect nothing except hardship in the way ahead of them. Today we want to consider the way to attain God's prosperity.

II. GOD'S PROVISION BEING CONDITIONAL

As believers we have to look to the Lord for our food, clothing, and other needs while we live on earth today. Without God's mercy, we cannot pass through our days on earth. This is true even for the rich ones; they have to look to the Lord also. During World War II, we saw many rich people stripped of clothing and food. One day many people will be in remorse over their wealth. Paul warned us not to depend on unpredictable riches. A greedy person is always an anxious person. Those who trust in the Lord may not have much in the way of savings, but the Lord will not leave them in difficulties. He can supply all their needs. However, we must also realize that God's supply is with conditions.

If God can feed the birds in the air, He can keep us alive. In reality, no one can feed all the birds or supply enough fertilizer to grow all the lilies of the field. But God has enough riches to keep the birds of the air and the lilies of the field alive. He also has enough riches to keep His children alive. God does not want to see us come short in anything. He does not want our living to be deprived in any way. Everyone who falls into deprivation falls because he has a problem in himself; he has not managed his wealth according to God's way. If we manage our money according to God's law, we will not be in poverty.

Let us read Luke 6:38. This portion of the Word describes the type of person God will supply. God is always willing to supply. When He supplies us, the supply can come in such abundance that it comes out of our mouth and even becomes loathsome to us, as described in Exodus. God has no problem in doing such a thing. We should never think that God is poor. The cattle upon a thousand hills are His, and the goats upon ten thousand hills are His. If everything belongs to Him, why are God's children poor? Why do His children experience lack? It is not because God cannot supply. Rather, we need to meet His requirements before we can receive His supply. We need to meet certain conditions before our prayers can be answered. Even our salvation had certain requirements to it—we had to believe. Every promise has conditions, and we must fulfill these conditions before we can receive the promise. Likewise, we need to fulfill God's requirements before we can receive His supply. His requirement is to give. The Lord says, "Give, and it will be given to you."

III. GIVE, AND IT WILL BE GIVEN

I have seen a few brothers and sisters who fell into dire need because they were unfaithful in the matter of giving. They were not actually lacking in income. The Bible shows us a fundamental principle—one must give to become rich and one becomes poor by accumulating riches. Whoever cares only for himself is destined to be in poverty. Whoever learns to give is destined to have riches. God's Word says it, and it is true. If we want to escape poverty, we have to give again and again. The more we give, the more God will give to us. Since we are willing to share our surplus with others, others will also be happy to share their surplus with us in the future. If we give one-twentieth to others, others will also give one-twentieth to us. If we give one-thousandth to others, others will also give one-thousandth to us.

With what measure we measure to others, with the same measure others will measure to us. In what capacity we treat our brothers and sisters, with the same capacity God will treat us. If we are willing to sacrifice our livelihood, others will also sacrifice their livelihood for us. If we only give others that which is totally useless, things which we never use, others will certainly give us totally useless and unusable things. Many people have problems with their income because they have problems with their giving. If a person has no problem with his giving, it is hard to imagine that he will have problems with his income. God's Word is quite clear. If we give to others, the Lord will give to us. If we do not give to others, the Lord will not give to us. Most people only exercise faith when they ask God for money; they do not exercise faith in giving money. It is no wonder that they have no faith to receive anything from God.

Brothers, as soon as we become Christians, we have to learn the basic lesson of financial stewardship. Christians have a unique way of managing their wealth: What we receive depends on what we give. In other words, the Christian way of financial stewardship is to receive according to what we give. Worldly people give according to what they have received, but we receive according to what we give. Our inflow depends on our outflow. Those who crave money and cling to it can never receive God's money; they will never receive any supply from God.

We should all look to the Lord for our needs, but God will supply the needs of only one type of people—those who give. The words *good measure,* which the Lord uses in Luke 6:38, are wonderful words. When God gives to man, He is never stingy. He is ever generous and overflowing. Our God is always generous. Our God's cup is always running over. God is never petty. When He gives, He says that it will be a good measure, pressed down, and shaken together. Consider the way in which we buy rice. Most rice merchants will not let us shake the measure. They do not allow the rice to settle before pouring it out. But the Lord said, "Pressed down, shaken together." Not only so, it is "running over." Our God is such a generous God. He gives by pressing down, shaking together, heaping up, and running over. However, He also says that with what measure we measure to others, it will be measured to us in return. If we are shrewd and exact in giving to others, God will only touch others to give to us in a shrewd and exact way.

We must give first to others, before others will give to us. Most people never learn to give. They always want God to answer their prayers. We have to give first before we can receive. If we have not received anything recently, it means that we have a problem in giving. I have been a Christian for more than twenty years, and I can surely bear witness to this principle. Whenever a person has a problem with his giving, he will experience a lack.

IV. TWO TESTIMONIES CONCERNING FINANCIAL STEWARDSHIP

A. Handley Moule's Story

Handley C. G. Moule of England was the chief editor of the magazine *Life and Faith*. He was a great man before the Lord in many ways. One of his outstanding achievements was his knowledge of the Bible. He trusted in the Lord for his living. Throughout his life, he experienced wants and trials many times, but because he knew Luke 6:38, he would tell his wife whenever he was in need, "There must be something wrong with our giving lately." He did not speak of the need in his house. Instead, his thoughts were on his giving.

Once his house was almost empty of everything. He did not even have flour, the main staple of the English diet. He waited for two days, but no one brought him anything. He then told his wife, "There must be something in our house that we do not need." He did not ask the Lord for flour. Instead he said, "There must be something excessive in our house. This is why the Lord does not give." They knelt and prayed and asked the Lord to show them any excess they had in the house. After praying, they looked through every item. They began with the attic, checking to see whether or not a particular item was redundant. They even went through their children's belongings and found that they had just enough of what they needed. Mr. Moule then told the Lord, "There is truly nothing excessive in this house. Lord, You have made a mistake in not supplying us with what we need." After a brief pause, he told his wife, "The Lord never makes mistakes. There has to be some excess in our house." They checked again. When they came to the cellar, they saw a carton of butter, which had been given to them many days earlier. Mr. Moule was happy when he saw the carton. He told his wife, "This must be the excess."

Both of them were rather elderly. They had for many years learned the lesson of giving. They knew the Lord's words: "Give, and it will be given to you." They were anxious to give away the carton of butter. But who should they give it to? Mr. Moule was a responsible brother in his church. After looking down the list of brothers and sisters who were poor, he decided to give every one of them a piece. The old couple cut the carton of butter into small pieces, wrapped them up, and sent them to these brothers and sisters. After sending out all the packets, he told his wife, "Now, we have cleared up this matter." They then knelt down and prayed, "Lord, may we remind You of what You have said: 'Give, and it will be given to you.' Please remember that we have no more flour."

That was perhaps a Saturday. Among those who had received the butter, there was a very poor sister who had been paralyzed and bed-ridden for years. For days, she had been eating her bread without butter and had been praying, "Lord, have mercy on me. Give me a little butter." Soon after this prayer, Mr. Moule came with the butter. She immediately thanked the Lord for this. A while later, she lifted up her head and prayed again, "Lord, although Brother Moule lacks nothing and has given me this butter, hear his prayer if he has any lack." Brother Moule had not told anyone about his lack, and no one knew about it. Some even rumored that Moule was a very rich brother, that he always gave things away, and that he had bought all that butter purposely to distribute to others. But this sister prayed, "If he has any lack, please answer his prayer." On that same day, probably within two or three hours, Mr. Moule received two sacks of flour. His problem was solved.

We have to believe in every word of the Lord. Most people have difficulty taking God's Word as God's word. Mr. Moule believed God's Word to be God's word. If you do not give, you definitely will not receive. If you give to others, others will surely give to you. This is why we need to learn to give. Giving is not the end; it enables God to give to us. This is the principle of Christian financial stewardship. Do not expect God to supply you with anything if there is excess in your house.

A co-worker once told me, "During the past twenty years, every time money has remained in my hand, there has always been a problem." If there is a problem in giving, there will be a problem in receiving. The more you want to keep, the less you will have. The more you want to give, the more you will have. Most people hold on tightly to all that they have, and so

God lets them hold on to that little amount. They have not learned to give. If the grace of giving is not in you, the grace of God will not be upon you. If you do not have grace for others, you will have little of God's grace for yourself.

B. Learning the First Lesson of Giving

I can give you many testimonies concerning giving. But I do not wish to do so. I will just speak about my first lesson in this matter. In 1923 Brother Weigh Kwang-hsi invited me to his place, Kien-ou, which was about one hundred fifty miles from Foochow. I was a student, and Brother Weigh was my classmate. When I was about to leave for Kien-ou, I asked Brother Weigh, "How much is the fare?" He said, "The fare by boat is several dozen dollars." I then said, "Let me pray about this. If the Lord wants me to go, I will go."

At that time I did not have any money in my hand. I prayed, "If You want me to go, You must provide me the money." After praying this way, the Lord gave me between ten and twenty dollars. In addition, I had more than a hundred silver dimes. But the total amount still fell short of the fare by more than half. Not long after this, Brother Weigh wrote me a letter and told me that everything was ready. I sent him a telegram and told him that I would go. I decided to leave on Friday. On Thursday I rose up early, and the word came to me: "Give, and it will be given to you." I was unsure within. If I gave my money to others and the Lord did not give any back, I would then not be able to go. I was quite troubled.

However, my feeling within grew stronger and stronger. I felt that I should give the dollars and keep the coins. Therefore, I thought about who should be given the money. Eventually, I had the thought of giving the dollars to a certain brother who had a family. I dared not tell the Lord that I would obey, and I dared not tell the Lord that I would disobey either. I just said, "Lord, I am here. If You want me to give to this brother, please let me meet him on my way." I rose up and walked out of the house. Along the way I met the brother. As soon as I saw him, my heart sank. But I was prepared. I went over to him and said, "Brother, the Lord has told me to place this in your hands." After I said this, I turned around and left.

When I was two steps away from him, my tears began to roll down. I said, "I have sent a telegram to Brother Weigh that I would go. Now the money is gone. How can I go?" But I also felt very happy within because the Lord said, "Give, and it will be given to you."

On my way home I said to the Lord, "Lord, You need to give to me. The time is short, and the boat is leaving tomorrow." No money came on Thursday. On Friday when I was about to leave, there was still no money. A brother came to send me off. But there was still no money. The brother took me aboard the boat. As soon as I stepped aboard the boat, I thought to myself, "I cannot go. I will never make it. I have never left Foochow before, and I have never gone inland. I do not know a single person west of Foochow." I had been praying since I left home that day. When I went aboard the boat I was still praying. I prayed until the brother left, and even until I laid down to sleep. I said, "Lord, I have given to others. Yet You have not given to me in return. It is now Your business." That day the boat took me to Hung-Shan Bridge, where I changed boats to Shui-Kou. While on board, I paced back and forth from the upper deck to the lower deck several times, thinking to myself, "In order for God to provide for me, I should make it easier for Him by walking around a few more times to see if He has arranged for me to meet someone." But this did not work out, and I did not find anyone whom I knew on the boat. Nevertheless, I repeated to myself, "Give, and it will be given to you."

This went on until the next day. At about four or five o'clock, the boat was about to reach Shui-Kou. After Shui-Kou, I had to change transportation again for a more expensive ship. After I paid the boat fare, I found out that I had only a little more than seventy dimes left. I was troubled, and I prayed, "Lord, I am now in Shui-Kou. Should I buy a ticket to return to Foochow?" Right then I resolved in my mind to simply go to Kien-ou and leave the rest to the Lord. I said, "Lord, I will not ask for money as long as You will take me to Kien-ou." After praying this way, I felt peaceful.

I was standing on the bow of the boat, and before the boat reached Shui-Kou, a little boat approached and the boatman asked me, "Sir, are you going to Nan-Ping or Kien-ou?" I said, "To Kien-ou." He said, "I will take you there." I asked him how much it would cost, and he said, "Seventy dimes." When I heard that, I knew the Lord had prepared the way for me. I agreed to go with him. He carried my luggage to his boat. The regular fare to Kien-ou was seventy or eighty dollars. I asked him, "Why are you letting me go so cheaply?" He replied, "The fare is so cheap because this boat has been chartered by a county officer. He is in the front cabin of the boat, and he has given me permission to carry another passenger so that I can earn some money to supplement my food." I clearly remember that day; I bought some vegetables and meat with the little money that was left and arrived at Kien-ou safely.

As the time for my return from Kien-ou grew near, I was once again in a quandary. I had only twelve dimes left. After spending about a dollar on shopping, I had only twenty cents left. I kept praying as the conference was coming to an end. One day Mr. Philips, one of the famous Cambridge Seven, invited me for a meal. He said, "Mr. Nee, we have been greatly helped by your visit. Is it all right for me to take care of the traveling expenses of your return trip?" When I heard this, I was overjoyed. But I felt it was not proper for me to accept the offer. I said, "Someone has already taken care of it." When he heard this, he said, "I am sorry to hear that," and did not mention the matter again. When I returned home, I regretted very much turning down the offer. But when I prayed I had peace within.

I waited for another day. On the third day, as I was getting ready to leave, I only had twenty cents in my pocket. This was not enough for the ticket. I was really in a dilemma. Brother Weigh's father and family all came to see me off. My luggage had already been taken away by the porter, and Brother Weigh was walking with me. I prayed, "Lord, You have brought me to Kien-ou. You have to bring me back home. It is Your responsibility and You cannot leave it to others. If I have committed any mistake, I am willing to confess it. But I do not believe that I have done anything wrong." I kept saying, "This is Your responsibility because You have said, 'Give, and it will be given to you.'" Halfway to the pier, Mr. Philips sent someone to me with a letter. I opened the letter, and it said, "I know someone is responsible for your fare. But God has impressed upon me that I should share your expenses. Please allow an elderly brother to have a little share in this and accept this small sum." I took the money and said to the Lord, "God, this has come right on time." I paid the fare with the money, and I still remember that there was enough money to print another issue of *The Present Testimony* when I returned home.

Upon my return I looked up my co-worker. As soon as I entered his house, his wife said, "Mr. Nee, when you left Foochow, why did you give my husband twenty dollars? Why did you walk away immediately after handing him the money?" I said, "There was only one reason: I had prayed for a whole day, and the Lord told me to give it to him. When I left my house and met him on the way, I simply gave him the money." She said, "That night we only had enough for one last meal. When your money came, we bought a load of rice and many pounds of firewood. The Lord did not supply us any more money until a few days ago. We had prayed and waited for three days on that occasion." I left without telling her my story. As I was walking down the hill, I said within myself, "It was good that I did not keep the twenty dollars for myself. The money would have died if I had kept it in my pocket. But now that it has been given away, it has become useful." I lifted up my head then and told the Lord, "This is the first time I have understood Luke 6:38." I consecrated myself to the Lord once again and said, "From this day forward, I will give. I will not let a single cent remain idle in my hand."

I only wish I could give more money so that it would work more miracles for the Lord. I would give money so that the prayers of others may be answered. I do not wish to hold on to my money, letting it remain idle and useless. I dare not brag about my experience in giving. Perhaps I have given a little more than others. Perhaps I have also received a little more than others. But this I can say: In the whole of China, it is hard to find another person who has received as much and given away as much as I have. You may take this as a word from "a fool" (2 Cor. 11:23, KJV). I would rather let my money work miracles and let it become answers to prayers, than see it remain idle and become useless. If I have no use for it today, I will give it away. When I have a need, it will come back, and when it comes back, it will come back more than what I gave.

A new believer must learn to manage his finances from the very beginning. I do not like to tell many stories about myself. However, I must testify that since 1923, I am behind no one in China with respect to using my last dollar. The Lord said, "Give, and it will be given to you." I am learning this constantly. As I give to others, the Lord meets my needs. I am convinced that a man will only receive when he gives. Time and again, I find that when I give liberally, the Lord liberally gives to me. I do not mind having the reputation of being rich. It is true; I am rich, because I always give. I always let my money go. It never stops, and when it returns to me, it is always multiplied many times. Our God is never stingy.

V. THE CHRISTIAN WAY OF FINANCIAL MANAGEMENT

The Christian way of managing money is not to hold on to money. The tighter you hold on to your money, the more it dies. The more you grasp it, the more it disappears; it will evaporate like vapor. But the more you give away, the more you will have. If God's children would learn to give more, God would have many ways to work out His miracles. Keeping back money only makes God's children poor. God will not entrust Himself to those who hold on to their money and who will not give. The more you give, the more God will give to you.

A. Sowing with One's Money

Please read 2 Corinthians 9:6, which says, "He who sows sparingly shall also sparingly reap; and he who sows with blessings shall also with blessings reap." This is also a scriptural principle of financial management. When Christians give, they are not throwing their money away; they are sowing. The Word does not say, "He who throws away his money sparingly shall also sparingly reap; and he who throws away his money with blessings shall also with blessings reap." It says, "He who sows sparingly shall also sparingly reap; and he who sows with blessings shall also with blessings reap." When you give, you are sowing. Do you want your money to grow? If you do, you need to sow. When you give your money away, it grows. When you do not give it away, it does not grow.

Brothers and sisters, can anyone be so foolish as to expect a harvest without sowing? How many times has God not answered your prayer for your needs? You are a "hard man," trying to reap where you have not sown and gather where you have not winnowed. This is impossible. Why do you not sow some of your money? There are many brothers and sisters who are in difficulty. Why do you not sow money upon them so that you may reap when the reaping time comes? The more a person holds on to his money, the less he will have. In the above portion of the Word, we see a very beautiful picture. The Corinthians gave to those in Jerusalem, remembering their needs, and Paul said that it was a kind of sowing, not a kind of throwing away. Please remember that money can be our seeds. If you see a brother or sister in difficulty, and you remember him or her, God will cause that money to grow and harvest thirtyfold, sixtyfold, and even a hundredfold. I hope that more of your money will be sown.

A new believer should learn to sow, so that when he has needs, he can reap what he has sown. You cannot reap what you have not sown. There are many brothers who are getting poorer and poorer. If you eat what you have, of course, there will not be anything left. But if you keep half of your seed for sowing, you will have a harvest next year. If next year you also keep half for planting, you will have another harvest the following year. If you want to sow anything, you must not eat all that you have. Some people always eat and never sow. They also never receive anything when they are in need. Suppose some young brothers sow some money upon other brothers, praying as they sow, "O God, I have sown upon the brothers. When I have needs, I want to harvest." If they do this, God will honor His own words.

B. Offering to God

This is not all. In the Old Testament, God said to the Israelites, "Bring the whole tithe to the storehouse that there may be food in My house; and prove Me, if you will, by this, says Jehovah of hosts, whether I will open to you the windows of heaven and pour out blessing for you until there is no room for it" (Mal. 3:10). Here we see the same principle.

At that time, the Israelites were in great poverty and difficulty. How could they carry out the words of Malachi 3:10? The Israelites might have asked, "If we cannot get by with ten loads of rice, how can we get by with nine? If ten bags of flour are insufficient, how can nine bags be sufficient?" These are words out of a carnal and foolish mouth. God reproached the people and told them that what is impossible with man is possible with God. He seemed to be saying, "Bring to My storehouse, and test Me if I will not open for you the windows of heaven and pour out for you a blessing that there shall not be enough room to receive it."

Ten loads are the reason for poverty, while nine loads are the cause for abundance. Man thinks that the more he has in his hand, the better off he will be. However, keeping things in one's hand is the very cause for poverty, while offering things to God is the very cause for blessing. If I have an additional load in my hands, it will become my curse. But if it is put in God's storehouse, it becomes my blessing. The principle with the Israelites was poverty for those who tried to hold back what was due to God. When you hold something back, you end up in poverty.

C. Scattering Money

Now read Proverbs 11:24: "There is that scattereth, and yet increaseth; / and there is that withholdeth more than is meet, but it tendeth to poverty." Many people have not scattered, and they are left with nothing. Many people have scattered, and they become prosperous. This is what God's Word shows us. This is the Christian principle of managing finances.

D. Giving All for God

Consider another wonderful portion of the Word—Elijah's prayer for rain on Mount Carmel (1 Kings 18). There was a drought, and it was so dry that even the king and his chamberlains had to go out to search for water. Elijah was repairing the altar on the mountain. He wanted to offer a sacrifice, and he asked men to pour water on the altar and the sacrifice.

How precious was water at that time! Even the king had to go out to look for water. But Elijah told the men to pour out the water. He told them to pour it three times until the water ran round about the altar like a river. Was it not a waste to pour out so much water before any rain came? Would it not have been a pity if no rain came after they poured out so much water? But Elijah told them to bring jars of water and pour them out. Next he knelt down and asked God to send fire to burn the sacrifice. God heard his prayer, received the sacrifice by fire, and sent the rain. We must first pour the water out before rain will come. The rain will not come if we are reluctant to pour out the water.

The problem of many people is that they hold on tightly to what they have and yet expect God to answer their prayers. Although God wanted to dispel the drought, man had to pour out the water first. The human thought is always to have some backup. If no rain came, at least there would be some jars of water. But those who count the jars of water on hand will never see rain. To see the rain, one must be like Elijah, willing to part with the water that is on hand. Everything has to go. If new believers are not delivered from the power and grip of money, the church will never be able to run a straight course. I hope that you will be a consecrated person and will offer up everything you have for God.

E. The Promise of Supply

Philippians 4:19 is a very special verse. The Corinthians were parsimonious in giving, while the Philippians were very generous. Paul received from the Philippians time and again. He told the Philippians, "My God will fill your every need according to His riches, in glory, in Christ Jesus." Do you see something special in Philippians 4? Paul emphasized, "*My God* will fill your every need." The God who receives the money and the gifts will supply the needs of the givers.

This is very clear. The Philippians had been caring for Paul again and again, and Paul's God supplied their needs. God will never supply those who do not give. Today many people hold on to Philippians 4:19, but they do not really understand it, because God does not supply those who ask, but those who give. Only those who give can claim Philippians 4:19. Those who do not give cannot claim this promise. You must give before you can say, "O God, today supply all my needs according to Your riches in Christ Jesus." God supplied all the needs for only the Philippians. God will only supply the needs of those who are practicing the principle of giving.

When your vessel is empty of flour and when your bottle is empty of oil, please remember that you must first make bread for Elijah with what little you have left. You must first feed God's servant. Take the little oil and flour and make bread for the prophet first. After a while, this little flour and oil will feed you for three and a half years. Who has ever heard of a bottle of oil feeding a person for three and a half years? But let me tell you, if you take your little flour and oil and make bread for the prophet, you will find the bottle of oil feeding you for three and a half years (cf. Luke 4:25-26; 1 Kings 17:8-16). What one has may not be enough to feed him even once. But when it is given away, it becomes the means of one's livelihood. This is the Christian way of financial management.

VI. LETTING GO OF OUR MONEY

Both the New Testament and the Old Testament teach us the same thing. The Christian way should not be the way of poverty. God does not want us to be poor. If there is poverty or want among us, it is because some people are holding back their money. The more you love yourself, the more you will go hungry. The more importance you attach to money, the poorer you will become. I may not be able to testify of other things, but I can surely testify of this one thing. The more one holds back his money, the more miserable and depleted he becomes. This is a sure principle. During the past twenty years, I have seen many such cases. I only wish that we could release our money and allow it to circulate around the earth, to work, and to become part of God's miracles and answers to prayers. Then when we have needs, God will supply us.

Not only are we in God's hands, but Satan is also in His hands. The cattle on a thousand hills and the sheep on ten thousand hills are His. Only foolish ones think that they have earned their own money. A new believer must see that tithing is our duty. We should give what we earn to take care of the poor saints. Do not be so foolish as to always receive. Do not try to save up your money or hide it away. The Christian way is the way of giving. Always give what you have, and you will find money becoming something living in the church. When you have any need, the birds in the air will work for you, and God will perform miracles for you.

Cast yourself upon the Word of God. Otherwise, God cannot carry out His word in you. First give yourself to God, and then give your money again and again. If you do this, God will have the opportunity to give to you.

CHAPTER TWENTY-NINE

OCCUPATION

Scripture Reading: 2 Thes. 3:10-12

Occupation is very important to a Christian. If one chooses a wrong occupation, he will not be able to go on in a positive way. A Christian must pay attention to the matter of choosing an occupation.

I. THE GOD-ORDAINED OCCUPATIONS ACCORDING TO THE SCRIPTURE

A. In the Old Testament Age

After God created man, He prepared an occupation for him. God assigned Adam and Eve the job of guarding and keeping the garden. The matter of occupation existed before man sinned. Adam and Eve's occupation in the beginning was that of a gardener; they guarded and kept the garden of Eden which God had created.

After Adam and Eve sinned, the earth no longer rendered service to them. They had to eat in the sweat of their face and till the ground so they could eat (Gen. 3:17-19). This shows us clearly that after man's fall, his God-ordained occupation was to be a farmer and to till the ground. Man has to till the ground in the sweat of his face in order for the earth to yield food to him. To this day farmers are still the most honest kind of people. In the beginning God ordained man to till the ground.

In Genesis 4 Cain was a tiller of the ground and Abel was a keeper of sheep. Here sheep farming came in. This shows us that shepherding is also an occupation that is acceptable to God.

After this, when men began to multiply on the earth, there

arose all kinds of craftsmen. There were blacksmiths, copper-smiths, makers of musical instruments, and artificers in brass and iron (4:21-22). By the time of the tower of Babel, there were bricklayers and carpenters (11:3-4). (Although building the tower of Babel was wrong, men were neverthe-less learning to build. Hence the coppersmith, blacksmith, maker of musical instruments, and craftsman are all proper occupations.)

In Genesis 12 God chose Abraham. He was a herdsman. He had many cattle and sheep. Jacob also had flocks of cattle and sheep. This shows that their main occupation was animal husbandry.

When the Israelites were in Egypt, they worked as crafts-men, burning bricks for Pharaoh. But after they came out of Egypt, God promised them a land flowing with milk and honey. Clearly, we see two occupations: raising livestock and farming. The grapes of the land required two people to carry them. This proves that there was farming. God said that if the Israelites disobeyed Him and worshipped idols, He would cause the heavens to be as brass and the earth to be as iron; the heavens and the earth would not work for the Israelites. This shows clearly that the occupations in the promised land of Canaan consisted of tilling the earth and raising livestock. These were the occupations in the Old Testament.

B. In the New Testament Age

The Lord Jesus' parables in the Gospel of Matthew show us that farming is a basic occupation in the New Testament age. For example, in chapter thirteen we have the parable of the sower, and in chapter twenty we have the parable of the vineyard. Luke 17 speaks of a slave coming back from plowing or tending sheep in the field. In John 10 the Lord said that the good Shepherd laid down His life for the sheep. Therefore, raising livestock and farming are the basic God-ordained occupations for men.

The Lord called twelve apostles, most of whom were fishermen. The one who was a tax collector was told by the Lord to drop his occupation. But it was as if He said to the fishermen, "Once you were fishermen. But from now on,

I will make you fishers of men." This shows that fishing is also an acceptable occupation.

Luke was a physician, and Paul was a tentmaker. Tentmaking is different from fishing. With tentmaking, labor is added to basic raw material. Tilling the ground produces material directly. Making fabrics, tailoring, or making tents add labor to raw material to manufacture finished goods.

I can only say that from the Old Testament to the New Testament, God has arranged certain occupations. The Lord's disciples were either farmers, shepherds, craftsmen, fishermen, or manufacturers. If there were any other occupations at all, the most we can include is "workmen" (not the workers who do spiritual work), because the New Testament says, "The workman is worthy of his pay" (1 Tim 5:18). A workman is one who labors manually or who sells his labor. Obtaining wages by manual labor is also an acceptable occupation in the Bible.

II. THE PRINCIPLE OF OCCUPATIONS

From these God-approved occupations in the Bible, we can see a basic principle: Man must receive or take from nature, or he must earn his wages in exchange for his time and labor. These are the principles of occupation outlined in the Bible.

A. Receiving from Nature—
Increasing Abundance

The sower sows a grain of wheat into the ground. After some time it bears many grains, a hundredfold, sixtyfold, or thirtyfold (Matt. 13:3, 8). One grain becomes a hundred, sixty, or thirty grains. One seed is sown into the ground, but it grows and bears many grains. This is to receive from nature. Nature is rich in its supply, and anyone can extract from it. God causes His sun to rise on the evil and the good and sends rain on the just and the unjust (5:45). This clearly hints that God sends these things for the purpose of farming. God intends for man to obtain his supply from nature. The same principle applies to livestock farming. One raises sheep which give milk or bear many lambs. This is an increase of production. It is something supplied by nature, not something acquired by other means.

In the New Testament we see fishing as an occupation. Fishing takes something from the rivers and seas. This again is to receive from nature. We do not make anyone poorer by fishing from the rivers and the seas. We can become rich by taking something from the rivers, and these riches will not make anyone poor. When my sheep bears six lambs or my cow bears two calves, no family becomes poorer because of this. When I till the ground, no one is hungry or suffers loss because my field has brought forth grain a hundredfold. The basic principle of a God-approved occupation is to gain without incurring loss to anyone. This is the kind of noble occupation that God ordains.

B. Manufacturing—Adding Value

The same principle applies to Paul's tentmaking. He did not receive directly from nature. Fishing, raising livestock, and farming receive from nature directly. But Paul manufactured something by adding value to his raw material. This increases the value of goods. A piece of fabric may cost one dollar. When I cut it, sew it, and make a tent out of it, it costs two dollars. Its value has increased, and my wage is the increased value of the good. I do not make anyone poorer by receiving money from the increased value. No one became poorer or suffered loss through Paul's tentmaking. When I increase the value of a piece of fabric, it is only proper that I receive my wages because I have put in time and skill. Therefore, another principle of a God-approved occupation is that it increases the value of goods.

C. Working for Wages

Another principle can be found in hired laborers, craftsmen, and medical doctors. In such cases one earns his money and wages through his own labor. This neither takes from nature nor adds value to raw materials, but one puts in his labor, pays a price, and provides a service to receive his income. The reward that comes as a result of one's labor is also acceptable to God.

D. What the Bible Disapproves of—Trading

There is one occupation of which the Bible particularly disapproves. Please pay special attention to this matter. If a new believer has the ability to choose his profession, I hope that he will not take trading as his occupation. Why? We should consider this matter from a broader perspective. Perhaps that will give us a clearer picture. Suppose there are one hundred persons here and each one has a million dollars. If we put them all together, we will have a hundred million dollars. Suppose I begin to trade as one of them. Naturally, I would want to make money. I would like my one million dollars to become two million dollars. Forget for a moment how I handle my business, whether it is done righteously or unrighteously. After a month I have two million dollars. This means that someone must have less money. This must be the case because there are only one hundred persons, each of whom had only one million dollars. Even if I conducted my business in the most righteous way, I would still have caused someone to lose money when I increased my money to two million.

I am a Christian, and let us say that you are a Christian also. You are my brother. Does it look good for me to make money and become richer by making you poorer? Certainly not. Even if you are a Gentile and a heathen, I am a Christian. I am a child of God, and I have my standing and status as a child of God. God's children should not cause an unbeliever to become poorer by increasing their own money. I would feel bad even if I employed righteous means to gain other believers' money. I would feel equally bad if I used righteous means to gain an unbeliever's money. This is what it is like to engage in trade. You cannot take money from another's pocket and put it into your own pocket. It does not matter how you do it. As long as you turn the money in another's pocket into your money, you are causing a loss to others. This is a fact.

Of course, the basic God-approved occupations in the Bible pose no such problem. Suppose I am a tiller of the ground, and I have harvested a hundred loads of rice. This will not cause another brother's possession to be reduced from ten loads down to nine loads. I cannot cause him to have any reduction. My hundred loads of rice will not reduce anything from anyone or cause anyone to become poorer. This is not making money; this is increasing the abundance of the land. We must completely differentiate between the two: Making money and increasing the abundance are two different things altogether. God does not want His children to make money just for the sake of making money. God wants our occupation to increase the abundance. This basic principle is quite clear. A new believer should not have his mind occupied with money day and night. Do not try to constantly consider how you can make money. Please remember that as long as you have made some money, others have lost money. The principle of trade is that when one's money increases, the money of others decreases.

III. CHOOSING FROM THREE DIFFERENT KINDS OF OCCUPATIONS

Here we see three different kinds of occupations. One is to trade, another is to work, and the third is to produce. The highest occupation God has ordained in the Bible is the one that produces. Since Adam, God's eyes have been on occupations that produce, because production increases the abundance of the earth rather than imposing poverty on others. If I raise a hundred sheep and after a certain number of years they have become four hundred, I have increased by three hundred sheep. This increase does not decrease a single dollar from any brother's or sister's pocket. How much money you have at home will not change. You will not have less just because my sheep has brought forth lambs. This is the basic scriptural principle of occupation. I should always be increasing and should always be adding to riches. I may sell my sheep and receive money. But in so doing, I have not made anyone poorer.

If a new believer has the chance to choose his own occupation, I hope he will choose one that will increase goods rather than increase his money. To increase money but not goods is very selfish. We need to learn to increase the things of the earth, not to increase our personal wealth. There is a great difference between the two.

Paul's tentmaking shows us another principle. He did not increase the amount of cotton, silk, or fabric. But because of his cutting, sewing, effort, and energy, he increased the value of the raw material. According to Bible scholars, tents at that time had to be dyed. Dean Alford told us that when Paul said, "These hands," in Acts 20:34, he was referring to the unavoidable stain of the dye of the tents on his hands. Paul's tentmaking was something that increased the value of goods.

It is good to increase the riches of the earth. It is also good to increase the value of goods. Suppose I make a chair from a piece of wood. This is good, because by doing so, I have increased the value of the wood. Although I have not increased the abundance in nature, the world has one more chair through me. The world had one more tent when Paul made a tent. This does not benefit oneself at the expense of others. One can make a tent; he can turn a cheap fabric into a valuable tent. Turning fabric into a tent increases the goods of this world. This is also an occupation that is acceptable to God.

A new believer must see that there are two criteria to a proper occupation. One must either increase the abundance of the earth or increase the value of goods. Actually, when one makes a tent, he is also increasing the abundance of the world. Because of the work of one's hands, the number of tents in this world has increased. Therefore, it is also right to say that this increases the abundance of the world. This is the basic principle of God's ordained occupations for men.

IV. AVOIDING PURE COMMERCE

I have studied economics a little. I know that there is the need for commerce. But I am a Christian; I am not an economist. While the Lord Jesus did say that we needed to do business until He comes (Luke 19:13), that verse means that we should give ourselves to our work like a businessman giving himself to his business. We know that a businessman has to devote himself to his business. He will get into any situation as long as there is money in it for him. The Lord meant that we should grasp every opportunity. We must give ourselves to our work in such a way.

Commerce began with Tyre, and it ends up in Babylon. We find this from Ezekiel 28 to Revelation 18. The one who invented commerce is the prince of Tyre. Ezekiel 28 shows us that the prince of Tyre represents Satan. "By the multitude of thy merchandise they have filled the midst of thee with violence, and thou hast sinned" (v. 16). Bear in mind that commerce always makes money for oneself at the expense of others and at the expense of decreasing the riches of the world. This is not the kind of occupation that God wants. This is the occupation which belongs to Satan. The principle behind such an occupation is wrong.

The principle of commerce is to increase the money in one's pocket by decreasing the money in another's pocket. Once the idea of making money comes into a person's mind, the result is very simple—one will get more money while another will have less. Once someone's money increases, there must be others whose money decreases. Suppose there are only twenty-one billion dollars in the whole world. Whether you are rich or poor, the total amount of money remains the same. The total amount of money in the world is limited. For my money to increase, I have to take it from others. This is pure commerce. I am not saying that after catching some fish, one cannot sell it. Neither am I saying that after harvesting a crop, producing a lamb, or making a tent, one cannot sell it. I am saying that making tents, raising lambs, harvesting crops, and catching fish are not pure commerce. Those occupations exchange production for money. I derive my benefit from nature. The abundance I receive comes from nature. It is nature that gives me the abundance; I do not become richer by making others poorer.

Christians must not try to make money from other people. Never harbor any thought of taking advantage of others. As God's children, we have a high standard. It does not look good for us to try to rack up the lowly money of the world. Suppose the president of a foreign nation comes to Kuling and finds a local native infected with malaria. Suppose he tries to sell him some quinine pills, saying, "I bought them for five dollars

per pill. Now I am selling them to you for six dollars per pill."
What kind of story would that be? It does not match the
status of a nation's president to earn a dollar from a coolie.
For a Christian to earn someone else's money is even worse
than a president taking money from a coolie. Our status is
different. We cannot make money from anyone.

Christians are noble people; we have our dignity, our
standing, and our principles. It is a shame for us to make
money from anyone. We cannot increase our wealth this way.
I would rather be a farmer who tills and plants. This is more
glorious than making money from others. God has prepared
nature to work for us, and we will be more noble if we do not
try to make money from others. Christians must have the
thought that they will not earn money at the expense of other
human beings.

Any occupation that increases the quantity and value of
goods is acceptable to God. But pure commerce is not acceptable to God. Please pay special attention to Ezekiel 28. The
principle of aggrandizement through trade began with the
prince of Tyre. God rebuked him, saying, "By the multitude
of thy merchandise they have filled the midst of thee with
violence." In Revelation 18 the world has come to an end and
the kingdom is about to begin. There we see Babylon being
judged. Commerce continues throughout history until the end
of Babylon. All the merchants of the earth weep and mourn
for Babylon. There we also see all the goods of the earth. The
first is gold and the last are the souls of men. Everything is
open for purchase and for sale, from gold to the souls of men.
Man always thinks of making money and becoming rich. But
brothers and sisters, we must flee from this low occupation.

V. PURE COMMERCE BEING DIFFERENT
FROM PRODUCTION

I hope you can differentiate between pure commerce and
production. Wheat, cows, sheep, tents, and fish can be sold.
This is not the commerce we are talking about. The so-called
commerce in the world means that today I buy one hundred
sacks of flour from another person. I store them until the
price goes up and then I sell them. Or I buy fifty tins of oil

and put them away until the price goes up and then sell them. The wheat or oil has not increased its volume because of me. The oil has not increased, neither has the wheat. But my money has increased. I have not increased the goods of the world, yet my wealth has increased. This is a shameful thing. This is one thing that believers should try to avoid at all cost.

It is all right to buy and sell for the sake of taking care of our production. But it is wrong to buy and sell for the sake of buying and selling. It is right for a brother to sell products from his farm. But it is wrong for the same brother to buy rice and then sell it again. Although both are selling, the principles are altogether different. If a brother buys ten tents and resells them, he does not have the same occupation as Paul's. If I make tents at night and then sell them in the morning, I have the same occupation as Paul's. The two are absolutely different. If you labor on something and then sell what you have labored on, this is something that can be blessed by God. But if you buy something and then sell it, hoping in your heart that you will make money in the process, you are engaging in the lowest occupation, not only from a Christian's point of view, but also from a Gentile's as well.

No brother engaging in pure commerce can be a responsible brother, for such a person can never be fully delivered from money. Our way is becoming clearer and clearer. God's children must be fully delivered from the power of mammon. This is the only way for them to serve God and for the church to have a way to go on.

VI. THE OCCUPATIONS WHICH ARE PLEASING TO GOD

Both shepherds and farmers are producers. Merchants belong to another category. There is a third kind of people who come in between these two. They are workers, like doctors and teachers, who work with their skills. These are also good occupations according to the Bible. Although they are not producing anything, they are not extorting anything from others either. They do not receive anything from nature, but they do not take anything from people either. They maintain their livelihood by utilizing their own contribution of time, energy, and mental power. The workman is worthy of his pay.

This is one scriptural occupation that is acceptable to God. We can say that the highest occupation is the occupation which produces. The second highest is the occupation that works with skills and that receives rewards by contributing intellectual or physical strength.

The producer takes from nature and receives nothing from men. The worker takes nothing from nature and receives nothing from men. The merchant receives nothing from nature but takes things from men. These are three totally different kinds of occupations. The producer obtains something from nature while taking nothing from men. This is the highest occupation in the Bible. The worker puts in his energy, whether mental or physical. He puts in his time and energy to earn what he deserves. He does not make others poorer. Others pay him for the service he renders, and the interests of both parties balance out each other. This is an occupation acceptable to God. The merchant who deals with pure commerce receives nothing from nature but receives something from men. He has no other motive than to make money. This is the lowest occupation according to the Bible.

Today the way is clear, and the principle is also clear. We hope that all the brothers would try to have a turn in their occupations.

VII. THE WAY TO GO ON

I do not wish to see anyone taking the extreme way. Do not condemn those who are engaged in commerce as soon as you meet them. They did not have the opportunity to choose their occupation. I knew a brother who was quite pure when he left school. After he went into business, his heart gradually became corrupt. He tried to make money day and night. If you wanted him to buy something for you, he would try to make some money in the process. He always tried to make some money from others. This is too poor. I believe such a person has been corrupted in his heart. We hope that anyone who can choose his own occupation will not go into pure commerce. We must open the eyes of those who are already in it and help them to have a change. Do not embarrass them, but at least show them the way clearly.

Pure commerce is never a good thing. We hope that ten or twenty years from now, it will be a tradition among us that no one goes into pure commerce. Hopefully, in the future all the brothers and sisters among us will build up the habit of shunning pure commerce. As God's children, we would rather be teachers or manual laborers; we would not go into pure commerce. We would till the land and harvest wheat, barley, or rice and then sell the harvest. We would raise lambs from our sheep and then sell them. We would have our hen lay eggs and then sell them. We would have our cow produce milk and then sell it. We would make fabric and then sell it. We can do all these things. The more we work and produce, the more God will bless. The worst thing that can happen to us is that our brothers and sisters simply make a great deal of money. Nothing could be worse than this.

Today our brothers and sisters are the poorest among all those in the other denominations. If we are not careful, we could become the richest. Because we are more honest, diligent, and frugal than others, and because we do not lie, smoke, drink, or live in big mansions, it is possible that within a short time, all of the brothers and sisters will become wealthy. John Wesley once said before he died, "I am concerned for our people in the Methodist assembly. They are honest, diligent, and frugal. Soon they will become the richest people in the world." Such a word has indeed come true today. The Methodists are the richest people in the world. But their testimony has been lost as a result.

We hope that all the new believers will earn their living by their own labor. We hope that they will not make money by taking in with one hand and taking out with the other. Our principle is to increase the abundance of the land, not the money in the world. If we do this, the money we receive will be clean, and when we offer it to God, it will be acceptable to Him. Every dollar will end up in a good place. Suppose a brother makes a basket and sells it and then offers the money to the Lord. This is much better than another brother who buys ten baskets, sells them, and then offers up his profit to the Lord. The amount of money offered may be the same, but the nature of the money is different. We hope that many brothers and sisters will see this principle. We must either labor with our hands or we must produce something. Both are according to the proper principles. I cannot forbid anyone from going into the business of pure commerce, but I would advise everyone to try his best to avoid pure commerce. This occupation will always drag a Christian down. We hope that the new believers among us will please the Lord in their choice of occupations.

CHAPTER THIRTY

MARRIAGE

In order to be a good Christian, one needs to deal with all the basic issues in a thorough way. If there is one basic issue that is not settled, whether it be the family or one's occupation, problems will eventually come back. As long as there is one unresolved issue, a Christian will not be able to take a straight path before the Lord.

Today we will cover the subject of marriage. A new believer should know what God's Word has to say about marriage. We need to consider this subject from various angles.

I. MARRIAGE BEING HOLY

The first question to address with regard to marriage is the matter of sex. We need to be clear that human beings have an awareness of sex in the same way that they have an awareness of hunger. Just as the consciousness of hunger is a natural demand of the body, the consciousness of sex is also a natural demand of the body. To feel hungry is natural; it is not a sin. But to steal food is sin; that is not natural. Likewise, having a consciousness of sex is natural and is not a sin. But if a person uses improper means to satisfy his demand, he falls into sin.

Marriage was ordained and initiated by God. Hence, the consciousness of sex also was given by God. Marriage is not something that was instituted after man's fall; it was there before man sinned. It was not instituted after Genesis 3; rather, God ordained marriage in Genesis 2. Hence, the consciousness of sex existed before, not after, sin entered the world. It is definitely not a sin for a person to have the consciousness of sex. There is no element of sin in this consciousness. Rather, it is a consciousness created by God Himself.

New believers must be clear concerning this point. I have contacted many young brothers and sisters in the course of my Christian life and service during the past thirty years. Many of them were troubled by the matter of marriage. They were unnecessarily condemned in their conscience because they were ignorant of God's ordination as well as God's Word. They had the consciousness and need of marriage, yet they thought that this was sin. Some brothers have fallen into serious doubts about God's work only because of their consciousness of sex. It is a heathen thought to treat sex as something sinful. We need to be clear about God's Word. Just as it is not sin for a man to feel hungry, the need for sex is not sinful; it is a natural consciousness.

Hebrews 13:4 tells us, "Let marriage be held in honor among all." Marriage is not only honorable but even holy. God considers sex not only natural but even holy.

Dr. Meyer, a co-worker of D. L. Moody, wrote many good books on edification. He once said, "Only the most filthy mind would consider sex as something filthy." I think this was well said. Man injects filthy thoughts into sex because he himself is filthy. To the clean everything is clean. To the defiled everything is defiled. Because man's mind is defiled, his thoughts also become defiled. We need to realize that marriage is clean. A God-ordained sex relationship is holy, clean, and undefiled.

In 1 Timothy 4:1-3 Paul said that in later times, there would be the teachings of demons, one of which is the forbidding of marriage. Here we see that even demonic teachings pursue holiness. G. H. Pember pointed out clearly in his writing how men would forbid marriage in the pursuit of holiness. They thought that this would make them holy. However, in his Epistle to Timothy, Paul told us that forbidding marriage is a doctrine of the demons. God has never forbidden marriage.

No one should be condemned unnecessarily in his conscience because of heathen religious teachings. The consciousness of sex is something natural and is not sin. It is only when one begins to deal with this consciousness that the possibility of it becoming a sin arises. It is not a question of the presence of this consciousness; the presence of this consciousness is natural and is not sin. It is the way a person deals with this consciousness that determines whether or not it is sin. This matter needs to be thoroughly cleared up. Otherwise a person's conscience will be condemned, and he will not grow. This feeling of guilt is, in fact, not sin at all but the result of ignorance.

II. BASIC ELEMENTS OF A MARRIAGE

A. Rendering Mutual Help

Marriage is ordained by God. In Genesis God said that it was not good for man to be alone. God said "good" to everything that He created. With the exception of the second day, God proclaimed that what He had created was good. God did not say that "it was good" on the second day, because the firmament was the place of Satan. Moreover, on the sixth day, God did not say that "it was good"; in fact, He even said that something was *not good* after He created man. God said, "It is not good that the man should be alone" (Gen. 2:18). This is not to suggest that man was not created well. It means only that it was not good because there was just one man. Only half of man was created.

God created a help meet for Adam on the sixth day. Eve was also made on the sixth day, and she was brought by God to Adam. She was made for the purpose of marriage. The words *help meet* mean "meet to help." This word in Hebrew means "someone that matches, someone that renders help."

In considering Genesis 2:18, many Bible readers think that when God created man, He created a male plus a female. However, the Bible says only that God created man. His creation of man was His creation of male and female. The male and female made a complete man. It was as if God created half of a man in the beginning and then the other half after seeing that this man was only one-half. The two halves were joined together to become one. Only when the two halves were joined together was man complete. This is why God did not say that "it was good" until Eve was made. This shows us that marriage is not initiated by man but by God. The institution of marriage did not come after man's fall but before it. Man did not sin on the first day of his creation; he was married on the first day of his creation. On the same day that God created Eve, He gave her to Adam. This is not something that happened after man sinned. Marriage is something initiated by God.

In Genesis 2 we see marriage in God's creation. In John 2, at the beginning of the Lord Jesus' ministry, there was also a wedding in Cana. During that wedding the Lord Jesus changed the water into wine. This shows that the Lord not only allowed marriage but even approved and endorsed it. The Lord Jesus not only attended the wedding but even enhanced it and made it better. It is clear that marriage was initiated by God and particularly approved by the Lord Jesus. Therefore, it is something entirely of God.

Here we see the place of marriage before God. God's purpose is to have a husband and a wife, who will mutually help each other. Thus, He called Adam's wife a help meet. *Help meet* in Hebrew means someone who is meet to help. Here we find that God wants man to live in a corporate way, to have mutual fellowship, and to render mutual help. This is God's purpose.

B. Preventing Sin

In the Old Testament God instituted marriage before sin came into the world. In the New Testament, Paul said that marriage not only is allowed but also is a necessity because of the presence of sin (1 Cor. 7).

Marriage can prevent sin. This is why Paul said that men should have their own wives and women should have their own husbands. This is to prevent the sin of fornication (v. 2). Paul did not condemn the consciousness of sex as sin. On the contrary, he showed us that both the male and the female should marry in order to prevent sin.

Paul said that we should make no provision for the flesh (Rom. 13:14). If a man constantly committed the sin of pride, Paul could not have said, "Since you always commit the sin of pride, you can be proud at home so that you will not be proud elsewhere! If you exercise your pride in one place, perhaps you will not exercise it elsewhere." Saying this would have been to make "provision for the flesh." God would never agree with his pride or my making some arrangement for him to exercise his pride. Consider a man who loves to steal. You should not say, "Since you like to steal, I will allow you to steal the things which belong to Brother So-and-so so that you will not steal from others." You should not say this; instead, you need to say, "You cannot steal at all." Stealing is definitely a sin, and we should not make any provision for it. Pride is definitely a sin as well, and we cannot make provision for it either. But sex is not a sin in an absolute sense. This is why men should have their own wives, and women should have their own husbands. If we do not understand this, we may think that Paul's word was making provision for the flesh. But we know that the apostle did not make provision for the flesh. Therefore, we cannot consider marriage to be a sin. Marriage is not God's provision for the flesh. We want to hold marriage on a high plane. It is something holy and ordained by God Himself.

Marriage is necessary because sin has entered. Marriage can prevent sin. This is not to make provision for the flesh. There is a clear difference.

In 1 Corinthians 7 Paul spoke about marriage. He began by saying that a wife does not have authority over her own body, and a husband does not have authority over his own body (v. 4). Paul's teaching is quite clear. Except for the purpose of devoting themselves to the service of the Lord, the husband and the wife should not be separated. This prevents fornication (v. 5). In order to prevent fornication, God ordains that male and female should marry and not be separated.

Paul used strong words to speak of those who have a compelling desire for sex. He said that they should marry in order to avoid burning with desire (v. 9). He did not reprimand such persons. Paul did not say, "You are wrong to have such a strong desire. You have sinned in having such a strong desire. Therefore, you have to make some provision for your flesh." Instead, he said, "If you have a strong desire, you should marry. It is better to marry than to live with such a strong desire." The Word of God is very clear concerning this. The consciousness of sex is not a sin. Even a strong sex urge is not a sin. But God has ordained that those who have a strong consciousness of sex should marry. They should not abstain from marriage on the one hand and fall into sin on the other hand. This is what the Lord has shown us.

The institution of marriage has a New Testament aspect and an Old Testament aspect. The Old Testament shows us that marriage provides help that is meet. The New Testament says that it is instituted to prevent sin. One aspect of the Christian marriage today is mutual help, and the other aspect is the prevention of sin.

C. Inheriting Grace Together

There is a third aspect. In his first Epistle, Peter said that the wives are "fellow heirs of the grace of life" (3:7). In other words, God delights to see husbands and wives serving Him together. God delighted to see Aquila and Prisca serving Him. He delighted to see Peter and his wife, Judah and his wife, serving Him together.

Therefore, there are three basic elements of a Christian marriage. First, there is mutual help; second, there is the prevention of sin; and third, there is the joint inheritance of grace of two persons in the presence of God. One should not be a Christian alone but a Christian together with another person. One should not inherit grace alone but together with another person.

III. THE QUESTION OF VIRGINITY

The Bible also shows us that even though there is the consciousness of sex, this consciousness is not very strong with some people, and so there is no need for such a one to fulfill this need. The Bible advises such persons to keep their virginity.

A. The Benefits of Keeping One's Virginity

Virginity does not make one more holy spiritually. However, a virgin can surely devote all his or her physical energy to the Lord's work. This also is spoken of in 1 Corinthians 7.

Paul shows us that there are three problems in marriage. First, marriage is a bondage. He says, "Have you been bound to a wife?" (v. 27). Often, a person is not free after he is married; once he is married he becomes occupied with many things. He is bound by his wife and has to take care of many things. Second, those who are married have affliction. Paul said, "But such ones will have affliction in the flesh" (v. 28). When a person is married, the affliction in the flesh increases, and it is hard for him to serve the Lord with a single heart. Third, those who are married care for the things of the world (vv. 32-34). In Matthew 13 the Lord indicates that these cares are like thorns which can easily choke the growth of the seed. The result can be barrenness (v. 22). In short, marriage brings in family problems, entanglements, afflictions, and anxiety.

Paul's words are not only for the co-workers but also for all the brothers and sisters. A person who keeps his virginity can be spared many difficulties. Paul did not command these ones to keep their virginity, but his words show his inclination toward this choice. Paul did not have any opinion of his own; he was merely telling the brothers the facts. Marriage is good, and it prevents the danger of sinning. But marriage also brings a person into family problems, entanglements, afflictions, and the anxieties of this world.

B. The Type of Person
Who Can Keep His Virginity

Following this, Paul shows us the type of person who can keep his virginity. He said some have the gift from God to keep their virginity. It is a gift from God to keep one's virginity. One person receives one kind of gift from God. Another person receives another kind of gift from God. If I need to marry, marriage is a gift from God; it takes a gift from God to marry. This is why Paul said, "But each has his own gift from God, one in this way, the other in that" (1 Cor. 7:7). Those who keep their virginity have the gift of God, and also those who are married have the gift of God.

The first condition for keeping one's virginity is that a person have only sex consciousness but no sex compulsion.

Some people have the compulsion of sex. Others have only the consciousness of sex but not the compulsion. Only those who do not have a compulsion for sex can keep their virginity.

Second, a person must have the desire to remain single and must be firm in his heart. Verses 36 and 37 say, "But if any one think that he behaves unseemly to his virginity, if he be beyond the flower of his age, and so it must be, let him do what he will, he does not sin: let them marry. But he who stands firm in his heart, having no need, but has authority over his own will, and has judged this in his heart to keep his own virginity, he does well" (New Translation, J. N. Darby). Paul shows us that to keep one's virginity, the person must have the intention and willingness to keep it. If anyone thinks that it is wrong to keep his virginity, he can marry. If a person has the intention and the inclination to remain single, and if he is firm in his heart to keep his virginity, he can keep it. Hence, firmness in heart is a necessary requirement.

Third, such a decision must not be in conflict with one's circumstances. Verse 37 says, "Having no need." Some have special considerations in their circumstances, and it is not easy for them to keep their virginity. Some may create many problems with their family if they keep their virginity. Hence, there must be the environmental provision before one can keep his virginity.

Paul shows us the three basic conditions for keeping one's virginity: They are (1) having no compulsion, (2) standing firm in one's heart, and (3) not creating problems in one's environment. Only when one meets all three conditions can he keep his virginity.

C. Virginity Being Related to
the Kingdom of the Heavens and to Rapture

Those who keep their virginity have much to gain before the Lord. Matthew 19 clearly shows that it is easier for a virgin to enter the kingdom of the heavens. We have to acknowledge that "there are eunuchs who made themselves eunuchs because of the kingdom of the heavens." Matthew 19 clearly speaks of the relationship between virginity and the kingdom of the heavens. We dare not say specifically what relationship there is between virginity and the kingdom of the heavens. However, we can say that keeping one's virginity definitely has its advantage in entering the kingdom of the heavens. The Lord tells us here that there are some who made themselves eunuchs, who keep their virginity for the sake of the kingdom of the heavens.

This is not all. Revelation 14 shows us that the firstfruits (the hundred and forty-four thousand) are virgins. They follow the Lamb wherever He may go. These hundred and forty-four thousand are the early raptured ones. Virginity definitely has something to do with rapture. We will find one day that virgins have a clear advantage in entering the kingdom of the heavens and in being raptured. What about today? Paul said that keeping one's virginity indeed reduces afflictions and enables a person to serve God well.

We can only present these facts to the brothers and sisters. Only those who do not have a compulsion for sex, who are firm in their heart, and who find adequate provisions in their environment can keep their virginity. We are presenting this matter in an objective and biblical way before the brothers and sisters. Everyone should make his or her own choice before the Lord.

IV. MARRIAGE PARTNERS

Concerning the matter of marriage, God has laid down definite guidelines on whom one can marry and whom one cannot marry. The Bible shows us clearly that the marriages of God's people should be restricted to those among themselves only. In other words, if one is to be married, his spouse must be sought from among God's own people, not from other people.

A. The Old Testament Commandments

There are sufficient commandments in the Old Testament to show us that we should not marry anyone outside of God's people.

Deuteronomy 7:3-4 says that the Israelites should not marry the Canaanites. They should neither give their daughters to the Canaanites' sons, nor take their daughters for their sons, because the Canaanites would turn them from following the Lord and would seduce them to serve other gods. God clearly shows through the Old Testament that one should look for a marriage partner among the Lord's people. One cannot look for a wife or a husband among unbelievers. The greatest problem with going after unbelievers is that the other person may turn one away from the Lord to serve other gods. It is easy for wives to follow their husbands to worship idols. It is also easy for husbands to follow their wives to worship idols. Since both are married, it is very easy for one to follow the other to worship other gods.

Joshua 23:12-13 warns the Israelites against marrying the people of the land. They were warned that the latter would become snares and thorns in their eyes. Their wives or their husbands would become their thorns, and they would be ensnared.

At the time of Nehemiah, the Israelites returned from captivity to the land of Judah. Many had married Gentile wives and could not speak the Hebrew language. Nehemiah charged them in 13:23-27 to sever all ties with the Gentile women and not to have any dealings with them. Here we see a basic problem in marrying a Gentile woman: Sooner or later the children will follow the mother and not follow the father to serve God. If you marry a Gentile, your children will easily follow your Gentile partner and go into the world. This is quite a problem.

Malachi 2:11 shows us that the Israelites committed treacherous sins and profaned the holiness of God because they took Gentiles to be their wives. In God's sight, marrying a Gentile woman is to profane the holiness of God. Hence, Christians should look for marriage partners only among the believers.

We can also take warnings from the failure of Solomon. Solomon was the wisest king, yet he fell into idolatry through marrying Gentile women.

B. In the New Testament

Paul's word in the New Testament is clear enough. In

1 Corinthians 7:39, he told the widows to marry those who were in the Lord.

Second Corinthians 6:14 is a well-known portion of the Bible. It says that believers and unbelievers should not share the same yoke. These words do not refer to only marriage. But they certainly speak also of marriage. Believers and unbelievers should not be engaged in the same business; they should not join themselves in one goal, like two animals plowing the field with one yoke. God does not allow this. He does not allow a believer and an unbeliever to bear the same yoke. In the Old Testament, an ox and a horse could not be yoked together, and an ass could not be equally yoked with a horse. You cannot have one that is fast and another that is slow. It is impossible to have one going one direction and the other going another direction, or one turning to heaven and the other turning to the world. You cannot have one seeking after spiritual blessings and the other seeking after worldly riches. It is impossible for one to pull in one direction and the other to pull in the other direction. If you do, the yoke will break.

Of all unequally yoked relationships, none is more serious than the marriage relationship. One may be unequally yoked with others in business ventures or in other things. But no yoke is more severe than the marriage yoke. When a believer and an unbeliever share the responsibility of a family together, the result will be nothing but problems. The ideal marriage partner is a brother or a sister. Never choose an unbeliever capriciously. If you pick out an unbeliever carelessly, you will surely encounter problems later. One will be pulling to one side, and the other will be pulling to the other side. One will turn to heaven, and the other will turn to the world. One will seek a heavenly gift, and the other will seek worldly riches. The difference between the two is tremendous. This is why the Bible charges us to marry those in the Lord.

V. IF MARRIED TO AN UNBELIEVER

But here is a problem: Suppose a brother is already married to an unbeliever, or a sister is already married to an unbelieving husband. What should they do? We mentioned earlier that a single person should seek a partner who is in the Lord. However, there are some who are already married. They already have an unbelieving wife or an unbelieving husband. What should they do?

A. If He Wants to Go Away

First Corinthians 7 has something to say about this matter. Verses 12, 13, and 15 address this point. They tell us what to do when a dispute arises in a family that has only one member who is a Christian. Please bear in mind that many such families today complain little, simply because the believers in these families are not absolute enough. The Lord Jesus predicted in the Gospels that there would be much contention within the family. If a believer is absolute, there is bound to be contention in the family. There are cases of "three against two and two against three," as in Luke 12:52, because some family members have become believers. Suppose a husband leaves his wife because she has believed in the Lord. Suppose he says, "You have believed in the Lord; I do not want you anymore." What should the wife do? The Lord's word in 1 Corinthians 7 is clear enough: "Let him separate" (v. 15). Therefore, if a husband wants to separate because the wife has believed in the Lord, or vice versa, the word is, "Let him separate."

However, one thing must be clear: You must not be the one who initiates the separation. You must not be the one who asks for the separation. The other party must be the one who asks for it. He is the one who is not happy with your faith in the Lord. He is the one who thinks that there is no future with you now that you have believed in the Lord. It is he who wants to go. If he wants to separate, "Let him separate."

B. If He Does Not Care, the Lord Will Save Him

Paul said that there is no need to separate if the other party does not care. How do you know that the Lord will not save him through you? If he does not care and wants to continue living with you, Paul said that you should be at peace with him and should not leave. He said that an unbeliever can be sanctified through a believer. He said also, "For how do you know, O wife, whether you will save your husband? Or how do

you know, O husband, whether you will save your wife?"
(v. 16). If the other party wants to leave, that is his concern,
not yours. But if he does not want to leave, you have to believe
that the Lord will save him. Paul said that it would be easy
for him to be saved. It may not be that easy for the Lord to
save others, but it would surely be easy for the Lord to save
one who is already yours. We need to deal with this matter by
taking such a stand.

VI. WHAT TO DO IF ENGAGED TO AN UNBELIEVER

Some brothers and sisters have another problem: They are
engaged to unbelievers. What should they do?

A. It Being Best for the Unbelieving Side
to Take the Initiative in Breaking the Engagement

It is clear that the Lord does not want us to marry unbelievers. If someone is already engaged to an unbeliever, the
best thing would be for the unbelieving fiancé or fiancée
to voluntarily break the engagement. The two are not yet
married; they only have an agreement to marry. If the Lord
opens the way for the unbelieving side to voluntarily break
the agreement because the other one has believed in the Lord,
that is the best solution.

B. Not Annulling Any Agreement Arbitrarily

However, it is often impossible to have such a solution.
Because a marriage agreement exists, the other party may
not easily let go just because you have believed in the Lord. At
such times, you need to realize that an engagement to a
person is a covenant with that person. Such a covenant is
a promise you have made before God. A Christian cannot
arbitrarily annul a covenant just because he has believed in
the Lord. Any covenant is holy in the eyes of God. You can
suggest a dissolution to the other party. The other party can
initiate such a dissolution, or you can initiate it. The proposal
need not be initiated by the other party. This is different from
the earlier case. In the case of a marriage, the other party
must initiate it. In the case of an engagement, you can initiate the dissolution of the engagement. If the other party

insists that you fulfill the marriage agreement, you have to fulfill it. Once something comes out of the mouth of a Christian, he has to honor it; he cannot annul it arbitrarily. We receive salvation because God honors His word. If God did not honor His word, there would not be any salvation at all. Therefore, you have to negotiate with the other party. If the other party is unwilling to dissolve the relationship, you have to marry him or her.

Psalm 15:4 says, "Should he swear to his harm, / He does not change." After the Israelites entered the land of Canaan, the Gibeonites deceived them with dry, moldy bread, old patched shoes, and worn garments. They said that they came from a far country, and Joshua promised not to kill them. Later, he found out that they were actually from a near country. Because a covenant had been made with them, God would not allow the Israelites to kill them. At the most, they were made woodcutters and drawers of water (Josh. 9:3-27). Honoring one's covenant is a serious matter in the Bible. It is all right for you to annul an engagement only if the other party is willing to annul it. But if the other party is not willing to annul it, you cannot annul it. The covenant with the Gibeonites produced serious consequences. Rain was withheld from heaven because Saul slaughtered the Gibeonites. David was forced to ask the Gibeonites what he should do for them. The Gibeonites demanded that seven of the sons of Saul be hung, and David had to comply (2 Sam. 21:1-6). God will not allow us to breach a covenant arbitrarily. We must learn to honor any covenant we make. We cannot do anything that is unrighteous.

C. Negotiating the Terms Beforehand

You have been engaged to someone, and now you have become a Christian. What should you do if the other party insists on marrying you? Here is something that you can do: Negotiate the terms with him ahead of time. You can say, "I will definitely marry you, but I would like to settle a few matters with you before marriage." What are the few matters? First, the other party must allow you to serve the Lord. You should not move into the other party's house with a false disguise; you should move in with an open banner. You are now a Christian. Even though you are marrying the other person, he must give you the liberty to serve the Lord. He must not interfere with your service to the Lord. Second, when you have children, they must be brought up according to the teaching of the Lord. Whether or not the other party becomes a Christian is up to him or her, but the children must be brought up according to the teaching of the Lord. You must settle this from the very beginning. Put this on the table first and have an agreement ahead of time. If you have an agreement, you will not face difficulties later. But if you do not make an agreement beforehand, you will face difficulties down the road. Marrying an unbeliever is always a loss. But you can minimize the loss and the headaches by coming to an agreement first. The other party must agree to give you the freedom to lead your children to the Lord. You have become a Christian. You will not go to the world. You will always be on the Lord's side. If the other party is agreeable to this, you can proceed with the marriage. If the other party does not like it, he can annul the agreement. We need to inform the other party about our future commitment. This will tend to reduce the problems that will eventually come.

VII. IF ONE NEEDS TO BE MARRIED YET CANNOT FIND A BELIEVER

This is a real problem; it is not an imaginary one. But we can only say that there is no teaching in the Bible concerning this matter. However, we need to touch Paul's heart. In 1 Corinthians 7 Paul wished that the widows would remain single if possible. But then, he also wished that the widows would marry those who are in the Lord (v. 39). Therefore, widows can remarry if there is the need. According to this principle, we can say that the best thing for a brother to do is to marry a sister in the Lord. If it is not possible to do this, it is best if he does not marry at all. However, if he must marry, we still would be happy to see him marry. Even if the other party is an unbeliever, we still would like to see him marry.

When we say this, we are not advocating, as the world says, "Choose the lesser of two evils." We are saying that we would rather see a person commit a sin against God's government rather than a moral sin. If by not marrying I fall into sin, I commit a moral sin. If I marry an unbelieving woman, I commit a sin against God's government. There are two types of sin; one is moral sin, and the other is sin against God's government. Please bear in mind that moral sin is more serious than sin against God's government. If a brother needs to marry and he cannot find a sister, the best thing for him to do is stay single. But if he must marry, we should let him marry even if it means marrying an unbeliever.

If you marry an unbeliever, you need to have your eyes open and realize that serious problems lie ahead. It is particularly hard for a believer to marry an unbeliever. The hardship is greater than that of an unbelieving couple in which one becomes a believer. A husband or wife who becomes a believer after being married may encounter hardship, but many times the Lord will bring him through. However, a believer who marries an unbeliever will face many difficulties. We need to warn him ahead of time, and he needs to open his eyes to the hardships ahead.

If a person marries an unbeliever, we must warn him of another thing: He should be careful not to be carried away. He has to remember that he is marrying an unbeliever, and if he is careless, he will be easily led away. Of course, those who are married or engaged have to be careful as well, but those who are considering marriage should exercise even more care. In other words, they need special protection, preservation, and prayer, so that they will not be carried away by the other party.

If you have no choice but to marry an unbeliever, you must also lay down the terms clearly beforehand. You need to tell the unbeliever, "I have already believed in the Lord. I will not force you to believe, but you cannot interfere with my faith. You must give me absolute freedom in this respect." You need also to bring up the question of children. "You must give me the freedom to lead our children to the Lord. I want my children to believe in the Lord. I do not want them to worship idols or to be conformed to the world." If you emphasize this point enough, perhaps you can get by with this issue.

I will speak a few words to the more mature brothers and sisters. When you see a new believer struggling with such a problem, you must be very careful. Do not open the door too wide. Do not allow him to arbitrarily marry an unbeliever. On the other hand, do not close the door too tightly. Do not keep him away from governmental sin while exposing him to moral sin. It is better to let someone fall into God's governmental hand than to let him fall into moral sin.

I have something more to say about this. We have many young brothers and sisters in every locality. Most of the problems in finding a spouse arise when too many saints have too many expectations concerning the background and status of others. A brother who has a higher social status does not want to marry a sister with a lower status, and the reverse is also true. Today there is no lack of brothers and no lack of sisters. But the question of status has caused many problems. I think this question would be easily solved if the brothers and sisters would change their concept about occupation. It would be easy for sisters to marry if they did not belittle brothers who are farmers. It would also be easy for brothers to marry if they did not belittle sisters who are farmers. Today we look down upon occupations which God honors and exalt occupations which men worship. This is what makes things complicated. Today we have no lack of sisters and brothers, but we do not have many matching pairs according to status. Since the matter of status is a worldly consideration, we need to have a complete turn in our concept concerning occupation in order to solve this problem.

VIII. WHAT TO DO WITH ONE'S CONCUBINE[*]

In the Bible there is no command telling man to separate himself from his concubine. Nowhere in the Bible does God ask man to send his concubine away. I am talking about concubines whom one took before he believed in the Lord. In the Bible I think there is sufficient indication of how God wants man to take care of concubines.

---

* Editor's Note: Watchman Nee dealt with the matter of concubines because of the problem at this point in China's history.

Perhaps we should look first at man's demand before considering the Bible's demand. Man's immediate thought is to send away all his concubines. If the concubine cannot be sent away, man's thought is for the husband to discontinue sexual relationships with her. This is a human concept, and unfortunately many brothers and sisters hold this concept. But this is not God's revelation; it is in fact a heathen thought.

A. The Bible Never Demanding That Concubines Be Sent Away

In the Bible no one took a concubine in a worse way than David. He not only took a concubine but even committed murder in taking that concubine. Uriah died because of his wife. David sacrificed Uriah to gain Bath-sheba. Solomon was born of Bath-sheba, and so was the Lord Jesus Himself. The Lord acknowledges this fact in the New Testament. Matthew 1 tells us about four women. Bath-sheba is included and is spoken of as the wife of Uriah. We must be clear about this fact: Those who have taken concubines should submit to God's disciplining hand; they should never chase their concubines away.

Why does the Bible not demand that the concubine be sent away? Please bear in mind that the sin of fornication and that of taking a concubine are two completely different things. If I steal a Bible today, I can return another Bible tomorrow. If I steal one thousand dollars today, I can return one thousand dollars tomorrow. But if I take a concubine today, I have no way to return her.

Some brothers think that all concubines should be sent away. This is a consideration from the male's point of view. All males should know that in God's eyes taking a concubine is equal to committing adultery. However, on the side of the concubine, when she marries a male, she is not married to two husbands. The male is married to two women, but the concubine is not married to two husbands. We have to see that the Lord never asks the man to send his concubine away.

I think the principle behind Solomon's mother is very clear. The Lord sent Nathan the prophet purposely to David

after David married Bath-sheba. Everything the Lord needs
to say concerning this subject has already been said through
Nathan; there is no need for you to add anything to his word.
Even if Nathan had missed anything, there would still be no
need for you or I to add a footnote to the subject three thousand years later. Nathan told David that his son would surely
die, and judgment would come to him. Others would commit
fornication with his wives in the sight of the sun, and the
sword would never depart from his house (2 Sam. 12:7-14).
Nathan did not ask David to send Bath-sheba away. If he
were to send her away, what would she do? Uriah was already
dead. Some are without their Uriah today, while the Uriah of
others is dead. What should they do? When God sent Nathan
to David, He did not ask David to chase Bath-sheba away. In
fact, God later caused her to give birth to Solomon (v. 24).
God did not cause any of the wives of David to give birth to
Solomon. He caused David's concubine, Bath-sheba, to give
birth to Solomon. Moreover, the first page of the New Testament says, "And David begot Solomon of her who had been
the wife of Uriah" (Matt. 1:6). The New Testament does not
say that one can take a concubine. But it does not say that
one needs to chase his concubine away either.

B. Her Duty of Marriage Not Being Diminished

Exodus 21:9-11 specifies that if a master betroths a maid
to his son, he shall deal with her after the manner of daughters. If the son properly marries another later, the maid will
become a concubine. God's ordination is clear: Her food, her
raiment, and her duty of marriage shall he not diminish. If he
does not do these three things to her, she shall go out free and
be a slave no more. Thus, if anyone thinks that he cannot
have intercourse with his concubine, he is not keeping the law
of God. I hope that you can be clear about this matter.

C. Such a One Not to Be an Elder

There is only one portion of the Word that addresses the
matter of concubines in the New Testament. In reading the
Bible, we love to see a certain matter that is mentioned only
once. If a certain matter is mentioned twice, we have to make

a comparison. If it is mentioned three or more times, we need to integrate the different portions before we can arrive at a conclusion about God's teaching. This is why every Bible student loves single-incident injunctions, because one needs to refer to only one case in order to know God's will. There is only one portion in the New Testament—1 Timothy—that only indirectly refers to the matter of concubines. There it says that an overseer must be the husband of one wife. This means that all who have concubines cannot be elders in the church. However, the New Testament does not say that such a one should send his concubine away or abstain from fulfilling her duty of marriage.

D. The Best Arrangement— the Concubine Being Saved and Deciding to Separate Voluntarily

If a concubine is saved and has no compulsion for continued sexual relationships, it is good if she is willing to separate from the husband. But this is something voluntary; it is not a commandment of the Lord nor a commandment of the church. The church should not demand anything concerning this matter.

God has put only two together, and this principle should be maintained. It is quite obvious that a person who takes a concubine will suffer more affliction in the body than one who upholds monogamy. This one will naturally experience more discipline from the Lord.

IX. DIVORCE

The Bible speaks of divorce, but divorce is sanctioned by the Scripture under only one condition. There are many ordinances regarding divorce among the nations of the world. Some countries have more than twenty ordinances on the subject. The Chinese also have many ordinances. For example, if either party is mentally unsound or if there is incompatibility of any kind, the couple can divorce each other. But the Bible gives only one condition for divorce—adultery. Factors such as mental instability or prolonged separation do not constitute legitimate reasons for divorce. The only reason for a divorce is extramarital sexual conduct. In Matthew 19 and Luke 16 the Lord Jesus shows us clearly that divorce is permitted only if adultery is involved.

A. What God Has Joined Together, Man Should Not Separate

Divorce is allowed in the case of adultery because man should not separate what God has joined together. In other words, the husband and wife are one in the sight of God. All divorces violate this oneness. What is adultery? It is the destruction of that oneness. If you commit sexual acts with someone other than your wife or your husband, you have committed adultery and have violated that oneness. A wife or a husband may be missing for years or may be mentally sick. There may be psychological harassment or other factors involved, but if one party turns away and marries someone else, he is breaking the oneness and has committed adultery in reality.

B. One Being Allowed to Separate Only When the Oneness Is Broken

Divorce is allowed in the case of adultery because the oneness has already been broken. Originally, the wife was one with her husband. When the husband commits adultery, she becomes free. When the oneness was there, she had to preserve it. Now that the oneness has been broken by the husband, the wife is free. Thus, adultery is the only condition for divorce. A wife can leave her husband if he has committed adultery. If a sister finds her husband committing adultery or taking another woman, she can divorce her husband, and the church cannot stop her. She can divorce her husband, and she can remarry. Anything that destroys the oneness is sin. A person can leave his or her spouse only where adultery is involved, because adultery has destroyed the oneness. Divorce is but a declaration that the oneness between a husband and a wife is gone. Since the oneness is gone, one can remarry.

Matthew 19 and Luke 16 are two clear passages concerning this subject, and we have to pay much attention to them. Divorce is based on adultery. Adultery breaks the original oneness between a husband and a wife. The two are no longer one, but have become two. Therefore, they can divorce. They can divorce each other because there is no more oneness between them. Actually a divorce has already occurred when one party commits adultery; it does not begin with the divorce proceedings. The so-called divorce proceedings are but a procedure. Marriage begins with the declaration of oneness, and divorce is a declaration that such a oneness no longer exists. This is why divorce is permitted where adultery is found. A divorce that is not based on adultery means that both parties are committing adultery. Suppose neither a husband nor a wife has committed adultery. They cannot have a divorce even if they cannot get along with each other. Once they divorce each other, they have committed adultery. If the oneness has not yet been broken when one tries to remarry, he or she is in reality committing adultery. Only when the oneness no longer exists can a person remarry.

We need to know what marriage is. Marriage means oneness; it means that two persons are no longer two, but one flesh. Adultery destroys this oneness, while divorce is but an announcement of the destruction of this oneness. Today if the oneness is gone between two persons, a remarriage is justified. But suppose the oneness is still there. The two may quarrel bitterly, they may not get along with each other, and they may threaten to divorce each other. The world and civic laws may even allow them to divorce each other. But in God's eyes, the two still cannot divorce each other. If they divorce each other, they have committed adultery in reality. Divorce is allowed only where adultery has already occurred. We must see that no one can separate what God has joined together. Since there is already a union, one must never try to break it for any reason at all.

X. WIDOWS

The Bible allows widows and widowers to remarry for the same reason. Marriage is something that lasts till death. In resurrection there is no marriage relationship. In resurrection men neither marry nor are given in marriage (Matt. 22:30). Marrying and being given in marriage are things of this world. The angels neither marry nor are given in marriage. Resurrected men likewise neither marry nor are given in marriage. Marriage is a thing of this age, not of the next age. Therefore, marriage ends with death. After one's partner dies, he or she may remain unmarried for the sake of cherished affection. But the Bible says nothing to forbid him or her from remarrying someone else.

Consider the teaching in Romans 7 which says that every Christian is a remarried person. We were remarried through the death and resurrection of Christ. Romans 7 shows us that a wife is bound by the law to her husband as long as he is alive. After the husband dies, the wife can marry another man. Whoever marries another man while her husband is alive is an adulteress. If we are not yet dead to the law or if we are Seventh-day Adventists, yet we are married to Christ, all of us are adulteresses. Thank God, we have only one husband. The Seventh-day Adventists have two husbands. Romans 7 says that we could not belong to Christ as long as the law was still alive; if we had belonged to Christ then, we would have been adulteresses. We were originally married to the law, and we belonged to the law. However, we have died through Christ. Today, when we turn to Christ, we are not adulteresses. All of us have been remarried to Christ. We are dead to the law, and we are not adulteresses. Romans 7 tells us that a wife is bound to her husband until his death. After the husband dies, the wife is free. It is wrong for anyone in the church to think that widows should not remarry. This is a heathen concept.

It is all right if a widow wants to remain single like a virgin. Paul said, "It is good for them if they remain even as I am" (1 Cor. 7:8). To live alone like a virgin for the sake of serving the Lord is right, but to remain unmarried because of criticism and social pressure is wrong. I hope that this concept can be removed from the church.

Paul told Timothy, "I will therefore that younger widows marry" (1 Tim. 5:14). The same applies to widowers. Today the issue is whether or not one has the need for marriage. Some have a physiological need. Others have a psychological need; they would feel lonely if they did not marry again. Some have a need because of their family. It is all right for a brother or a sister to remarry after his or her spouse has died. No Christian should criticize another on this matter. We need to eradicate all heathen concepts from our mind.

XI. ON COMMITTING SIN

In the Bible God acknowledges the validity of sex. There is nothing wrong with the consciousness of sex or sex itself. The consciousness of sex is not sin; in fact, it is holy. However, this is true only within the context of a marriage. In a marriage, sex is good and holy. But any sexual consciousness or sexual act outside the bounds of oneness is sin. Have you seen the difference? What is sin? It is sex outside of marriage. Why? Because sex outside of marriage is a breach of the oneness of a marriage. Therefore, sex is a sin only when it destroys the oneness. Sex has nothing to do with sin when it is sex alone. Sex itself is not sinful. We must see this clearly before the Lord.

In Matthew 5:28 the Lord Jesus said, "But I say to you that every one who looks at a woman in order to lust after her has already committed adultery with her in his heart." The word *looks* here involves the will. It is not just seeing a woman but looking at her. Seeing is passive, while looking is active. This looking is followed by the phrase *in order to lust after her*. It is not a passing lustful thought that comes to one's mind when he sees a woman, but a look at a woman that is for the purpose of lusting after her. Lusting comes first, and then looking. This look is the second look, not the first look. The first look is a random look at a woman on the street. The second look is to actually *look* at her. Between the first look and the second look, a lustful thought has come in. The second look is therefore for the purpose of lusting after a woman. The second look is the third step in the process. The Lord Jesus is not talking about the first look, but the look which is the third step. When some see a woman on the street, they do not control themselves and lust after her. Satan injects lustful thoughts into men, and they turn and look the second time. The second look is sin. Sin is having lustful thoughts and looking at someone the second time.

Matthew 5 says that everyone who looks at a woman in order to lust after her has already committed adultery with her in his heart. The Lord Jesus is not referring to the first look. It is wrong to involve the first look in this discussion. Suppose I see a woman on the street by accident. Satan may inject lustful thoughts into me. If I reject them, that is the end of it. But if I turn and look at her again, that is sin. Please bear in mind that the consciousness of sex is not sin. It becomes sin only when there is the consent of the will. When such a consent of the will happens outside the context of marriage, the oneness is destroyed by the will. It is sin to destroy the oneness in one's conduct. In God's eyes, it is sin also to destroy the oneness in one's will.

In the Old Testament, only adultery is spoken of as sin; fornication is not mentioned as sin. The Old Testament forbids only adultery, because man did not have enough knowledge of himself yet. What is adultery? Adultery is sin committed by those who are married. What is fornication? Fornication is sin committed by those who are not married. The act is the same, but the sin is not the same. We can say that a prostitute commits only fornication, but not adultery, because she is not married. We have to realize that God does not want man to commit fornication. The Old Testament speaks only of the sin of those who are married; it does not speak of those who are not married. It does not mean that there is no such thing in the Old Testament, but the term is not there. Here we see that the act that destroys oneness—adultery—is sin. But the act that does not destroy oneness—fornication—is sin as well.

We need to see that adultery is sin and that fornication is also sin. To destroy the oneness of the married ones is sin. Fornication, which happens to those who are not married and which seemingly does not destroy oneness is also sin. Christians should not commit adultery; neither should they commit fornication. We must see that sex is holy; sex consciousness is not a sin. Sex within marriage is holy and is not a sin. But if you are married and have sex outside of marriage, that is adultery. If you are not married but have sex, that is fornication. As believers we must not commit adultery, and we must not commit fornication.

CHAPTER THIRTY-ONE

CHOOSING A MATE

Scripture Reading: Gen. 2:18

I. THE IMPORTANCE OF CHOOSING A MATE

When God created man, He considered Adam to be one half and Eve to be another half. Man was not a complete man until the two halves were put together. Everyone needs to be married. The only exceptions are those who have received God's gift of keeping their virginity. Most Bible teachers agree that to God's children, mating means searching for the other half. God has created you as one half, and He has also created another half for you. You have to find that other half in order to become a whole. Mating means to make up the "whole." The two halves are useless if they remain halves. You must find the other half. If the two halves come together yet remain as two halves, something is wrong with that marriage. We believe that what God has put together should not be separated (Matt. 19:6). This is why we should find God's match.

Marriage among our young people has much to do with the church; therefore, the older brothers and sisters in the church should not ignore this matter. We must recognize the importance of this matter and help the young ones to make the right choice. If they do not make the right choice in their marriages and something happens later in life, the problems in their families will become the problems of the church. This will put a heavy burden upon the church.

We hope that the young brothers and sisters will open up their hearts before the Lord concerning the matter of marriage. They should drop all prejudices and consider the matter calmly. Do not look at it too subjectively, but consider it objectively. If one becomes too subjective, his heart and head will be too hot to see everything soberly or clearly. Learn to be calm and objective, and learn to bring everything to the Lord and consider everything properly. Do not be stirred up by your emotion, and do not leap hastily into anything. Please remember that a Christian can jump into a marriage, but he can never jump out of it. Worldly people can jump in and out of a marriage easily. But you cannot jump out of it. This is why you must consider it carefully before you jump in.

Let me mention some basic factors affecting marriage. I would like the young brothers and sisters to consider these factors calmly and deal with them one by one. Do not gloss over them lightly.

II. FACTORS AFFECTING THE CHOICE OF A MATE

A. Natural Attraction

It was easier for Jacob to marry Rachel than for him to marry Leah. We must never belittle natural attraction. I would never say that anyone would do for a spouse as long as he or she is a brother or a sister. The matter of attraction is not involved in being a brother or a sister in the Lord. But if two persons marry each other, they must consider all the factors that constitute a marriage. One of these basic factors is attraction.

Dr. Bevan of the American Christian and Missionary Alliance had a proper word for this. He said, "Mutual attraction is the highest expression of love." Such a great servant of the Lord also said, "When the Lord makes you a brother or a sister to all the believers, the question of attraction is not involved. But when He tells you to marry a person, the question of attraction comes in."

Even Paul himself did not forget this matter in 1 Corinthians 7. He said that if one thinks that he should marry and he wishes to do so, he should go ahead and do it. This shows us that marriage must be something that is produced out of one's own willingness. One must feel that he wants to do it. Natural attraction is a prerequisite to a successful marriage. Of course, no one needs to teach this, because the young brothers and sisters know this already. They are very much aware of the factor of natural attraction in a marriage. We mention this so that they will see that the older brothers in the Lord recognize this fact and acknowledge its legitimacy. All marriages that are void of natural attraction will not work well. Such marriages are reluctant matches.

If you want someone to be your marriage partner, you must want to be with him (or her) and must enjoy his (or her) presence. You must not endure his company but must like it. There are many people whose presence you endure; you cannot say that you enjoy their presence. But if you want to marry someone, you must cherish and treasure his company. You must be happy about being together with him. If you do not like his company, or if it is not something of an enjoyment to you, you should not marry him, because you are short of one basic factor of marriage. The delight and enjoyment of one's company must not be something that is temporary; it must be a permanent sentiment. You should have the assurance that thirty years or fifty years from now, you will still enjoy his company. This enjoyment should not be gone after three or five days. This attraction is one of the basic conditions of a good marriage.

B. Physical Health

Second, physical health must be taken into consideration. It is true that great love overcomes physical weaknesses. We know that some people marry for the purpose of attending to the physical weakness of their spouse. One brother in England wanted to marry a sister because she was blind. There are many cases like this in church history. Where love is great, physical weakness is overcome.

But we must realize that under normal circumstances, not everyone will have such great love. Normally, physical weakness can become a damaging factor to the success of a marriage. As the physical weakness of one party becomes more acute, the need for sacrifice in the other party becomes more severe, and this spontaneously leads to the possibility of failure in the marriage.

There are only two possible scenarios for a married person who is handicapped in some way and who is being cared for by the other party. Either he is very selfish, or he is self-conscious. A selfish person only receives; he does not give. He only takes but does not spend. If a handicapped person is selfish and always thinks of his own need, after some time this selfishness will become apparent to the other party. The other party will despise such a person and will think, "My husband (or wife) is so selfish. He (or she) thinks only of himself (or herself) and not of others." She (or he) will begin to despise the other half.

Perhaps such a person is not selfish but is very self-conscious. This will also pose a problem. When a person is very self-conscious, he will feel guilty about his spouse's constant service and sacrifice for him. It will be hard for him to receive this service or special treatment. This is why under normal circumstances, illness affects the success of a marriage.

Let us turn from the recipient's side to the serving one's side. There are also two possibilities with the one who is rendering the service. Either he sacrifices willingly, or he is willing to sacrifice with certain limitations. Human patience easily runs out; there is always a limit to it. Problems will flare up in the home when patience runs out. Sometimes patience has not run out, but there is an unwillingness to sacrifice. Sometimes you may discover that the opposite party is too selfish. You may begin to despise him or her. If the opposite party is self-conscious, you will burden him with a sense of indebtedness. This is like lending money to others. If the borrower is selfish, he will continue to borrow. But if he is self-conscious in any way, your giving will only make him feel worse. I would like to point out this matter to you. Although physical weakness is not an insurmountable problem, it will become a big issue in the family sooner or later. Physical weakness may not be a problem at the time of marriage, but it will certainly be a problem after marriage.

I know of a brother who has a severe sickness and whose wife has to work to sustain the family. The wife works during the day and takes care of the household chores when she comes home at night. Such a situation can last only for a short period of time; it cannot go on for a long time. The wife may work for one or two months, but she cannot go on this way forever. Under normal circumstances, no one can be overburdened.

I believe that a man and a woman should be comparable in health for a marriage to be successful. You cannot have one party who is healthy and the other party who is seriously ill. Otherwise, it will be hard and unbearable for the couple to go on during times of special trials. One must pay attention to the health of the other party when it comes to marriage.

C. Heredity

Marriage must be viewed as a long-term endeavor. As such, the matter of heredity must be taken into account. One should consider the health of the individual as well as the health of his or her progenitors.

Heredity is not only medically valid, but it is also spoken of in the Bible. God's law says that God is a jealous God. God will visit the iniquity of those who hate Him until the third and fourth generations. He will also show loving-kindness to the thousandth generation of those who love Him and keep His commandments. Many live dissipated and lawless lives in their youth because their fathers or grandfathers before them sowed to whirlwinds. The Bible says that those who sow to whirlwinds are those who walk in a wanton way. They may be forgiven and saved and they may receive new life one day, but some who are qualified for salvation may not be qualified for marriage. The Lord may forgive their sins and conduct and may save them. But if they marry and bear children, the children may not be saved easily. They will transmit their evil seed to the next generations, but they cannot transmit their regeneration to them. They can only sow the seed of sin but not the life of God; they cannot pass their regeneration on to their children.

Many times when such persons bear children, the next generation falls into gross sin and serious lawlessness. This brings much sorrow to the parents. I am not saying that this will occur when they are first married. I am saying that they will have a difficult time with their children during the latter years of their life. Some have wondered how some spiritual persons could have given birth to the kind of children they have. You may wonder why a sister has such an undisciplined daughter. You should realize that there is such a thing as the law of heredity. In many cases the second and third generations inherit the evil seed of the first generation. What one sows in the whirlwind he will reap in the whirlwind. Your next generation will reap the seed that you have sown. On the one hand, this sowing will give the church one more difficult sinner to work on, and on the other hand, it will give you one more rebellious son in your family. This can present quite a problem to everyone.

What should be done if there are some who have a hereditary problem but who are already married? They have to ask God for mercy so that they would be delivered from God's governmental hand. This has to do with God's governmental hand and His arrangement. They should pray that God's governmental hand will pass over them and spare them these dire consequences.

Young brothers and sisters should pay attention to the factor of heredity in the opposite party, because it has much to do with the rest of their life.

D. Family

Fourth, one has to pay attention to the family of the other party. There is a familiar expression in the West, which says, "I am marrying So-and-so, not her family." But please remember that there is no such thing. When a person marries a girl, her whole family comes along. Once a person marries another person, the whole family of the other side comes along, because a person is more or less a part of his family. All you need to do is to see if the other side's family has a high standard of morality or a lofty set of values. What is their view toward many things? Do they have a strict standard for everything? How do the males treat the females in this family? And how do the females treat the males? Simply consider these matters a little and you will know what your family's future holds.

A young person has been under his family's influence for

over ten or twenty years. He may not be satisfied with his family, but after he is married, his family's traits and ways will unconsciously surface in his new family. Sooner or later these traits will be made manifest. I dare not say that this will be so ten out of ten times. But I dare say that it will be so seven or eight out of ten times. Although the traits may not surface all at once, the other party's family will gradually creep into your own family.

If a father is very strict with his children, the sons and daughters of that family will not be too affectionate. Children from stern families are often lacking in affection. If a family is warm and the parents are full of love, the children from this family will spontaneously be gentle and easygoing. If both the father and the mother in a family are strict, the children from that family will be introspective and inward. It is all right if you want a husband from such a family, but do not expect to find a warm husband. If you find a daughter from such a family, she will be introspective and inward. If a family carries a certain trait, seven to eight out of ten times, the children will carry the same trait. Family traits always resurface in the second generation.

This is why some say, "If you want to marry the daughter, take a good look at the mother." This word may not be altogether true, but there is some truth to it. By looking at the way the mother treats the father, you will know how the daughter will treat her husband in the future. She has been watching her mother for over twenty years, and this is what she has learned. Daily she has been observing the way her mother treats her father. How can she not treat her husband in the same way? It will be hard for her not to do the same things. I would not say that, in ten out of ten cases, a daughter will be the same as her mother. But I would say that you can expect this to happen seven or eight out of ten times.

For example, some people have a very strong character. They can be very gentle when you speak to them. But they grew up in a family with strong character. Sooner or later these overbearing traits will surface in them. If a family is close, and there is little quarreling or fighting in the family, the one who comes from this family will spontaneously be congenial and quiet. They will not argue or engage in physical fights easily. Children who come from such families will at least consider quarreling to be wrong and serious. To ask them to engage in a brawl would be like asking them to climb over a high mountain. If a brother or a sister grows up in a family that argues or quarrels every day, he or she may be courteous with you today, but this courtesy is undependable; it is only a temporary mask. One day when he lets down his guard, all of the skills that he learned from his family will come out. To him, cursing will require no effort, neither quarreling, and you will not be able to do anything about it.

Before you decide to marry someone, you should study the other party's family, and decide whether you like it or not. If you like it, seventy to eighty percent of the problem is solved. If you feel that something is wrong there, do not expect your future spouse to be an exception.

Please remember that one's habit is different from one's view. One's view may be one way, but his habit may turn out to be something else. If there are arguments, fights, and bad habits in a family, sooner or later the children will argue and fight. It is not easy to change anyone's habit. When one marries a sister, he is marrying her whole family. When one marries a brother, she is also marrying his whole family. This is why one must carefully consider the other person's family.

E. Age

Generally speaking, women mature and age faster than men. In a marriage, the man should generally be five, six, or even seven to eight years older than the woman, as far as physical age is concerned. The woman matures five years ahead of the man and ages about ten years faster than he does. This is true as far as physiological development is concerned.

On the other hand, there is the mental development of the human life. Man has an intellectual age. It is possible for a person to be physically matured yet remain intellectually a child. It is possible for him to be old in the body but young in the mind. A man can be in his thirties physically but act as if he were in his twenties mentally. In that sense he is still young. Among Christians, if a brother's mental maturity exceeds that of a sister, it may not be a matter of concern for the brother to be younger than the sister in age.

The matter lies in whether one pays more attention to the physical age or the mental age. If physical age is the primary concern, it is better for the brother to be older than the sister. If mental age is the primary concern, it is all right for a sister to be older than a brother. This is something we cannot decide for a couple; they have to consider it for themselves. Some pay more attention to the physical aspect and others to the mental aspect. There is no regulation or law as far as age is concerned.

F. Compatibility in Personality, Goals, and Interests

The above five items are related to the physiological aspect of human life. Now we want to talk about the psychological aspect of a person. In other words, we want to talk about the question of personality.

For a marriage to be healthy, there must be not only natural attraction but also compatibility or agreement in personality. One can also say that there must be compatibility in interests or likes. If there is no compatibility in personality or interests in a marriage, sooner or later there will be no peace in the family, and both parties will suffer. A new believer must realize that natural attraction is temporary, but compatibility of character is something that lasts.

Among unbelievers, the kind of love described in their romance novels is always a matter of natural attraction. But this is not the kind of love spoken of in the Bible. Love does include natural attraction, but natural attraction may not be love. There is natural attraction in love, but there is also compatibility of personality in love. There are two basic conditions or, you may say, two basic ingredients of love: One ingredient is natural attraction; the other ingredient is compatibility and similarity of personality and interests.

Someone may be attractive to you as far as outward appearance is concerned, but you may not like him at all because what he does is totally the opposite of your taste. He may not like what you like, and you may not like what he likes. This shows that there is an incompatibility in personality.

1. Warm versus Cold

A husband or wife may be very affectionate in a family. He or she may like people very much and be very generous to people. He or she may go out of the way to provide warm hospitality to people. But the other party may be quite cold toward people. He or she may not be completely void of love, but an equal amount of affection is not found in him or her. Immediately, we can see that the problem is with their personalities. Suppose you are a person who is very affectionate toward others. You are generous and warm. Suppose you marry a husband who is also very loving and affectionate towards people. Both of you will find great interest in meeting people. You will feel that life is easy. Whenever you turn to the west, you will find the tide flowing to the west. You will always be riding in the direction of the tide. But if the other party is cold and frigid toward people, he will pull in one direction while you pull in the other direction. You will feel that you are tolerating him, and he will feel that he is tolerating you. When you behave a certain way, he may feel that it is too much and that he is tolerating you. When he behaves a certain way, you may feel that he is too stingy and that you are tolerating him. This is not very good.

2. Kind versus Harsh

Some people are not only affectionate but also kind. They do not want to hurt or offend anyone and are always considerate of others. If one chooses a husband or a wife who is also kind and considerate, who is happy to preserve the pride of others, and who never wants to embarrass others, he or she will always feel happy and optimistic. When he moves in one direction, the tide will seem to follow him in the same direction. Life will be easy for him. But suppose the other party is totally different. Suppose she always turns the opposite direction and is harsh and demanding toward everyone and everything. He will face many problems in his marriage. Sometimes a person is kind not only toward people but also to cats and dogs. If such a one has a wife who always beats the dogs and cats, they will face problems. Some people are kind to people as well as to things. Others are insensitive to everything, not just to cats and dogs but also to people. It is quite a big problem for two persons with different personalities to live together. It is hard for one side to pull in one direction and the other side to pull in the other direction.

3. Generous versus Stingy

Consider another example. A brother may be very generous towards people and willing to give away anything. If a brother or sister comes to his house, he will bring out everything he has in the house. But suppose such a one marries a wife who cringes whenever people come for a meal, and who is worried that others will eat everything that she has. One would expect difficulties in such a marriage. This is not a moral failure but a personality problem. The personality of some people is such that they cringe when they have to share a little food with others. When guests come, they purposely serve poor things and hold back the good things. This is clearly a problem of personality, not of morality. This person always leans in one direction. If the generous person marries a wife who likes to give away everything just as he does, he will feel that he is sailing downstream; he will be happy. But if there is any incompatibility in personality, the two sides will be pulling in opposite directions, and the couple will live in heated arguments all the time. This will become quite a problem.

4. Candid versus Cautious

Some people are very candid by nature. They not only are frank but they also like to be candid. Other people are cautious by nature. They not only are cautious themselves but they also like other people to be cautious. Problems will occur if these two come together. Please remember that there is nothing wrong with being candid, and there is nothing wrong with being cautious. This is not a problem of morality but of personality. Here is a person who is cautious, quiet, and introspective. Next to him is one who is candid and open in everything. The cautious one should not criticize the candid one, nor should the candid one criticize the cautious one. Both are wonderful people. This is not a matter of morality but of personality. One loves to be candid, while the other loves to be cautious. The candid one feels that the other person is too slow, while the cautious one feels that the other person moves too fast. Both suffer. If a candid person meets another candid person, both will go on happily. If a cautious person meets another cautious person, they will also get along with each other smoothly.

5. Thoughtful versus Impulsive

Some people are very thoughtful; they weigh everything carefully and consider it thoroughly. But others are impulsive in everything they do. They act first and think and talk about it later. Again, this is not a matter of morality but of personality. A thoughtful one should not criticize an impulsive one. Rather, he should find a thoughtful wife. An impulsive one should find an impulsive wife. In this way, both will live in peace. If a thoughtful person marries an impulsive wife, it will create quite a problem because each one will be pulling in the opposite direction.

6. Exact versus Careless in Words

Some people are very exact in what they say. They are so exact that their exactness terrifies others. Every word they say has to be exactly right. Other people may not be inaccurate on purpose, but they are not as careful in their words. Again, this is not a matter of morality but of personality. If you put these two kinds of people together, one may criticize the other for telling lies while the other may say that it is better to keep quiet than to speak as the other one does. To be fair, if every word had to be so accurate, perhaps no more than twenty sentences a day would be spoken in the world. You can see that incompatibility of personality is indeed a big problem.

7. Active versus Quiet

Take another example. Some people are very energetic, while others are very quiet. Both are right since this is not a matter of morality. But when a very lively person marries a very quiet one, even though one is a brother and the other a sister, it will no doubt spell trouble for the marriage. Sooner or later, a personality problem will be turned into a moral problem. They will magnify each other's peculiarity. The quiet husband will feel that his wife is too outgoing. The lively wife, in turn, will feel that she has married an insensitive man. A big problem will arise in this family. I know a husband who likes to stay at home, but he is married to a sister who likes to visit others in this place and that place. The husband finds it unbearable. He cannot stand going from place to place with his wife all the time, yet he feels imprisoned at home if he does not follow her. When he comes home, she is never there. He continuously tries to endure. If the situation goes on unresolved in this way, trouble will break out. Again, this is not a matter of morality but of personality; it is something that was overlooked at the time of their marriage.

8. *Clean versus Sloppy*

One sister cares very much about cleanliness at home. Everything in her house has to be very clean. She walks behind her husband with a rag and cleans up everything. But the husband takes pleasure in sloppiness. One day I visited their home and found her husband throwing a pillow on the floor, turning over a chair, and shuffling everything around. I asked him why he was doing this. He said, "I am so happy today because my wife has gone to her parents' house." He had been so frustrated by her cleanliness that he reveled in sloppiness. This is not a matter of morality. There is nothing wrong with being a little neat, and there is nothing wrong with being a little sloppy.

9. *Compatibility of Personality Being the Most Important Factor in Maintaining a Good Marriage*

A new believer must see that there are two basic conditions for love. One is natural attraction, and the other is compatibility of personality. When you want to choose a mate, you must first choose one who attracts you. A marriage that has no attraction will not work. Second, choose one whose personality is similar to yours. The mature ones should help the young ones to know their personality. Do not neglect the matter of compatibility in personality just because there is natural attraction.

I know of a couple in Shanghai who are always quarreling. I asked the husband why he married her in the first place. He replied that when he first saw her, he was attracted by her dark eyes. This is natural attraction. He just liked her dark eyes. But soon after they were married, the whiteness and the darkness of her eyes were forgotten. He only remembered that she liked to be tidy, and that he did not like to be tidy. She liked to be cheerful, but he liked to be quiet. She liked to be fast, while he liked to be slow. Please remember that personality is something permanent, while natural attraction is something temporal.

In choosing their mates, young people should not consider only natural attraction. No doubt there should be natural attraction. I like to see young brothers and sisters paying attention to natural attraction. There is nothing wrong with this. But natural attraction is not enough. You must consider also the compatibility of your personalities. This is something altogether different. If personalities clash, natural attraction will soon disappear. Natural attraction may induce you into a marriage, but it will never sustain your marriage. These are actual problems that we must be made aware of.

Some have said that a person can have two heavens or two hells. A person may go up to one heaven and down to one hell. He may also go up to two heavens or down to two hells. The happiest place on earth is a happy family; it is like heaven. The most terrible place on earth is a sad family; it is like hell. When a family is happy, one feels as if he were in heaven. When a family is sad, one feels as if he is in hell. A believer may have one heaven and one hell. An unbeliever may have two hells. He has a hell when he lives on earth and another hell when he dies and goes into hell. There are many Christians who live in hell today but who will go to heaven in the future. They live this way because the harmony of personality is missing from their families.

I recall the case of a brother whose wife fought and quarreled with anyone anywhere. She could be very spiritual when she wanted to be, praying beautifully and acting very spiritual. But when her temper flared up, no one could talk to her. She fought with her neighbors all the time, and no one could do anything about it. Her husband had to go around and apologize to this and that family all the time. Every time he came home, he had to find out whom she had quarreled with in order to apologize to that person. She was in trouble every day. Actually, if that brother had married a quiet sister or that sister had married an active brother, everything would have been fine. When an energetic sister marries a quiet husband or a quiet brother marries an active wife, trouble certainly will arise in the family.

10. Not Expecting the Other's Personality to Change

Many people have a wrong concept. They think they can change someone else's personality. Please remember that this is not possible. It takes a long time for even the Holy Spirit to change a person. How much can you do? Please remember that marriage does not bring with it the power to change a person's nature. Many brothers and sisters know that their spouses have a different personality, and they want to change it. But after two or three years, they find that there is still no change. If there is one hope in the world that is doomed to failure, this is certainly the one. I have yet to see a husband who has managed to change his wife. Neither have I seen a wife who has changed her husband. I once said that in marriage, one can only purchase ready-made goods, not made-to-order goods. Whatever a person is, that is what you get. You cannot order a person to be a certain way. You must first find out if you can accept such a brother's or sister's personality. You can only find out one's present personality; you cannot expect to change it. If you harbor such a hope, you will surely be disappointed. We hope that God's children will pay attention to this matter. This will spare them many headaches.

During the ten years that I worked in Shanghai, one-fourth of my time was spent in counseling family problems. I advise you emphatically not to put brothers and sisters with different personalities together. If they are put together, the result will certainly be serious. Children from such families will certainly be affected also, because they will not know which side to take when the parents are on a see-saw. It is also clear that it will not be easy for their children to be saved either.

G. Weaknesses

Now let us consider the matter of weaknesses. The above discussion referred to differences in personality and did not involve any moral issue. But human beings have not only differences in personality, but also weaknesses.

1. Moral Weaknesses

What is a weakness? Some are lazy, while others are diligent. Diligence is a virtue, while laziness is a weakness. Some are accurate with words; accuracy is a virtue. Others not only are a little careless with their words but also constantly lie. They love to exaggerate what they say. This is a weakness in personality. Some are tight-lipped and do not like to talk much; this is a virtue. Others like to criticize and correct others; this is a weakness. They gossip about this and that family. This is not a matter of personality, which does not involve moral values. When a character trait involves a moral issue, it is a weakness, and it needs to be dealt with before God. Some people do things quickly while others act slowly; this is a matter of personality. But if a person is so quick that he becomes impatient, he has a weakness. Some people are so slow that they become untrustworthy. This is also a weakness. Being impatient is a weakness, and being so slow as to become untrustworthy is a weakness as well.

2. Discovering the Other's Weaknesses

What should one do about the weaknesses of the other party? This is rather hard for any outsider to decide. Before young brothers and sisters marry, they need to find out each others' weaknesses. They must do this before they are engaged, not after. It is wrong to look for weaknesses after you are married; it is, in fact, very foolish to do this. It is too late to look for weaknesses after you are married. It is better for the husband and the wife to be as foolish and deaf as possible. If you try to discover the other person's weaknesses after marriage, you are too late, because you are already living together every day. You will see many things without even trying. If you purposely try to search for weaknesses, you will surely find more. The purpose of marriage is not to provide you with an opportunity for finding faults. Do not open your eyes after you are married. Before you are engaged, while you are still choosing your mate, do not be blinded by natural attraction. Do not allow natural attraction to veil you from the weaknesses of the other person. Do not be so hot as to overlook the weaknesses in the other party.

3. Some Weaknesses Being Unbearable

Let us consider the problem of weaknesses. There are two ways to deal with weaknesses. Some weaknesses are intolerable. They are like difficult personalities, too hard for some to accommodate. A marriage will not be successful if there is the presence of such weaknesses. Others weaknesses are bearable. After considering, one may decide that he can live with such weaknesses. Of course, he must try to discover the other party's weaknesses before they are engaged. Some try to discover their spouse's weaknesses after they are married. It is useless to find faults then; this will only damage the family, because no one can change those weaknesses. It is impossible to change them. One must take note and consider well *before* he enters into a marriage whether or not he is able to live with the other party's weaknesses.

4. Weaknesses Should Not Be the Same

Here is a word of reminder: Do not presume that those with similar weaknesses can get along with one another. Many people think that those with different weaknesses cannot get along with one another, and that those with similar weaknesses can. This cannot be farther from the truth. Some couples who have the same weaknesses argue, quarrel, and fight with each other all the time. One has a hot temper, and the other also has a hot temper. You may think that it is wonderful for both to have the same temperament. Actually difficulty is compounded when both have the same weaknesses. When there is a difference in personality, the conscience is not involved. When there is a matter of weakness, the conscience is involved. When both the husband and the wife are believers, any weakness in one party will be consciously felt by both parties. The burden of responsibility will be compounded, and the problems will be compounded as well. This is why we say that a couple should have similar personalities but different weaknesses.

I remember a husband who carelessly left things around the house; he never tidied up his room. His wife was the same. One made messes and the other made more messes. You would think that they would have been at peace with each other. But the two of them quarreled every day. The husband would say, "Do you not think that leaving things around like this is messy?" The wife would reply, "Why do you not tidy them up? Do you not know that I am very busy?" Please remember that one burden is heavy enough; two become unbearable. The result will be a compounding of family problems. Never assume that trouble will be less when both parties have the same weaknesses. Similar weaknesses result in problems. In fact, the problems will be doubled. When the weakness is with one person, he can bear it alone. But when both have the same weakness, the burden becomes too heavy. It is hard enough for one to bear his own burden. It is impossible for him to bear the other's burden on top of his own.

Young brothers and sisters should realize that some weaknesses can be tolerated even when found in both parties. But some weaknesses are compounded when they are found in both parties. Such weaknesses are intolerable. It is better that the weaknesses of the two persons be different. Of course, sometimes even couples with similar weaknesses can get along with each other; there is no rigid rule concerning this. One simply has to watch for himself.

H. Character

For a marriage to be successful, both parties must have character attributes that the other one appreciates. The wife must not despise the husband, and the husband must not despise the wife. Once there is contempt of any kind, the family is finished. Both sides should respect the other's character. The husband must respect his wife's character, and the wife must respect her husband's character. Hence, we have not only the matter of personality and weakness, but also the matter of character.

For example, it is excusable for a wife to hide things occasionally when she speaks. But it becomes a problem of character if she lies all the time. Some husbands by nature are somewhat selfish; they care only for themselves and not others. But they cannot carry their selfishness so far as to lose their wife's respect. Within a family, the husband must have some character traits that the wife respects. This is different from the matter of compatibility of personality. It is difficult enough for a couple to adjust to friction and conflict in personality. If, in addition to this, there is any contempt in character, the very foundation of the family is shaken. Then nothing can be done to save the situation.

Sometimes we see husbands who are very obnoxious. At other times we see wives who are very calculating; they will do things that are profitable only to themselves, and nothing more. Clearly these are character flaws. They are not merely weaknesses. This is a matter of contempt and disrespect. Once such elements exist, the basic ingredient of a marriage is gone. This is why we have to ask ourselves whether we can tolerate the other side's character.

Some people are quite cruel. They are harsh to others, no matter who they may be. They are insensitive to others' problems and feelings. They only want to express their own feelings, caring little if others are hurt. This is not a matter of incompatibility of personality but of a character flaw which opens the door for disrespect.

Some people have no control over themselves. They do not have any self-discipline. They are wild in everything, including their temper. When a problem arises, their anger flares up. Why does a person lose his temper? He loses his temper because he is selfish and because he is only after his own satisfaction. In the final analysis this is not a problem of temperament or weakness, but a problem of character. Once this element comes in, contempt and disrespect also come in.

Therefore, before two persons marry each other, they have to discover the admirable attributes in the other party. This is particularly true with marriages among God's children; there should always be some noble traits on each side. If a man has nothing in him that others can appreciate, this man is not qualified to marry. You must have at least one or two noble traits in the eyes of God before the other party will respect you.

I. Getting Along with Others

There is another aspect of personality and human consideration that we have to take care of. When you contemplate marrying a person, you must ask whether that person can get along with others. Marriage means a living together, and it is a big question whether or not a person can live together with others. Some people are by nature very individualistic. They cannot live together with others. If a brother is at odds with his father, mother, brothers, and sisters, you can only expect an unhappy marriage if you marry him. If a sister cannot get along with anyone and is always in conflict with others, you can be sure that there will be little happiness if you take her for your wife.

Everyone who wishes to marry must meet one basic requirement—he (or she) must be able to get along with others. Because marriage is a living together, if one cannot get along with others, he surely cannot live with you. If he cannot get along with others, how can you expect him to get along with you? The chances are very slim; it will be very difficult for him to change. If he has no respect for anyone in the world, can you imagine that he will have respect for you? If you wait until you are married, you will see that he also will have no respect for you. It is difficult for such ones to marry. In choosing a spouse, you must make sure that the other party has the basic human factors necessary for a marriage. You must find out whether he can get along with others.

Suppose a sister has reached the age of marriage. If she goes around and tells everybody, "My mother is terrible. My father is terrible. My brothers and sisters are all terrible. Everyone in the family treats me terribly," you can be sure that she will complain later; she will say also that you are terrible. Such a person lacks the ability to get along with others.

Please remember that if you can get along with others easily, the chance of success in marriage will be high. If you cannot live with anyone, the chance of success will be low. I am not saying that no one will be able to live with such a person. But I am afraid that it will not be an easy thing. This is a very important factor.

J. Being Consecrated

We have covered the matter of physical health, the matter of character, and the matter of the soul. Now we want to cover the matter of the spirit. Spiritually, a person must be consecrated to the Lord.

We should not marry a non-Christian. However, more is involved than just this; we should have a higher vision before the Lord. A successful marriage must not only be one with natural physical attractions and compatible personalities, but also be one in which both parties have the same spiritual goals. This means that both must want to serve the Lord. Both must be totally given to the Lord. One lives for God; so does the other. In all things great or small, both are for the Lord. This means that there is the need of consecration. Consecration is more important than good character. Once a couple is consecrated, the marriage will have a solid foundation. In such a marriage both sides will have a strong common interest before God.

In such a family, there is no question as to who should be the head and who should obey. Instead, both will say that Christ is the Head, and they will both obey Him. Then there is no need for any side to save his "face." Many times the wife argues with the husband, not because she is right or he is wrong, but because she wants to save her "face." It has nothing to do with right or wrong. She is merely trying to "save face." But the question of "face" will not come in if both are consecrated. Both can lose their "faces" before the Lord. Both can confess their faults before the other. We are those who are for God's will. Any problem can be resolved if both parties are for God's will.

In a family, if both the husband and the wife are fully consecrated to the Lord, and if both of them serve the Lord in one accord, the chance for such a marriage to be successful will be very high. Even though there may be natural differences, and even though physical attraction may fade away, none of these will become hindrances to them, and the family will still go on in a positive way.

These ten factors have to be considered in choosing a mate. They can be classified under physical (or outward) attributes, psychological (or character) attributes, and spiritual attributes. We must take care of all three things. We have to pay attention to a person's physical attributes, personality, and spirituality. All three must be placed in their proper perspective. We must consider all three things and study them one by one.

III. PAYING ATTENTION TO CHOOSING A MATE

Before you consider marrying someone or entering into an engagement, you should jot down all his attributes one by one. What about the natural attraction of such a person? What about his physical health? What about his heredity? How is his family? Everything needs to be written down in detail. This is a serious matter. Do not do it carelessly. You should write down every attribute one by one. What is his personality like? What are his weaknesses? How many attributes can you find in such a person that you can appreciate? Is he able to get along with people? How well does he relate to his family? How is his relationship with his friends? Does he have any friends? Please remember that those who have no friends make very poor wives and husbands. A person who cannot relate well to others has little chance of relating well to you. You must observe privately how he treats people, friends, family members, younger brothers and sisters, children, and parents. Then you need to know whether he is fully consecrated and whether he wants to live for the Lord. Find out how much he has given up for the Lord and how much spiritual experience he has.

The mature ones who oversee the young ones must also write down every point concerning the two persons and make a comparison. They will then have an idea of whether or not the two will quarrel or argue in the future. Many become aware of problems only after the problems have surfaced. We must study this carefully beforehand. This will tell us the chance of a couple's future success.

I would like to say emphatically that the family life of our next generation has much to do with the church life of our next generation. I want to speak a word to the elderly ones: You must take care of the families of our next generation. The church life of the next generation will be strong only if you take care of this matter well. If our next generation has terrible families, the church will suffer great drawbacks. Today those who already have families have no way to change their families. We can only ask them to exercise more forbearance, endurance, care, and love. But we hope that those who are not yet married will exercise themselves to build up a good family. This is indeed an excellent endeavor. In the coming days may God bestow His grace to the church so that many young families will be raised up in which both the husband and the wife serve the Lord and walk in His way together in one accord. How beautiful such a picture will be!

CHAPTER THIRTY-TWO

HUSBAND AND WIFE

Scripture Reading: Col. 3:18-19; 1 Pet. 3:1-7; Eph. 5:22-23

We have already covered the subject of choosing a mate. That word was for the young brothers and sisters. However, not everyone among us is young. In the future some new believers among us will be married ones. The Bible has clear teachings for those who are married. Some portions of the Word contain teachings for husbands, and some portions contain teachings for wives. Before a person is married, he should do his best to choose someone with the fewest number of weaknesses. However, after a person is married, he or she has to learn to behave in a way that avoids causing problems to the family or the church.

I. SPENDING TIME TO LEARN TO BE A HUSBAND OR A WIFE

The first thing a married person must realize is that it is a serious matter to be a husband or a wife. Everyone needs a certain amount of preparation before taking a job. For example, a doctor needs five, six, or seven years of training before he can practice medicine. A teacher has to spend a few years in a teaching college before starting to teach. An engineer also needs to spend four years in the university before launching his career. Even a nurse needs to study for three years in preparation for her career. But the interesting thing is that no one spends a day learning how to be a husband or a wife. It is no wonder that there are so many bad husbands and wives. They have never sat down to consider how to be a proper husband or a proper wife. I would be very hesitant and uneasy about asking someone to treat my illness if he had never studied medicine. Likewise, I would be very hesitant and uneasy about using a nurse who had never studied nursing before. I would be fearful and uneasy about hiring a teacher who had never been trained. If I wanted to build a house, I would only want to hire a civil engineer. I would worry and be afraid if he were not a trained civil engineer. Similarly, I have doubts about those who have become husbands or wives without ever being trained.

Our parents never taught us to be husbands or wives. When we grow up, we find a job. When we have the ability to support a family, we find a partner and get married. Please remember that many difficulties arise between the husband and the wife because neither has undergone any preparation. When two persons are drawn into a marriage unprepared and suddenly find themselves husband and wife, how can they expect anything but problems for the family? Everything we do with our life requires training; we dare not jump into anything rashly. We prepare for our work and try to learn something about it before we plunge into it.

We must see that no job is more difficult than the job of being a husband or a wife. All jobs have fixed working hours. This is the only job that takes up all twenty-four hours of the day. Every job has a retirement age except this one. This is a very serious vocation and a very important one.

For now we will put the past behind us. Even though you were not prepared when you became a husband or a wife, you have nevertheless become one. You are already married and have reached this point in your life. Perhaps your looseness in the past has ruined your family. Today you have to see that the family is a very serious matter. You have to go back and learn your lessons all over again. The husbands need to go back to learn how to be husbands, and the wives need to go back to learn how to be wives.

It may not work for a person to try to apply the same earnestness he adopts in his job to his family. The truth, however, is that many people are far more careless toward their family than they are toward their jobs. This invites inevitable failure into their family. We have to pour all of our energy into building our family. We have to be more conscientious with it than with our jobs. If we behave carelessly and do not consider being a husband or a wife a serious occupation, our family will end up with nothing but failure. If we want our family to be a successful family, we have to cherish it as a job and spend time with it. We have to try our best to make it work. This is serious business, and we have to make it work at all costs. Those who are careless about their marriage and have no intention of making it a success will never have a successful marriage.

All married brothers and sisters must learn this lesson. We must spend time before the Lord to deal with this matter in a responsible way. This is a more difficult job than any other job. We need to spend time before the Lord to learn our lesson well. I hope that we will start learning it today.

II. CLOSING ONE'S EYES
TO THE OTHER PARTY'S WEAKNESSES

After a person is married, he should learn to close his eyes so that he does not see. In a marriage two persons live together as husband and wife. They do this day by day, year by year, without any leave of absence or separation. There is plenty of time for each one to find the other person's weaknesses and faults. You have to learn before the Lord to close your eyes the day you are married. The purpose of a marriage is not to discover the weaknesses in the other party; it is not to discover the other party's flaws. Your wife is not your student, and your husband is not your disciple. There is no need for you to seek out his faults in order to "help" him. Never look for weaknesses and never try to correct. If you take heed to this warning, your family will be on a firm foundation.

As I mentioned earlier, one has to open his eyes wide to discern and consider all the faults of the other party carefully before entering into a marriage. But after he is married, he should not try to know anything more. From the day he is married, he should forget about trying to understand anything. If he tries to find faults, he can easily find some. However, God has put the two together. They may have the next fifty years together. Each side will have all the opportunities he or she wants to find out the weaknesses of the other party during those fifty years. This is why the first thing to do after being married is to close your eyes to the other person's faults and weaknesses. You know a great deal already. If you intentionally try to find out more, you will end up with nothing but trouble.

When God puts two persons together as husband and wife, His intention is that there be submission and love between the two. He has no intention for them to discover each other's faults or to correct each other. God has not made you a teacher or a master. None of the husbands are the teachers of their wives, and none of the wives are the masters of their husbands. No one needs to correct her husband, and no one needs to correct his wife. Whatever type of person you have married, you should expect them to continue in the same way. There is no need to look at the faults and weaknesses of others and try to change them. A motive of trying to change the other party is basically wrong. Those who are married must learn to close their eyes. Learn to love the other party. Do not try to help or correct them.

III. LEARNING TO ACCOMMODATE

One must learn to accommodate as well. This is the first lesson one must learn after he is married. No matter how much alike the husband and the wife are, and no matter how compatible their characters are, sooner or later they will discover many differences between them. They will have different opinions, different likes and dislikes, different ideas, and different inclinations. Sooner or later they will discover many differences between them. This is why a person must learn to accommodate the other person as soon as he is married.

What does it mean to accommodate? The meaning of accommodation is to meet someone halfway. We need to take note that it is something mutual. The best thing is for both sides to give in. If it is not possible for both sides to give in, at least one side must try to go halfway. Even if one sees many problems, he should still try to move away from his own position to the other party's position. It is best to move over completely. But at least one should meet the other halfway. In other words, after two people are married, both must learn to change at least half of everything they do. It is best to change completely. But at least they should change half of what they do. Always go out of your way to meet the other party. To accommodate means to not insist on one's own view and to be willing to drop one's ideas. A person may have a certain view, but he compromises his view for the other's sake.

If a young couple would learn to accommodate each other during the first five years of their marriage life, they would have a peaceful and happy family after these five years. Accommodation means one side goes halfway and the other side also goes halfway. It means one side moves halfway across and the other side also moves halfway across. The husband gives in to the wife, and the wife gives in to the husband. If neither party knows the meaning of this during the first five years of their marriage life, it will be difficult for the family to go on harmoniously. Marriage is not a simple matter. In order to have a good marriage, one must put much effort into it to make it good.

Accommodating others means sympathizing with the other person's limitations. Some people are very sensitive to sound. Others are very afraid of silence. Some cannot stand noise, while others cannot live without noise and excitement. That is why you have to learn to accommodate. If one person likes to be quiet and the other person lowers his voice for this one's sake, both have gone halfway, and there is accommodation. Suppose one is extremely clean, while the other is extremely lazy. If the lazy one has to go along with the clean one all the way, he will throw down his pillows and clothes and sing for joy when his wife leaves for her parents. On the other hand, if the tidy wife always has to go along with the lazy one, she will want to move back to her parents' home when she cannot put up with the mess.

As Christians we should learn to deny ourselves. Self-denial makes one an accommodating person. Both the husband and the wife have to learn to accommodate each other. In this way the family will have peace, even if they do not yet have happiness. If there is self-denial in the family, there will surely be accommodation in the family. If there is no self-denial in the family, no one will be accommodating.

Accommodation is needed not only in a few things or a

dozen things but even in hundreds and thousands of things. We cannot expect anything less. This is the discipline God gives to us in the family. Because we have to accommodate others in the family, we are disciplined through the family. This is the way we learn discipline. We must learn to put our views aside and accept the views of others. We must learn to accommodate.

IV. LEARNING TO APPRECIATE
THE VIRTUES OF THE OTHER PERSON

Once we are married, we have to learn to appreciate each other's virtues. In a family we need to learn to close our eyes to each other's faults and accommodate each other on the one hand, and we need to learn to appreciate each other's virtues on the other hand. This means that when the other person does something good, we must be sensitive to it. If a husband does not know how to appreciate his wife or vice versa, he or she opens up a big gap in the family. This does not mean that the husband has to flatter the wife or that the wife has to do something special to please the husband. It means that both must learn to appreciate the other person's virtues, goodness, and beauty.

I know a brother who is taking responsibility in a local church. All the brothers and sisters in that locality think that he is a very good brother. But if you ask his wife about him, she will tell you that he is hopeless. The sister constantly criticizes her husband, saying that he is not qualified to be a responsible brother. In that local church, all the brothers and sisters are submissive, with one exception—his wife. You will find that this kind of family will not go on well.

We also know of cases involving the opposite circumstance, in which everyone says that a certain sister is very good, but her husband does not. One year I was in Peking talking to a few people. Everyone there spoke highly of a certain sister. Halfway through the conversation, her husband came in. As the conversation about the sister went on, her husband remained silent. He seemed to be saying, "You do not know her. I have married the wrong person." The thought that one has married the wrong person has destroyed many families.

A husband must not be behind others in his appreciation of his wife. He may not need to excel above others in his appreciation, but he must not be behind others. You are not a proper spouse if your level of appreciation is less than that of others. If you feel that your husband is wrong, why did you marry him in the first place? This proves that you were firstly wrong. In order to have a good family, the husband must know how to appreciate the wife, and the wife must know how to appreciate the husband. One must not say something bad while others are saying something good about his or her spouse. You must discover his or her virtues. You must be sensitive to his or her merits. Whenever the opportunity arises, you must publicly acknowledge his or her virtues and speak your feelings. You are not telling lies. You are telling facts. When you appreciate your husband or your wife, your family will become more united, and your relationship more solid. If you do not do this, you will bring many problems to the family. Many misunderstandings and problems in the family arise as a result of neglecting this matter.

In England, a sister once married a brother, but the brother never said anything good about her all her life. This sister was always worried, saying, "I have failed as a wife. I have failed as a Christian." She worried so much that she contracted tuberculosis and later died. Before she died, her husband said to her, "If you die, I do not know what I will do because you have done so much for me. If you pass away, what will happen to our family?" The wife asked, "Why did you not say this earlier?" Then she went on, "I have always felt that I was not good, and I rebuked myself for it. You have never once said that I was good. I was sad and worried and always thought that I was wrong. That is why I became sick and am about to die." This is a true story. The husband told her how he felt only on her deathbed. Please remember that there is always a place in the family for kind words. We should learn to speak more kind words. We should learn to appreciate our wives and our husbands.

I know of some brothers who do not do well because their wives never appreciate them. The wives always think that their husbands are useless. They say to their husbands,

"Among all the brothers, you are the only useless one." These brothers become self-condemning. They say, "I cannot do anything. My wife says that I am no good. The person who knows me the most says that I am no good." As a result, they actually turn out to be no good. Whether or not one has a happy family life depends not only on closing our eyes to the others' weaknesses, but also on finding out the other party's virtues and appreciating them. Sometimes we have to tell the other party about it or acknowledge it in public. If we do this, many problems in the family will disappear.

V. BEING POLITE

One also must exercise politeness in the family. It is repugnant for anyone to be impolite to others. You should treat everyone politely, no matter who he or she may be. No matter how familiar you are with a friend, you should never give up your manners. As soon as you give them up, you will lose him. No matter how close you are to others, you will lose them the moment you give up your manners. In 1 Corinthians 13 Paul told us that love does not behave unbecomingly. Love does not allow anyone to give up his manners. Please remember that problems at home often arise because of small matters. It is often at home that a person behaves with unbecoming manners. Most people think that they can throw away their manners because their wife or husband is so familiar to them. Please remember that the joy and pleasure of human relationships have much to do with manners. As soon as you throw away proper manners, the ugly side of human nature will surface. No matter how familiar people are with one another, they must maintain proper manners between them. A brother put it aptly once when he said that manners are like the lubricating oil in a machine. The machine will run smoothly only with the lubricating oil. When two persons are together and manners are lacking, friction will arise and uncomfortable feelings will breed.

A. Words

In the home, we have to learn to always say, "Thank you" and "I am sorry." We should take care of polite words such as *thank you, may I, I am sorry,* and *please.* If you do not know how to use these words, you cannot even make friends, let alone succeed at home. Christians must remember that love does not behave unbecomingly. You must learn to say, "I am sorry," "Thank you," and "May I" at home. Learn to speak polite words in the family.

B. Dress

In the family not only must our words be proper and polite, but even the way we dress has to be proper and tidy. Everyone wants to dress properly in front of their friends. But one should dress properly in his family as well. You must dress neatly and be proper with your clothing. Love does not behave unbecomingly. Do not be loose through familiarity. Once you become familiar, you become loose, and it is easy to act impolitely. Familiarity breeds disrespect and contempt. Husbands and wives are already very familiar with each other. If propriety is absent, more familiarity will breed. Therefore, be proper in the way you dress yourselves. Do not save your sloppy dress for wearing at home.

C. Conduct

One must also be proper in his conduct. Whenever one serves something, it is best to serve it on a plate and to offer it to others with both hands. If he has only one hand to spare, he should still be proper in his attitude. When he passes a knife to others, he should avoid pointing the sharp end at others. When he passes a pair of scissors to others, he should avoid giving the others the pointed end. When he serves others something, he should present it properly and not throw it at them. We have to pay particular attention to these little gestures around the house. The difference between throwing something at others and handing it to them is only three seconds. But what a great difference it makes! Therefore, learn to have manners.

I cannot say that I have known many families, but I cannot say that I have known few either. When a person is discreet at home, his family will have less problems. I have observed that when a husband and wife are polite to each other, there is more peace and less noise from the plates and chopsticks. Where manners are wanting and things are thrown around, the family is full of friction. If a husband and wife are polite to each other at home, they will at least be able to maintain a peaceful family.

I believe that if many wives treated their friends the way they behaved in their family, no one would want to come to their houses. I also believe that if many husbands treated their colleagues the way they behaved at home, none of their colleagues would want to work with them. I want to tell the brothers that their wives have been very tolerant with them. They have tolerated what no colleagues would tolerate. I also want to tell the wives that their husbands have been very tolerant with them. If they treated their best friends the same way, their friends would desert them. Being impolite is an expression of crudeness. No Christian may be crude. A person who has learned the proper lessons will never be an impolite person.

D. Voice

There is another factor crucial to our manner—our voice. We may say similar things, but the way we say it may be different. Our tone can be different. When a boss speaks to his subordinates, he has one kind of tone. When friends speak to friends, they have another kind of tone. When people are in love, there is love in their tone of voice. When a person hates, there is hatred in his tone of voice. The problem with most people today is that they have exhausted their nice tone of voice before they get home. When they come home they have only an ugly tone of voice left. We are polite to our colleagues in the office, we are tolerant of the patients in the hospital, and we speak carefully to students in the school. But we speak bluntly when we are at home. If you spoke in the office with the tone of voice you have at home, you would be chased out of your office in two days. Many people have a very crude tone of voice at home. They use the crudest language in their homes. It is no wonder that they cannot maintain a proper family life.

We must see that the family will not be peaceful as long as

the tone of voice is wrong. Any tone of voice that is improper, strong, harsh, or proud must not be allowed in the family. Any tone of voice that is self-pitying, self-loving, or that gives the impression of a self-pronounced martyr must not be found in the family. If you speak in other places with the tone of voice that you use at home, you will ruin your career. Yet you allow such a tone of voice to remain in the family. It is no wonder that you are experiencing trouble at home. Therefore, we need to learn to be polite. Love does not behave unbecomingly, even in one's tone of voice. Do not speak loosely. If one is careless with his tone of voice in the family, his family will not go on well.

VI. ALLOWING LOVE TO GROW

In order for a family to go on well, love must grow. One must not allow love to die. Often young people ask, "Is it possible for love to die?" I will answer today, "Yes, love can die, and it dies easily." Love is like anything organic; it needs feeding, and it needs food. Love dies without food. If you starve it, it will die. But if you feed it, it will grow.

Love is the foundation of a marriage. It is also the foundation of the family. Love leads two people into marriage, and it keeps them together in the family. Love grows easily if you feed it properly. However, it dies easily if you starve it. Many people love each other before they are married, and so they marry one another. But after they are married, they begin to starve their love, and their love gradually dies.

Marriage without love is a painful thing. A family that is without love is an even more painful thing. If a family is without love, it may not feel the pain of it now. It may not feel anything before the couple reaches middle age. But when they become old, you will find that something is wrong with this family; it is too cold! The difference between a family that has love and one that has no love is very great. Learn to feed your family with love before you reach middle age. Try your best to feed it and nourish it. If you do this, your home will be full of love.

Another point which needs much attention: Every married person should find out the things that the other person is most afraid of. Do not indulge in your own carefree lifestyle. Every person has something which he or she hates or fears the most. This hatred and fear may be related to a moral weakness. Husbands and wives must learn to accommodate each other and learn to adjust themselves in this case. One person may fear and abhor something that is not at all related to a moral weakness. In this case the other party should learn to compromise completely.

Let me give one or two examples. A few years ago I read a story about a husband in America who sued his wife for abuse. This story may sound funny, but it is also scary. This husband could not stand monotonous sounds. He simply could not tolerate them. Originally, he and his wife were deeply in love, but the marriage came to a crisis after two years. His wife loved to knit, but he could not bear the sound of it. For the first year or two, he tried to tolerate it. But gradually it became worse. By the seventh year, he could no longer tolerate it, and he sued her for mental abuse. The judge declared that it was not a crime to knit and did not grant them the divorce. The husband told the judge, "Before I was married, she was like a lamb to me and I loved her. After a year of marriage, I found out that she was addicted to knitting. Each time she completed a piece, she would take it apart and knit it back all over again. She just loves to knit. Today I cannot bear the sight of any woolen yarn. I cannot even bear the sight of a lamb; as soon as I see one I try to kill it. If you do not grant me the divorce, do not blame me for killing someone else's lamb." Do you see the problem here? It is a real problem. His wife felt that there was nothing wrong with her knitting, but her husband hated knitting so much that he was driven to kill any lamb that he saw.

Please remember that everyone has things that he does not like and things that he fears. These things may have nothing to do with morality. A person may hate monotonous sounds; this is his peculiarity. Everyone has his own peculiarity, which has nothing to do with morality. For any family to be successful, the husband and the wife must never do anything which the other party considers obnoxious, even though he or she may not have the same feeling about it. If you do something which the other party cannot stand, yet have no feeling about it, you will end up having problems in your family.

In Shanghai I had many occasions to talk to families. During my travels, I also talked to many families. The things that a family fights over are often very small matters. To outsiders and friends, they may be small matters. But when these so-called small matters happen with such frequency that it exhausts a person's patience, major problems occur in the family.

We must realize before God that it is a very delicate thing for two persons to live together. This is not an easy task. Never think that we can be loose in this. What you consider inconsequential may be intolerable to the other party. You will be mentally torturing the other party if you do what he or she cannot stand.

VII. NOT BEING SELFISH

There is another consideration which is very important for the family: One must not be selfish. If you are married, you must live like a married person. You should not live like a bachelor. First Corinthians 7 says that a person marries to please the other person (vv. 33-34). Selfishness is probably one of the chief causes of family problems.

I remember a pastor in America who conducted the marriage of more than 750 couples during his lifetime. In every wedding he would advise the newlyweds to take note of one thing—not to be selfish. After they were married, they had to love each other and not be selfish. When the pastor was old, he wrote to all the couples asking how they were doing. All of them replied that they were able to have a happy family life because they took his advice about not being selfish. This is very unusual in America. At least twenty-five percent of American marriages end up in divorce today. But these seven hundred or more couples had lived happily with each other.

We must see that selfishness is a big problem. We must learn to feel what the other person feels. We must learn to feel his pain, his joy, his dislikes, his problems, and his inclinations. A person cannot be a good husband or a good wife if he or she is subjective. Those who are subjective are selfish. In fact, self-love is the most subjective thing.

A basic condition for marriage is self-sacrifice. Sacrifice means learning to please the other person. If you want to please the other person, you must be objective, not subjective. It is not a matter of your likes and dislikes, but of the other party's likes and dislikes. Learn to discover what the other party likes. Learn to understand him and his views. Learn to stand on his side, and learn to understand him and yourself from his perspective. Learn to sacrifice your own feelings, your own opinions, and your own views as much as possible. Try to understand and know the other side. Pursue self-sacrifice and love. If you do this, you will have fewer problems in the family.

Many married men think that they are the center of the universe. They think that the whole universe revolves around them. When they marry a girl, they receive her into the family for their own welfare and benefit. Those who think this way surely bring problems to their family. A wife may also think that she is the center of the universe and that everyone exists for her sake. She may think that everyone is for her happiness, and that when she found a husband, she actually found a slave. For her, everyone else is peripheral and she is the center. She marries a husband only for the purpose of achieving her goal. Such a marriage will surely fail. It serves nothing but self-interest. Brothers and sisters, your family will have problems unless you pay attention to this matter.

VIII. ALLOWING THE OTHER PARTY THE FREEDOM TO KEEP SECRETS AND HAVE PRIVATE POSSESSIONS

In a home, you must allow the other person to have a certain amount of freedom and confidentiality. You must also allow the other person to keep his or her private possessions.

In many homes wives do not have any rights. In other homes husbands do not have any rights. These kind of families are bound to have problems. You may be a husband or a wife, but bear in mind one thing: Anybody in the world can be loved except one type of person—a jailer. No one can love a jailer, a prison warden, or someone who imprisons him. No one can love those who take away his freedom. Many husbands are like prison wardens to their wives. For them to expect their wives to love them is like expecting a prisoner to love the prison warden; nothing can be more impossible than this. They hope for the impossible. Many wives are prison wardens to their husbands. They are asking the impossible when they want their husbands to love them. Prison wardens are objects of fear, not objects of love. You can never completely take away a person's own freedom. Although marriage does take away a man or a woman's freedom, not all freedom should be sacrificed. The husband does not have to give up all his freedom to the wife, nor does the wife have to give up all her freedom to her husband. If you expect your wife to give up all her freedom to you, this is the same as saying that you want her to fear or hate you.

No one likes to lose all of his freedom; this is human nature. Even God gives us freedom. The biggest proof of this is that there are no fences around hell. The tree of the knowledge of good and evil was not surrounded by the fiery sword of the cherubim from the beginning. If God did not want man to have any freedom, He would have surrounded the tree of the knowledge of good and evil with the fiery sword of the cherubim in the first place, and Adam and Eve would not have eaten the fruit. But God does not infringe upon man's freedom. For this reason, every husband should leave room for the wife, and every wife also should leave room for the husband. If you take away all freedom and make all the decisions, it is only natural that the other party will fear you. If you are not careful, the other party may go further; he or she may hate you. As soon as freedom is gone, hatred comes in. At the minimum, fear will come in.

The husband must learn to give the wife some freedom, and the wife must learn to give the husband some freedom. Allow the other party to have his own time, his own money, and his own possessions. Do not think that you can borrow your wife's time for your use just because you are her husband. Both the husband and the wife have to learn to keep their place. When you waste your wife's time, you are taking away her freedom. Small matters can become serious problems later.

Every husband and wife should have his or her own

secrets. This is a legitimate thing. The right hand does not need to know what the left hand does. If he is the left hand, it is not necessary for you as the right hand to know what he is doing. Learn to respect individuality. Do not make two persons one. If you keep this rule, you will avoid many problems in the family.

IX. THE WAY TO SOLVE FAMILY PROBLEMS

What should we do when there are disputes between the husband and the wife? How do we solve family disputes? It is inevitable for husbands and wives to encounter problems and enter into arguments. However, since both are adults and are children of God, they must learn to know what the other person's problem is, and where they differ. Before they can solve any disputes, they must know where the problem lies.

A. Any Settlement Needing to Be Fair

Any settlement must be fair. If it is not fair, it will not last. Do not expect one party to endure to the end. One out of ten Christians may endure to the end. But the other nine will not able to endure to the end. If a solution is not fair, sooner or later the problem will come back again. When I was in Shanghai, I arbitrated in some family disputes. Many people wondered why tiny matters could be blown up to such a big scale. You must realize that when small matters are blown up, they are not blown up because of the matters themselves but because of history. It is the accumulation of a series of things that leads to the explosion. The explosion may be ignited by small matters, but the underlying cause may have been an accumulation of grudges over the years. Do not consider any matter to be trivial. Problems surface today because they were not dealt with in a fair way in the first place, and patience ran out in the meantime.

B. Holding Conferences between Husbands and Wives

It is best for outsiders to stay out of family disputes. Let the couple hold their own conference. Let them settle their own disputes when they get into an argument. Do not allow news to leak out of the family, while the family itself is left in the dark. Sometimes, news regarding the husband is heard twenty miles away and yet he does not know about it himself. Sometimes news about the wife travels the same way. Let the wife tell her own husband about their own affairs, and let the husband tell his own wife about their affairs. In this way both are clear. Our experience tells us that husbands seldom know what their wives are thinking about and vice versa. Everyone else knows what they are thinking about, but they themselves do not know what each other is thinking about. Therefore, allow both to have the opportunity to speak to each other, and each should wait for the other to finish before he or she speaks. Do not allow the talkative side to dominate the talk. The husband must listen to the wife, and the wife must listen to the husband.

Many times, problems are solved as soon as the husband hears a word from the mouth of his wife, or the wife hears a word from the mouth of her husband. Many wives will only speak but will not listen to their husbands. If they would just listen, their problems would go away.

Both husband and wife should sit down and discuss the matter in an objective way, not in a subjective way. Once they become subjective, the discussion will fall apart. While they are talking, they should try to find the right judgment and the right feeling. They may not know who is right, but they should try to find out what is right. They should try to understand what each one is saying. Both must do this objectively, not subjectively. Both should speak, and after speaking, they should pray together. Always seek settlement through prayer. Ask the Lord to clearly show them where the problem lies. If they can follow this advice, the problem will be more or less settled by the time they pray together a second time. Many problems arise because they have not sat down to listen to each other and to listen objectively. As soon as they sit down and listen objectively, half of the problem is solved. As they sit and listen some more, they will discover where the problem lies.

During the first few years of a marriage life, a family should have this type of meeting two or three times a year.

Each side will then learn where problems lie and how to deal with them. Many families need to learn this lesson. It will surely solve many problems within the family.

X. THE NEED FOR CONFESSION AND FORGIVENESS

Between the two persons in the family, there must be confession and forgiveness. Many mistakes need to be confessed, not just ignored. Do not be careless about your own faults; you must always confess them. As for the faults of the other party, you must forgive them.

When a Christian does something wrong, the basic principle is to not cover it up. It is not enough to just repent for it. When a Christian does something wrong, the basic principle is to confess. A Christian does not cover up or turn away from a sin; this is not enough to be called a Christian. When a Christian does something wrong, he must confess and say, "I was wrong in this." Every wrong must be confessed. Whenever there is any wrong between the husband and wife, there must be confession. One must acknowledge, "I have done wrong."

You confess when you are wrong. But what happens when the other person is wrong? You have to treat it the same way that you treat all Christian relationships. When there is any wrongdoing, learn to forgive. Do not delve into the matter and do not be vindictive. Love does not take account of evil. This means that it does not remember the sins of others. Learn to forgive them before the Lord. Once you forgive, you should forget. You have to lay aside what you have forgiven. Do not be like Peter, who tried to count the number of times others offended him (Matt. 18:21-22). As long as you are counting, you are not forgiving. Real forgiveness does not count the number of times one forgives. As soon as you forgive, the matter is over. In order for a family to go on, there must be forgiveness.

XI. CONSENT OF BOTH PARTIES
IN SEEKING HELP FROM THE CHURCH

When a family has a problem, it must try to solve it first by calling a family meeting. In some cases one should forgive. In other cases one should confess. It is difficult for a third party to settle disputes within a family. The disputes between two persons are most easily solved between themselves. When a third party is involved, the situation becomes complicated. We should try to settle any dispute in as simple a way as possible. Do not look for complicated solutions. Referring a dispute to a third party is like adding mud to an injured leg. An injured leg without any mud is easily treated. But when mud is added, it is hard to deal with the wound. Disputes between two persons are more easily solved when a third party is not involved. As soon as a third party is informed, the problem is complicated. Therefore, a couple should learn to solve their own problems and should not try to inform a third party about it.

However, sometimes one needs to refer a certain matter to the church. Please remember that a person should not bring the matter to the church alone. The husband must seek the consent of the wife and vice versa before they can bring their dispute to the church. The two persons must have exhausted their means of handling the situation, and they now want the church to step in to help them. They should not come with their quarrels, but as those who are seeking help from the church. Both must come, and both must speak. Suppose both are willing to come to the church and say, "We are Christians. There is something between us. We would like the church to point out what is wrong." One will tell the church how he feels, and the other will tell the church how she feels as well. When both do this, it is easy for the church to step in to solve the problem. This is not an occasion for vindication. It is not the time for each person to expose the other's faults. Neither is it a time to get into a brawl. The purpose of telling the church is for both parties to sincerely discover where the problem lies.

XII. LIVING TOGETHER BEFORE THE LORD

In order to settle family problems and to have a good family life, there is also the need of positive influence. In particular, families with children should set aside a time for prayer together, a time for waiting upon the Lord and for fellowshipping about spiritual matters. Both the wife and the husband should be open to judgment from God's light concerning many matters. Neither the husband nor the wife should try to save his or her "face." Both should be willing to come under the judgment of God's light. There should be many spiritual transactions in the family. The members of the family should spend much time in prayer and spiritual fellowship together. This is especially true for families with children. They must seek opportunities to come more often to the Lord. In order for a family to go on properly, the husband and the wife should both live before the Lord. As soon as they do not live before the Lord, their family will have problems.

XIII. THE PROPER CHURCH LIFE BEING MAINTAINED THROUGH A PROPER FAMILY LIFE

I have mentioned twelve items. I hope that you will learn these lessons in the family. Do not be careless or foolish in these matters. If you do not learn your lessons well, family problems will soon become church problems. If a man cannot live together with his wife at home and cannot be one with her, he can never be one with the brothers and sisters in the church. This is a fact. A person cannot possibly fight at home with his wife and come to the church with hallelujahs in his mouth. One can only be a good brother in the church when he is a good husband and father at home. A good church life is maintained through good families. The husbands have to be good and the wives also have to be good. Then the church life will be free of problems.

CHAPTER THIRTY-THREE

PARENTS

Scripture Reading: Eph. 6:1-4; Col. 3:20

I. THE RESPONSIBILITIES OF PARENTS

Apart from the book of Proverbs, the Old Testament does not seem to give us much teaching concerning parenting. In the New Testament, however, Paul wrote something about being parents. Most books in the world teach children how to be children; not many books teach parents how to be parents. Most people pay attention to teachings for children. But the New Testament pays much attention to teachings for parents. It does not pay much attention to teachings about being children. Although it does teach us something about children, the emphasis is not on children. Both Ephesians 6 and Colossians 3 put more emphasis on parents than on children. We should learn to be proper parents because God pays more attention to parents than to children.

If we try to summarize the words in the Bible concerning parenting, the main thing parents should do is nurture their children in the teaching and admonition of the Lord and not provoke them to anger or discourage them. This means that parents must exercise self-control and must not be loose in any way. This is Paul's teaching concerning the subject.

As difficult as it is to be a husband or a wife, I hope you will realize that there is something more difficult—being a parent. Being a husband or a wife involves only two people; being a parent involves more. Being a husband or a wife is a matter of personal happiness; being a parent is something that affects the well-being of the children of the next generation.

The responsibility over the future of the children of the next generation is on the shoulders of the parents.

We have to realize how serious this responsibility is. God has placed a person's body, soul, and spirit, even his whole life and future, into our hands. No individual influences another individual's future as much as parents. No one controls a person's future as much as parents. Parents almost have a say in whether their children will go to hell or to heaven. We must learn to be good husbands and good wives, but above all we must learn also to be good parents. I believe that the responsibility of being a parent is more than that of being a husband or a wife.

Here we will consider the Christian way of parenting. The knowledge of this will save us from many headaches.

A. Sanctifying Oneself for the Sake of the Children

First, all parents must sanctify themselves before God for the sake of their children.

1. The Lord Sanctifying Himself for the Sake of the Disciples

What does it mean to be sanctified before God? The Lord Jesus said, "For their sake I sanctify Myself" (John 17:19). This does not refer to being holy, but to whether or not one is sanctified. The Lord Jesus is holy and His nature is holy. But for the sake of the disciples, He sanctified Himself. There were many things that He could have done which were not contrary to His own holiness; nevertheless, He refrained from doing them because of weakness in the disciples. In many matters the disciples' weakness directed the Lord and restricted His freedom. The Lord could do many things, but He did not do them because He did not want the disciples to misunderstand or be stumbled. As far as the Lord's nature was concerned, He often could have acted a certain way. But He refrained from doing so for the sake of the disciples.

2. Not Walking in a Loose Way

Similarly, those who have children should sanctify themselves for the sake of their children. This means that we should refrain from doing many things which we could do for the sake of our children. There are many things which we could say, but for the sake of the children we do not say them. From the day we bring our children into our family, we should sanctify ourselves. If you do not restrict yourself, you will not be able to restrict your children. The looseness of those who do not have children, at the most, results in trouble for themselves. But for those who have children, looseness results in damage to their children as well as to themselves. Once a Christian brings a child into the world, he must sanctify himself. Two eyes, sometimes four, are watching you all the time. They will follow you all your life. Even after you have left this world, they will not forget what they have seen in you; the things you do will remain inside of them.

3. Acting according to Standards

The day your son is born is the day you should consecrate yourself. You must set a standard for yourself in morality, in conduct at home, and in all moral judgments regarding right and wrong. You must set a high standard for what is ideal, and you must also set a standard for yourself in spiritual matters. You must act strictly according to these standards. Otherwise, you will have problems for yourself, and you will spoil your children. Many children are ruined by their own parents, not by outsiders. If parents are lacking in ethical, moral, and spiritual standards, they will ruin their children.

A young person makes decisions and judgments in his future life according to the training he received during his early years with his parents. A child may remember or forget what you say, but what he sees surely will remain in him forever. He develops his sense of judgment from you, and he also develops his system of values from you.

Every parent must remember that his actions will be repeated in his children; his actions will not stop with him. When you do not have children, you can do whatever you like when you are happy and give up and forget about everything when you are unhappy. But once you have children, you have to restrict yourself. You have to act according to the highest standard of conduct whether you like it or not. The whole life of Christian children depends on the behavior of their parents.

I remember a brother who said something when his son got into trouble. He said, "He is just a replica of me and I am just he." When a parent sees something in his children, he must realize that he is seeing himself. He must see that they are his very reflection. They are just reflecting him. Through them he can see himself.

This is why every couple should consecrate themselves anew to God as soon as they have a child. They should come to the Lord and consecrate themselves to Him again. From that time forward, the Lord has committed a human being, with his entire spirit, soul, life, and future, into their hands. From that day forward, they have to be faithful to the Lord's commitment. Some people are committed to a work for one or two years when they sign a contract. But this work lasts for their entire life; there is no limit to the term of this commitment.

4. The Sense of Being Entrusted

Among believers in China, no failure is greater than the failure of parenting. I think this is due to the influence of paganism. Failure in one's career cannot be compared to failure in parenting. Even failure in being a husband or a wife cannot be compared to failure in parenting. A husband or a wife can protect himself or herself, because both are over twenty years of age. But when a child is placed in your hands, he cannot protect himself. The Lord has entrusted a child to you. You cannot go to Him and say, "You have entrusted five children to me, and I have lost three." You cannot say, "You have entrusted ten to me, and I have lost eight." The church cannot go on if parents do not have a sense of being entrusted. We do not want to see our children being rescued back from the world. Suppose we beget children, lose them to the world, and then try to rescue them back. If we allow this to happen, the gospel will never be preached to the uttermost part of the earth. Our children have been taught many teachings, and we have been taking care of them for years. At least these children should be brought to the Lord. We are wrong if we do not take care of our children. Please remember that it is the parents' responsibility to ensure that their children turn out the right way.

Please give me the liberty to say this word. Throughout church history, the greatest failure among Christians is the failure in parenting. This is something no one cares much about. The children are young; they are in your hands and can do nothing much themselves. If you are loose with yourself, you will also be loose with them. We must realize that parents must exercise self-control, sacrificing their own freedom. God has committed a human body, along with his soul, into our hands. If we do not exercise self-control and give up our freedom, we will have a difficult time answering to our God in the future.

B. The Need to Walk with God

Second, parents must not only realize their responsibility and sanctify themselves for the sake of their children; they must also walk with God.

One sanctifies himself for the sake of his children. But this does not mean that he can be loose and careless when he is by himself. He should not exercise self-control merely for the sake of his children. The Lord Jesus was not short of holiness in Himself. He did not sanctify Himself just for the sake of His disciples. If the Lord Jesus sanctified Himself merely for the sake of His disciples, but was not holy in Himself, He would have been a total failure. In the same way, parents must sanctify themselves for their children, but they themselves must also walk with God.

No matter how much zeal you show in your children's presence, they can easily see through you if you are not genuinely zealous. They are very clear, but you may not be that clear. You may be a very loose person yet act carefully in their presence. In reality you are not the person you pretend to be. Please remember that your children can see through you easily. If you are a careless person and you try to act in a discreet way before your children, they will easily detect your carelessness and pretension. You must not only sanctify yourself before them for their sake, but you must also be genuinely holy in yourself, walking with God as Enoch did.

I would like to draw your attention to the example of Enoch. Genesis 5:21-22 says, "Enoch lived sixty and five years, and begat Methuselah: and Enoch walked with God after he begat Methuselah three hundred years, and begat sons and daughters." Before Enoch was sixty-five years old, we do not know his condition. After he begat Methuselah, we know that he walked with God three hundred years. Then he was taken up by God. This is a special case in the Old Testament. Before Enoch begat children, we do not know anything about his condition. But after Enoch begat Methuselah, the Bible says that he walked with God. When the burden of the family was upon him, he started to feel his weakness. He felt that his responsibility was too great and that he could not manage it by himself. So he began to walk with God. He did not walk with God just in the presence of his son; he walked with God even when he was by himself. He felt that if he did not walk with God, he would not know how to raise his children. Enoch begat not only Methuselah but also many other children; nevertheless, he walked with God for three hundred years. His responsibility as a parent did not hinder him from walking with God; rather, it caused him to walk with God. Eventually, he was raptured. Please remember that the first person who was raptured was a father. The first person to be raptured was one who had many children and yet who still walked with God. The way one bears his responsibility in a family is a reflection of his spiritual condition before God.

We must see that in order for us to bring our children to the Lord in a genuine way, we need to be a person who walks with God. We cannot send our children to heaven merely by pointing our fingers to heaven. We have to walk in front of them. Only then can we ask our children to follow us. Even though Christian parents want their children to be better than they are in the hope that their children will not love the world and will go on in a positive way, there are many bad families because the parents themselves draw back. If this is the case, they will never realize their goal no matter how hard they try. We must remember that the standard of the children cannot be higher than the standard of their parents. This does not mean that we should set a false standard. We should have a standard that is genuine and spiritual. If we have this, our children will come up to our standard.

Please forgive me for saying something that sounds simple and elementary. I once went to visit a family and saw the mother beating her child because the child lied. However, both the father and the mother in this family also lied. I learned that they lied on many occasions. But when their child lied, he was beaten. Honestly speaking, the child's real mistake was only a deficiency in his technique of lying; he was caught lying. The only difference between the child and the parents was that one was caught lying while the others were not. It was not a matter of whether one lied, but a matter of skill. One lied, and he was caught and punished. If you have a double standard, how can you raise your children? How can you tell your children not to lie when you are a liar yourself? You must not have one standard for your life and another standard for your child's life. This will never work. Suppose your children see and receive nothing but lies and dishonesty from you. The more you punish them, the more problems you will have. Some fathers tell their sons, "Wait until you are eighteen, and I will let you smoke." Many children say in their heart, "When I am eighteen, my father will let me lie. I am not yet eighteen, so I cannot lie. But when I am eighteen, I will lie." This pushes your children into the world. You must walk with God as Enoch did, in order to raise your children as Enoch did. If you do not walk with God, you cannot expect to raise your children the way Enoch did.

Please remember that your children will learn to love what you love, and hate what you hate. They will learn to treasure what you treasure, and condemn what you condemn. You must set a moral standard for yourself and your children. Whatever your moral standard is, that will be their standard as well. Your standard of loving the Lord will be their standard of loving the Lord. There can be only one standard in a family, not two.

I know of a family whose father is a nominal Christian. He never goes to church, but he wants his children to go every

Sunday. Every Sunday morning, he gives a little money to each of his children and tells them to go to church. The money is for the children to make offerings. Later in the day, he plays a game of mahjong with his three friends. His children, however, spend the money on snack food. They play until the pastor is almost through with his sermon, and then they sneak into the building to hear a verse or two. When they go home, they give their father a nice report. They have snacks, they get to play, and they make a report. This, of course, is an extreme case.

I hope we can see that God has committed our children to us. There can be only one standard in the family. Whatever we forbid our children to do, we should not do. There must never be two standards in a family, one for the children and another for us. We must keep the same standard for our children's sake. We must sanctify ourselves to maintain a standard. Once the standard is set, we must maintain it. I hope we will all take good care of our children. They are constantly watching us. Whether or not they behave well depends on whether we behave well. They are not merely listening to us; they are watching us as well. They seem to know everything. They know if we are pushing them around, and they know if we are acting in front of them. We should not think that we can deceive our children. No! They cannot be deceived. They know how we feel, and they are clear about the true picture. Whatever we demand of our children, we must take the same position in that matter.

After Enoch begat Methuselah, he walked with God three hundred years. What a beautiful picture this is! He begat many children, yet he could walk with God three hundred years. He was a genuine father without any pretense. Such a walk is altogether proper in the eyes of God.

C. Both Parents Being of One Mind

Third, the father and mother must be of one mind in order for a family to be healthy. They must be of one mind in sacrificing their own freedom for God's sake and in raising up a strict moral standard. The father must not have one view while the mother has another. I am talking about the case where both parents are Christians. It is another matter if one of them is not a Christian.

A father and mother often do not take the same stand. As a result, they give their children the ground to sin freely. It is not easy for children to have an absolute standard if their parents are not of the same mind. If the father says yes in regards to a certain matter but the mother says no, or vice versa, the children will go to the parent they like and the one they feel most comfortable with. If it is more convenient to ask the father, they will go to the father, but if it is more convenient to get an answer from the mother, they will go to the mother. This immediately creates a big discrepancy.

I know of an old Christian couple who held different views. One would have one opinion and the other would have another. Their relationship as husband and wife was poor. As a result, they also became poor parents. Their children would ask the mother about things she agreed with, and they would ask the father about things he agreed with. They manipulated their requests in this way. If the mother came home and asked the children about their behavior, they would say, "We have checked with Father." If the father came home and asked the children about their behavior, they would say, "We have checked with Mother." As a result, their children had complete freedom by manipulating their way through their parents' inconsistencies. Twenty years ago I said to the father, "If this kind of condition continues, your children will surely turn away from the Lord." He said, "That will not happen." Today all of their sons have graduated from college, and some have gone overseas for further study, but none have believed in the Lord. They all are very undisciplined.

It is a different matter if one of the parents is an unbeliever. If both are believers, however, they have to expect God's heavy hand upon them. If one is not a believer, either the believing husband or the believing wife can pray specifically for mercy. But if both are believers and they pull their children in different directions, they can expect nothing but trouble down the road.

Whenever children get into trouble, the parents must exercise themselves to be of one mind. They must have the same mind before their children. Whatever the children ask, the husband's first answer should be, "Have you checked with your mother? What did she say? If your mother says yes, you can do it." If you are the wife and your children ask for something, you first should answer, "Have you checked with your father? Whatever he says, I will say the same." Whether or not the other person is right is a different story. You must maintain the same stand. If there is any dispute, both of you must go into your room to discuss it. Do not open a loophole for them. They will become loose once there are loopholes. Children always like to look for loopholes. If the husband sees a fault in the wife or vice versa, any question as to why something was said to the children must be asked behind closed doors. It is important to clarify any disagreement, but you must not allow your children to find loopholes in you. If the parents are of one mind, it will be very easy to lead the children to the Lord.

D. Respecting the Rights of Children

Fourth, there is a basic principle in the Bible that children are given by Jehovah (Psa. 127:3). According to the Bible, children are entrusted by God to man. One day you must render your account of this trust to God. No one can say that his children are his and his alone. The thought that one's children are his own, that one can do whatever he wants with them, and that he has absolute control over them is a pagan concept; it is not a Christian concept. Christianity never teaches that children are ours. Rather, it acknowledges that children are God's trust and that parents cannot exercise despotic control over their children throughout their childhood.

1. Parents Do Not Have Unlimited Authority

Some people hold on to the concept that parents are always right. They hold on to this concept even after they have become Christians. Please remember that many parents are not always right. Many times the parents are quite wrong. We should not pick up pagan concepts, and we should not assume that we have unlimited authority over our children.

Please remember that parents do not have absolute authority over their children. Children have their own spirit and their own soul, over which the parents have no control whatsoever. Since children have their own spirit and soul, they are under their own control. They can go to heaven, or they can go to hell. They must be responsible for themselves before God. We cannot treat them as an object or as property. We should not assume that we can exercise unlimited authority over them. God has not given us such absolute authority. God has given us unlimited authority over dead things, but He has not given us unlimited authority over human beings who have their own spirit and soul. No one can have absolute authority over another person with a spirit and a soul. The thought of absolute authority is a pagan concept. It is related to pride and should not be found among us.

2. Children Are Not the Means by which Parents Vent Their Wrath

We are reasonable with our friends and with other members of our family. We are courteous and reasonable with our colleagues and are even more courteous and respectful to our superiors. We try to get along well with every kind of person. But we treat our children as if they are our personal property, forgetting that they also have a spirit and a soul and that they are gifts from God. It is possible for us to vent our anger on them and treat them as we please. Some people think that they need to be courteous to everyone in the world except their own children. They seem to regard their children as the means of venting their anger. I know of parents who are this way at home. They seem to think that a man must be courteous and gentle and yet, at the same time, have a strong temper. It seems that they are not complete if they do not lose their temper. Nevertheless, they realize that they will be in trouble if they lose their temper with others. Their superiors will fire them if they lose their temper with them, and their friends will despise them if they lose their temper with them. They think that there is only one place where they can lose their temper without suffering punishment—with their children. Many parents have a terrible temper toward their children. It is as if their children were the cultivating ground for their temper.

Please forgive me for saying such strong words. I have seen many parents shout at their children over dinner and then turn toward me and say, "Mr. Nee, please take some of this food. It is delicious." When this happens. I have no heart for the food. These things often happen within a span of just a few minutes. On the one hand, they scold their children, and on the other hand, they say, "Mr. Nee, please eat." The problem with some parents is that they consider their children to be the rightful means for venting their anger. Did God give us children so that we have a place to lose our temper? May God be merciful to us!

Please remember that God has not denied all rights of children. He has not annulled all the self-esteem, personal freedom, or independent constitution of the children. He has not put them in our hands for us to beat them and scold them. There is no such thing. This is a non-Christian thought; it is not a Christian concept. Please remember that the same standard of right and wrong equally applies to us and our children. There should be only one standard for us and our children. We cannot have one standard for ourselves and another standard for them. Let me say a word to the new believers. You must be tender and gentle to your children. Never be rude to them. Do not scold them or rebuke them arbitrarily, much less beat them at will.

Please remember that such conduct leads to indulgence. Everyone who wants to know God must learn to control himself. In particular, he should control himself when it comes to dealing with his children. This kind of self-control comes from a proper respect of a child's soul. No matter how small or weak a child is, remember that he has his own personality. God has given him a personality and a soul. You must not damage his character, destroy his personality, or despise his soul. You must not treat him in an arbitrary way. You must learn to respect him as a person.

At the same time, our children are entrusted to our family. Their standard of morality must be our standard of morality. Whatever applies to them must also apply to us. Parents have no right to vent their wrath on their children. A Christian should not lose his temper with anyone, not even with his own children. It is wrong for us to lose our temper with anyone, no matter whom it may be. We should be reasonable, and we should only reason with our children. What is right is always right and what is wrong is always wrong. Do not intimidate them just because they are small and weak. Those who oppress the weak and the small are the most cowardly people in the world.

3. Do Not Become a Cross to Your Children

Two students were once talking to each other in school. The girl said to her classmate, "I know my father. He is willing to die for me." Listen to what she said! This is the comment of a child about her father. Her father was a Christian. This was the kind of father he was to her. The other girl was also from a Christian family. Her father was harsh and lost his temper with his daughter easily. Once she heard a sermon at school. When she arrived home, her father asked her what she had learned. She answered, "I now know that the Lord has given you to me to be my cross." Both fathers were Christians. But what a difference between them!

I would say to the parents: Be slow to demand obedience from your children. Instead, first demand that you yourselves be good parents before the Lord. If you are not good parents, you can never be good Christians. God does not give us children for the purpose of making us their crosses. God gave us children so that we will learn to honor their freedom, personality, and soul before the Lord.

E. Not Provoking Children to Anger

Fifth, Paul showed us an important thing that parents should not do—they should not provoke their children to anger (Eph. 6:4).

1. Not Exercising Authority Excessively

What does it mean to provoke children to anger? It means the excessive use of authority. One can overpower his children with physical strength. This is always possible because parents are stronger than their children. Or one can try to subdue his children with financial power. He may say, "If you do not obey me, I will not give you any money. If you do not listen to me, I will take away your food and clothing." Since the children depend on him for their living, he overpowers them with his money by threatening to withdraw his support. Some parents dominate their children with physical power, and others dominate them with their iron will. This can provoke their children to anger. When they are provoked, they will wait for the chance for their freedom. One day they will break their bondage and seek total freedom.

I know a brother whose father gambled, smoked, and behaved rudely at home. He embezzled public funds and was involved in many other unscrupulous businesses. But he still went to church, and he wanted all of his children to go to church. He would rebuke and punish them severely if they did not go. He ruined his children's taste for the family, all the while insisting that they go to church. Later, the brother said, "I vowed that when I grew up one day, I would never go to church. As soon as I could support myself, I was going to turn away from the church." Even though he swore this way, eventually he was saved. Thank God! Otherwise, he would have become another anti-Christian proponent. This was a very serious matter. The father did not try to make his children love him, yet he demanded that his children go to church. This never works. This provokes children to anger. Parents should not exercise excessive authority over their children or provoke them to anger. They must never make their children hardened and rebellious toward them.

I remember another man who is not saved. Not long ago I saw him. He was forced to read the Bible when he was growing up at home, and he was forced to read the Bible when he went to a parochial school. I am not saying that parents should not charge their children to read the Bible. I am saying that you must attract them and be an example to them yourself. It will never work if you merely tell them that the Lord is precious, yet constantly abuse them. There was a mother who was a nominal Christian. She had a terrible temper. She insisted that her son read the Bible and go to a parochial school. One day he asked when he could stop reading the Bible. His mother replied, "When you finish secondary school, you can stop reading the Bible." On the day that he received his high school diploma, he took his three copies of the Bible and burned them in the backyard. You must draw children in a natural way. Otherwise, when their anger is provoked they may do anything. You want them to be good, but they will rebel against you when they become free. This is what is meant by provoking children to anger. Do not provoke your children to anger. You must learn to be proper parents, to have love, tenderness, and a proper testimony before them. You must also be an attraction to them. Do not exercise your authority excessively. Authority can only be exercised under self-control. If you are excessive in your use of authority, you will stifle your relationship with your children.

2. Showing Proper Appreciation

In addition, you should show proper appreciation for your children when they perform well. Some parents only know how to punish and scold; they know nothing else. This easily provokes their children to anger. Please remember that many children do have a desire to be good. If you have nothing for them except punishment and rebuke, they will become disheartened, according to Paul's word in Colossians 3:21. They will say that it is useless to do good because their parents will not acknowledge it. You must encourage your children when they perform well. You can say to them, "Today you have done well. I will reward you. I want to give you something special." Children do need to be disciplined, but they also need to be rewarded. Otherwise, they will become disheartened.

I read of a story about a little girl whose mother only knew how to beat and scold her children. The child had a good disposition when she was young. Since she felt that her mother did not approve of her, she decided that she would work especially hard one day to try to please her. When evening came, her mother undressed her, put her to bed, and began to walk away. As the mother was walking away, the daughter called to her. The mother asked what she wanted. She did not say anything. When the mother started to walk away again, the daughter called again. When the mother asked her again, the daughter said, "Mother, do you not have anything to say?" This is one of the stories told by Mr. Bervin. After the mother left, the girl cried for two hours. Her mother was too insensitive. She only knew how to beat and scold her daughter; she was insensitive to everything else.

Please remember that the New Testament has more teaching for parents than for children. The whole world speaks of the mistakes that children make, but the Lord spoke of the mistakes that parents make. Since the world speaks so much about children's mistakes, we do not have to say too much about them. The Bible tells us parents can indeed provoke their children to anger and dishearten them through their insensitivity. This is why it speaks so much about parenting. This occupation is more difficult than any other occupation in the world. Those who are parents must devote all their energy and mind to be proper parents. Please do not be insensitive to your children.

F. Being Accurate with Words

Sixth, parents' words are very important to children. You must not only be a pattern to your children but also realize that your words are very important to them.

1. Not Making Empty Promises

Please remember that parents should not say anything to their children that they cannot carry out. You must not make empty promises to your children. Do not promise them something if you do not have the ability to fulfill your promise. Do not make a promise to them if you cannot fulfill it. If your children want you to buy something, you have to consider your financial ability. If you can do it, do it. If not, you must say, "I will do my best. I will do what I can do. But I cannot do what is beyond my ability." Every word of yours must be reliable. You should not think that this is a small matter. You must not allow your children to doubt your words. Not only must they not doubt your words, but they also must have the assurance that your words are accurate. If the children find their parents' words to be unreliable, they will grow up acting carelessly. They will think that since one can be careless with his words, he can be careless with anything. Some expressions can be used only in politics; they are not factual. Parents should not use such expressions. Many parents are apparently too kind to their children. They promise whatever their children ask, but nine out of ten times they cannot fulfill their promises. Such wonderful promises produce only one result in the children—disappointment. You must promise only things that you can do. If you cannot do a certain thing, do not promise it. If you are not sure whether you can do it, tell them so. Your words must be accurate.

2. Orders Needing to Be Carried Out

Sometimes you are not making a promise, but giving an order. If you open your mouth to ask your children to do something, you must make sure that it is done. You have to make them realize that you mean what you say. Many times you give a proper order, but you forget about it. This is wrong. You should not tell your children that it is all right if they do not carry out your order this time, just as long as they do it the next time. If you excuse them, you are not doing them a favor. You should show your children that once you say something, they must carry it out whether or not you remember it. If you say it once, you can say it a hundred times. If your word counts for one thing, your word should count for a hundred things. You should not nullify your own words. Show them from their youth that words are hallowed, whether they are a promise or an order. For example, if you tell your child to sweep his room every morning, you must first consider whether or not it is within his ability to do it. If he does not do it today, you must make sure that he does it the next day. If he does not do it the next day, you must make sure that he does it the third day. You must uphold your order this year, and you must uphold it next year. You have to show your children that your words are not uttered lightly and that once they are uttered, they have to be carried out. If they find that your words do not count, your words will become ineffective. Hence, every word out of your mouth must be practical and principled.

3. Correcting Exaggerated Words

Sometimes you exaggerate your words. You must find an opportunity to tell your children that you exaggerated your words on that particular occasion. Your words must be accurate. Sometimes you see only two cows but you say that there are three, or you see five birds but say that there are eight. You must correct yourself immediately. In speaking to your children, you must learn to always correct yourself. You should learn to say, "What I just said was not that accurate. There are two cows, not three." You must show them that words should be sanctified. Everything that happens in the family should be for the building up of Christian character. You must sanctify your words. When your children speak, they should also sanctify their words and be accurate with them. When you say something wrong, you must make a point to admit your mistake. In this manner you will train your children to sanctify their words. Many parents say five when they mean three or three when they mean two. They speak loosely and do not set up good patterns at home. As a result, their children never realize that words are sacred.

All these problems occur because there is a lack of discipline from the Lord. We should experience the Lord's discipline and lead our children to the Lord's discipline. At least we should show them that words are sacred. Every promise should be realized and every order should be carried out. Every word has to be accurate. If we do this, our children will receive proper training.

G. Nurturing Children in the Discipline and Admonition of the Lord

Seventh, you must nurture your children in the discipline and admonition of the Lord (Eph. 6:4). The discipline of the Lord is telling a person how he should behave himself. You must consider your children as Christians, not Gentiles. The Lord's discipline tells a person how he should behave as a Christian. The Lord intends that all of our children become Christians. He has no intention that any of them be a Gentile or an unsaved person. You should plan on all of them becoming not just Christians, but good Christians. You should tell them what a proper Christian is by teaching them the discipline of the Lord. Here we must briefly cover a number of points.

1. Helping Children to Have Proper Aspirations

The biggest thing about a child is his aspirations. Every child has an aspiration when he is young. If the government allowed every child to print his business card, I think many children would print "President," "Chairman," or "Queen." Parents must help their children to have proper aspirations. If you love the world, your children will probably want to be the president, a millionaire, or a great academic. How you live affects the aspirations of your child. Parents must learn to channel the ambitions of their children in the proper direction. They should aspire to be a lover of the Lord. They should not aspire to love the world. You should cultivate such an ambition within them while they are young. Show them that it is an honorable thing to die for the Lord, that it is a precious thing to be a martyr for the Lord. You have to be an example to them, and you have to tell them your ambitions. Tell them what you want to be if you are given the opportunity. Tell them what kind of Christian you want to be. In this way, you will channel their ambitions in the proper direction. Their goals will change, and they will know what is noble and what is precious.

2. Not Encouraging the Pride of Children

Children have another problem: They are not only ambitious and aspiring but also proud of themselves. They may boast about their own cleverness, skill, or eloquence. A child can find many things to boast about. He may think that he is a very special person. Parents should not discourage them, but neither should they cultivate their pride. Many parents cultivate their children's pride and encourage them to go after vainglory by heaping praises upon them in front of other people. We should tell them, "There are many children who are like you in this world." Do not try to encourage their pride. We should enlighten children according to the discipline and admonition of the Lord. They should be able to think, to speak, and to learn all the skills. But you have to tell them that there are many who are like them in this world. Do not destroy their self-esteem, but do not allow them to become proud. You do not need to hurt their self-esteem, but you must point out their pride to them. Many young people leave home only to find out that they have to spend ten or twenty years in the world in order to learn how to do things properly. By then it is too late. Many young people have a wild temper at home. They are so proud that they cannot work properly. We do not want our children to become disheartened, but neither do we want them to be proud or to think that they are somebody.

3. Teaching Children to Accept Defeat and to Learn Humility

A Christian needs to know how to appreciate others. It is easy to be victorious, but it is hard to accept defeat. We can find champions who are humble, but it is rare to find losers who are not bitter. This is not a Christian attitude. Those who are good in some areas should learn to be humble and not boastful. At the same time, when a person is defeated he should learn to accept his defeat. Children are very competitive. It is all right for them to be competitive; they want to win at ball games, track meets, and in their school work. You have to show them that it is right for them to study well at school, but they have to learn to be humble. Encourage them to be humble. Tell them that there are many other students who may be better than they are. When they are defeated, you need to teach them to accept their defeat with grace. A child's problem often has to do with these attitudes. After a game the winner is proud, while the loser will complain that the judge was not fair or that he made the wrong judgment because the sun was glaring in his face. You should help them to develop a humble character. They should be under Christian admonition and should develop Christian character. They can win, and when they lose they can also appreciate others. Admitting defeat is a virtue. The Chinese are greatly lacking in this virtue. Most Chinese blame others when they are defeated instead of conceding with grace. You must nurture your children in the discipline and admonition of the Lord.

Many children say that their teacher plays favorites when others do well on tests. When they do not do well themselves, they say their teacher does not like them. Here we see the need for humility. Christians must have the virtue of accepting defeat. If others are good, we have to say promptly that they are good. We also have to accept defeat and concede that others are smarter, more hard working, or better than us. It is a Christian virtue to accept defeat. When we win, we should not look down upon everyone else. This attitude is unworthy of a Christian. When others are better than us, we have to appreciate them. Others may jump higher or be stronger than us. We should train our children to acknowledge achievement in others, while they are still living at home with us. This training will help them understand themselves when they grow up as Christians. We should know ourselves and appreciate those who are better than us. If our children are this way, it will be easy for them to experience spiritual things.

4. Teaching Children to Choose

I hope that we will pay attention to this matter. In many aspects we have to teach our children according to the discipline of the Lord. From their youth, we should give them a chance to make their own choices. We should not make every choice for them until they reach the age of eighteen or twenty. If we do, it will be impossible for them to make any decisions when they grow up. We have to always give them the opportunity to make decisions. Give them the chance to choose what they like and what they do not like. We have to show them whether their choices are right. Give them the chance to choose and then show them the right choice. Let them see it for themselves. Some like to wear short dresses. Some prefer one kind of color, while others prefer another kind of color. Let them make the choices by themselves.

Some people do not give their children the opportunity to make choices. As a result, when their children reach their twenties and marry someone, they do not know how to be the head. You can tell them that the husband is the head of the wife, but they will not know how to be the head. You must not allow them to wait until they are married to find out that they do not know how to be the head. If at all possible, give your children plenty of opportunity to make decisions. When they grow up, they will then know what to do. They will know what is wrong and what is right. Give a child opportunities to make choices from the time he is young. I will say a word to all those who have children: "Give them a chance to choose." Otherwise, many Chinese children will be damaged when they grow up. The damage is often manifested when the children are between the ages of eighteen and twenty. They act in irresponsible ways at this age because they have never been called upon to make any choices. We must teach our children according to the discipline of the Lord. We must teach our children to make choices rather than making all the choices for them. We have to let our children know whether they have made the right choices.

5. Teaching Children to Manage Things

We must also teach our children to manage things. We must give them the opportunity to take care of their personal belongings, to manage their own shoes, socks, and other affairs. Give them a little instruction and then let them try to manage things by themselves. Let them know how things should be handled from their youth. Some children have a bad start because their fathers love them blindly and do not know how to train them. As Christians, we have to train our children to manage their things properly.

I believe if the Lord is gracious to us, we will gain half of our increase from among our own children and the other half from the "sea" (i.e., the world). If all the increase is from the sea and none is from among our own children, we will not have a strong church. Paul's generation could be saved directly from the world, but the generation after Paul, men like Timothy, came in through their families. We cannot expect our increase to always come from the world. We have to expect the second generation, men like Timothy, to come from our own families. God's gospel does save men from the world, but we also need to bring in men like Timothy. Before the church will be rich, there must be grandmothers like Lois and mothers like Eunice who raise, edify, and nurture their children in the discipline

of the Lord. If there are no such people, the church will never
be rich. We must give our children the opportunity to manage
things from their youth. We must give them the chance to
learn to arrange things by themselves. Hold family meetings
frequently and allow the children to make decisions. If we
have to rearrange the furniture, involve them in its rearrangement. If we have to rearrange the cupboard, involve them in
its rearrangement. Teach them to manage things. Whether
we have daughters or sons, we have to teach them to manage
things. Then they will become a good husband or a good wife
in the future.

What is our situation today? Girls should be cared for by
their mothers. But many mothers do not take care of them,
and the burden is turned over to the church. Boys should be
cared for by their fathers. But many fathers do not take care
of them, and the burden is also passed on to the church. As a
consequence, as men are saved and brought into the church,
the business burden of the church doubles. This is because
those who are parents do not live properly as Christian parents. After the church preaches the gospel and saves men, it
has to deal with all kinds of family problems associated with
these men. But if parents are responsible for the proper nurturing of their children, and if the children are brought up in
the church, the church will be relieved of half of its burdens.
In Shanghai I have often felt that the workers should not be
handling the many affairs that they handle; those affairs
should be handled by the parents. The parents do not teach
their children well, and these children drift into the world. As
a result, we have to rescue them back from the world and pick
up the burden of teaching them ourselves. This creates much
work for the church.

H. Leading the Children
to the Knowledge of the Lord

Eighth, we must lead them to the knowledge of the Lord. A
family altar is indeed necessary. In the Old Testament the
tabernacle was linked to the altar. In other words the family
is linked to service and consecration to God. No family can go

on without prayer and the reading of the Word. This is especially true with families that have children.

1. Meetings That Are on the Level of the Children

Some families fail in their prayer and Bible-reading time because their family meetings are too long and too deep. The children do not understand what is going on. They do not know why you are asking them to sit there. I do not like it when families invite us to their homes to speak about deep doctrines and then force their children to sit with them. Some home meetings go on for one or two hours about difficult doctrines. This is indeed a great suffering for the children. Yet many parents have no feeling about this. The children sit there, but they do not understand. For example, if the topic is on the book of Revelation, how can they understand it? The home meetings must suit the children. These family meetings are not designed for you; your meeting is in the meeting hall. Do not impose your standard on your family. What you do in the family must suit the taste of your children and must be on their own level.

2. Encouraging and Attracting

Another problem with some home meetings is that there is little love in them. It is neither the father's attraction nor the mother's attraction that draws the children to these meetings; it is the whip that keeps them there. They do not want to join. But they come because there is the threat of the whip. If you take away the whip, they will not come. This will never work. You must think of some ways to attract them and encourage them. Do not punish them. Never beat your children for not attending your family worship hour. If you beat them once, you may create a problem in them for the rest of their lives. Parents must attract their children to the family worship hour. Do not force them to come. This will only result in terrible consequences.

3. Meeting Once in the Morning and Once in the Evening

We suggest having two home meetings a day, one in the

morning and one in the evening. The father should lead the
morning time and the mother should lead the evening time.
Get up a little earlier. The parents must not remain in bed
after the children have taken their breakfast and gone to
school. If you have children at home, you have to wake up earlier. Have a little time together before the children go to
school. Your meeting should be short, living, and never long.
Perhaps ten minutes is enough. Fifteen minutes is the longest
it should be. Never exceed fifteen minutes and do not be
shorter than five minutes. Ask everyone of them to read a
verse. The father should take the lead to pick out a few
phrases and speak about them. If the children can memorize
something, ask them to memorize. Do not quote a whole verse.
Ask them to remember the meaning of a sentence. At the end
of the meeting the father or the mother should offer a prayer
for God's blessing. Do not offer lofty or deep prayers. Pray
about things that children can understand. Do not be long. Be
simple. Then send them to school.

Every time you sit down for your meal, you should thank
the Lord for it. Whether it is breakfast, lunch, or dinner, you
should be sincere in your thanksgiving. Help your children
to give thanks. The evening meeting should be a little longer,
and the mother should lead it. It is not necessary to read the
Bible at night, but the family needs to pray together. In particular, the mother has to gather the children together and
talk to them. While the father is sitting next to her, the
mother should encourage the children to speak up. Ask them
whether they had any problems that day. Ask whether they
fought with one another and whether anything was bothering
them. If a mother cannot make her children speak up, something must be wrong. It is a failure of the mother to allow a
barrier to exist between herself and her children. The mother
must be at fault if the children are afraid to speak to her.
They should be free to speak up. The mother must learn to
bring out the things that are in her children's hearts. If they
do not want to speak up that day, ask them the next day.
Guide the children. Let them pray a little and teach them
to say a few words. This meeting must be living. Ask them to
confess their sins, but do not force them. There must not be

any pretense. Everything must be done in a very natural way. Let them take some initiative themselves. If they have something to confess, let them confess. If they have nothing to confess, do not force them. There must not be any pretense. The pretense found in many children is the result of pressure from strict parents. Children do not tell lies, but you can force them to tell lies. The parents should lead them to pray in a simple way one by one. Make sure that everyone prays. Finally, conclude with a prayer of your own. But do not be long. Once your prayer becomes long, children become bored. Feed them according to their capacity. Once you try to do too much, you will overburden them. Pray a few sentences with them and then let them go to sleep.

4. Paying Attention to Their Repentance

Let them know the meaning of sin. Everyone sins. You must pay attention to the matter of their repentance and then bring them to the Lord. After some time you should ask them to receive the Lord sincerely. Then bring them to the church and let them be a part of the church. In this way you will lead your children to the knowledge of God.

I. The Atmosphere in the Family Being Love

Ninth, the atmosphere in the family should be one of love. Some become psychologically abnormal or withdrawn because they do not have love at home.

The way a child grows up depends on the atmosphere in his family. If a child does not receive any loving nurturing as he grows up, he will become stubborn, individualistic, and rebellious. Many people cannot get along with others in their adult life because they did not experience love in the family as a child. They saw only quarrels, arguments, and fights in the family. Children from such families grow up abnormally. Those who come from such abnormal families surely grow up to be lonely people. They will be antagonistic toward others. Because they feel inferior in their heart, they try to boost their self-image by considering themselves better than others. All those who have an inferiority complex have a tendency to exalt themselves. This is their means of offsetting their own inferiority.

Many bad elements in society such as robbers and rebels come from families which are void of love. Their personality becomes warped, and they turn against their fellow man when they grow up. When they come to the church, they bring their problems with them. I feel that half of the work of the church can be done by good parents. But this work falls upon our shoulders today because there are few good parents. New believers should see that they should treat their children in a proper way. A family must be filled with an atmosphere of love and tenderness. There must be genuine love. Children who grow up from such families will become normal persons.

Parents must learn to be friends to their children. Never allow your children to distance themselves from you. Never make yourself unapproachable. Please remember that friendship is built upon communication; it does not come by birth. You must learn to approach your children. Be happy to help them so that they will tell you when they encounter problems and seek your counsel when they are weak. They should not go to others when they are weak. They should be able to tell you their successes as well as their failures. You should be their good friend, the approachable and helpful one to them. They should look to you when they are weak and fellowship with you when they are successful. We have to be friends to them. When they are weak, they should be able to come to us for help. We should not be a judge on the throne but a help to them. We should be there whenever they need help, and we should be able to sit down with them and discuss problems with them. They should be able to seek counsel from us as from friends. In a family the parents must earn so much trust from their children that they become their friends. If a parent will do this, he or she will have done the right thing.

You have to learn this lesson from the time the children are young. How dear and near your children are to you depends on how you treat them the first twenty years of their lives. If they are not near to you the first twenty years of their lives, they will not be near to you when they are thirty or forty years old. They will drift further and further away from you. Many children do not like to be near their parents. They are not friends to them and there is no sweet relationship between them. They go to their parents when they have problems in a way that resembles a criminal going before a judge. You must work to such an extent that your children will come and seek your advice first when they have problems. They must feel comfortable confiding in you. If you can achieve this, you will find few problems in your family. In fact, all problems will be solved.

J. The Matter of Punishment

Tenth, there is the matter of punishment. When a child has done something wrong, he or she must be punished. It is wrong not to punish.

1. Being Afraid of Beating the Children

The most difficult thing is to punish someone. Those who are parents must be afraid of beating their children. They must consider it as serious as beating their own parents. No children should beat their own parents. One can be forgiven for beating his own parents, yet he will not be easily forgiven for beating his own children. You must learn to be afraid of beating your own children and must consider it as serious as beating your own parents.

2. Beating Being Necessary

However, beating them is sometimes necessary. Proverbs 13:24 says, "He that spareth his rod hateth his son: / but he that loveth him chasteneth him betimes." This is Solomon's wisdom. Parents should chastise their children with the rod. Beating is necessary.

3. Beating Justly

If you beat, however, you must beat justly. Do not lose your temper, and do not beat in anger. No one may beat their children in anger. Something is wrong with you when you are angry. Brothers and sisters, when your children do something wrong, and you beat them in your anger, you should realize that you also should be beaten. You must calm down first before God. As long as you are angry, you cannot chastise anyone.

4. Pointing Out to the Children Their Fault

Some problems must be settled by beating. But you must show the child what you are beating him for. If you need to beat him, you also need to show him his fault. You must show him his fault each time you beat him. You must tell him what his fault is. It is not enough to try to stop his fault by beating him. You have to explain to him that you are beating him because he is wrong in certain things.

5. Beating Being a Serious Thing

Every time you beat a child, you must not do it in a common way. You must show him that beating is a big thing. The whole family has to know about it. All the adults and children have to come together. The father or the mother has to carry out the beating like a surgeon performing an operation. A doctor does not cut with a knife out of anger; he cuts to remove a problem. In the same way a parent must not punish in anger; he or she must be calm. Parents must never beat their children in a state of fury. On the one hand, they must point out the fault. On the other hand, they must not be angry in any way.

How should you do it? I have a suggestion. By the time you have a cane in your hand, the child must have committed some very serious wrong. While you are holding the cane in your hand, you should ask the child's brother to fetch a pail of warm water and his sister to fetch a towel. Then you have to show the child what he has done wrong. You have to tell him that anyone who has done something so serious must be punished severely. He should not flee from his mistakes. Fleeing from punishment is wrong as well. A person must be bold to receive punishment if he is bold to commit sin. Tell him that he has done something wrong and that you have no choice but to punish him. The beating is for him to realize his wrong. You may beat him two times or you may beat him three times. Perhaps the child's hand will bruise and bleed from the beating. You should then ask his brother to soak the bruised hand in the warm water to relieve the blood circulation. Afterward you should wipe the child's hand with the towel. You have to do this ceremoniously. Show them that there is only love in the family; there is no hatred. I believe this is the right way to punish.

Today much of the punishment in the family is the result of anger and hatred, not love. You say that you love your children, but who will believe you? I will not. You must let them know where they are wrong. Let them know that their father is not beating them in hatred. When you beat, do it properly. After you beat them, you should take them to bed. If the offense is too serious, the mother or the father can share two of the child's stripes. You have to tell the child, "This matter is too serious. I have to beat you five times. But I am afraid that you cannot take it if I give you five stripes. So your mother will share two of them and your father will share one of them on your behalf. You yourself must still take the other two stripes." You have to show him that this is a serious and grave matter. He will remember not to sin freely for the rest of his life.

This is the Lord's discipline; it is not the discipline of your temper. It is the Lord's admonition, not the admonition of your temper. I do not stand with the temper of any parent. The temper of the parents will ruin the future of their children. The parents must learn to have true punishment for their children. But, at the same time, they must also learn to love. This is the proper way to have a Christian family.

II. GREAT CHILDREN COMING OUT OF GREAT PARENTS

Finally, I would say that many men whom God used in this world came from great parents. Beginning with Timothy, we find numerous men used by God who came from great parents. John Wesley was one of them. Another one was John Newton. There are many hymns in our hymnal written by Newton. John G. Paton was another one. He was one of the most famous missionaries in the modern world. I can think of no other father like his father. In his old age Paton still remembered, "Every time I wanted to sin, I remembered my father, who was always praying for me." His family was very poor. There was only one bedroom, one kitchen, and another small room. He said, "I trembled every time my father prayed and sighed in the small room. He was making petition for our souls. Even though I am so old now, I can still remember his sighing. I thank God for giving me such a father. I cannot sin, because when I sin, I transgress against my heavenly Father as well as my earthly father." It is difficult to find a father like Paton's father, and it is difficult to find a son as great as Paton.

I cannot tell you how many strong believers would be raised up in our second generation if all the parents of this generation would be good parents. I have always wanted to say this: The future of the church depends on the parents. When God bestows grace on the church, He needs vessels. There is the need for more Timothys to be raised up. It is true that we can save men from the world, but there is a greater need for raising up people from among Christian families.

CHAPTER THIRTY-FOUR

FRIENDS

Scripture Reading: James 4:4; 2 Cor. 6:14-18; Psa. 1; 1 Cor. 15:33

I. THE BIBLE
NOT EMPHASIZING FRIENDSHIP

One thing special about the Bible is that it does not say much about friendship among God's children. This does not mean that the word *friend* is never used in the Bible. The word is used numerous times in the Old Testament; we find it in Genesis and especially in Proverbs. In the New Testament we find the word in Matthew and Luke. But the friendship spoken of in the Bible primarily refers to friendship outside of Christ; the Bible does not say much about making friends with those who are in the Lord. If I remember correctly, the word *friends* is spoken of twice in Acts in relation to Christians. In the first instance, some among the Asiarch leaders were Paul's friends. They entreated Paul not to venture into the theater (19:31). In the second instance, Julius treated Paul kindly and allowed him to go to his friends to receive care (27:3). In addition to these two verses, 3 John 14 says, "The friends greet you. Greet the friends by name." As far as I know, these are the only three places in Acts and the Epistles that speak about the subject. This shows us that the Bible does not say much about the matter of friendship.

The Bible does not emphasize friendship but instead emphasizes our relationship as brothers and sisters. It emphasizes the relationship of the brothers and sisters in the Lord. This is the basic and primary relationship. The Bible puts much more emphasis on this than on friendship.

II. FRIENDSHIP BEING
THE MOST IMPORTANT RELATIONSHIP IN THE WORLD

What does friendship mean? An old man can be a friend to a young man. There can be friendship between husbands and wives. Fathers and sons can be friends with each other, and brothers and sisters also can be friends. Being a friend to someone means loving and communicating with that one; this is the only relationship that counts in a friendship. Among the different kinds of human relationships, there are blood relationships. This kind of relationship exists only between relatives. Friendship, however, is different from such relationships; it is sealed in mutual love. Friendship disregards all other relationships and binds two persons together through love. Friendship often exists between husband and wife, father and son, mother and daughter, or teacher and student. Friendship can develop between people of similar age, similar social standing, or similar era.

Friendship is an important relationship for a person who has not believed in the Lord Jesus. Before a person accepts the Lord as Savior, he does not share any spiritual relationship in the Lord. This is why friendship is the most important relationship in the world to him. But among us, friendship is no longer the most important thing. Friendship is rarely mentioned in the New Testament. Our emphasis is on the relationship that exists between us as brothers and sisters in the Lord. Our relationship as friends in the Lord is much less significant. Friendship is not important among God's children.

Before we believe in the Lord, we do not have a spiritual relationship. We only have father and son, mother and daughter, teacher and student, and master and servant relationships. This is why friendship is an important matter to those who have not believed in the Lord. Two persons can be father and son to each other, but they can still have differences in standing. The same can be said of a mother and a daughter, a husband and a wife, and a master and his servant. Everyone can have his or her own standing. Blood relationships, however, are limited in number. Most persons can have between three and five blood relationships; those who have eight and ten such relationships are considered unusual. Other than these relationships, all other contacts are with friends.

Man cannot be satisfied with family relationships alone. He cannot be satisfied with the teacher-student relationship or any other social relationship alone. Man needs friendship. Friendship is based on love, not on the blood relationship. Many of our human relationships are inherited from birth; only friendship is by personal choice. This is why friendship is a most important matter to an unbeliever. Everyone has friends. A person can have three, five, eight, or ten friends. He can have dozens or hundreds of friends if he is sociable enough. He can enjoy companionship, love, and fellowship among these friends. Friendship indeed occupies an important place in an unbeliever's life.

If an unbeliever does not have any friends, he must not be a very likable person. He may be somewhat abnormal or have a sick personality; he may be very hard to get along with; or perhaps his untrustworthiness or peculiarities have discouraged others from making friends with him. Under normal circumstances, a man always has friends.

III. GOD'S COMMAND BEING FOR US
TO TERMINATE OUR WORLDLY FRIENDSHIP

God, however, has ordained that we terminate our friendships after we have believed in the Lord Jesus.

A. Friendship of the World Being Enmity with God

James spoke of friendship of the world (James 4:4). The world here means "worldly people." "The friendship of the world is enmity with God." Please remember that the love for the Father is not in us if we love the world (1 John 2:15). To be a friend of worldly people is to be an enemy of God.

A new believer must be very clear that as soon as he becomes a Christian, he has to replace all of his friends. If you have just accepted the Lord, you must replace your friends. This is the same as changing one's attire and everything else when one believes in the Lord. Friends also need to be changed. One has to have an entirely different set of friends. I know what I am talking about. A new believer will live a poor and shallow spiritual life if he does not change his friends. A person should terminate all of his old friendships as soon as he believes in the Lord. It is wonderful to note that when God's love comes in, man's love departs. When the Lord's life comes into us, the world can no longer be a friend to us. But our Lord did not say that we have to hate the world in order to love God. This does not mean that we have to ignore the world or that we can no longer greet our friends on the street. Rather, it means that whoever befriends the world is at enmity with God. We do not have to treat the world as our enemy, but our deep friendship and our devotion to fellowship with it must be terminated. We may still love our friends, but now our goal should be to save them. We may still treat them as friends, but our goal should be like that of Cornelius—to bring them the gospel. Cornelius invited two groups of people when Peter came to his house: his relatives and his intimate friends (Acts 10:24). He knew that God wanted him to invite Peter, and he invited his relatives and intimate friends as well to listen to the gospel. This is the goal of our continued acquaintance; it is not to maintain our former ties. A man cannot stop knowing a person whom he has known already. A friend is still a friend. One cannot cut off his relationship with those who have been acquainted with him for years. Dealing with our friendship means that we have a turn in the Lord. It means that all former relationships cease. From this point forward, we still talk to our friends when we see them. We still discuss things with them if we have problems. But we have a new life, while they do not have such a life. Our relationship should not ignore this change in life. A person becomes a friend by first becoming acquainted with another, then by loving him, and finally by socializing with him. If we continue such a relationship with our friends after we are saved, we are at enmity with God, and spontaneously we will not be able to go on in a proper way.

In running a race, the lighter the weight one has on his body, the better it is. The more one deals with sins, the lighter his weight will be. The more recompenses one makes, the lighter his burdens will be. The more friends you leave behind, the less weight you will have. If you add a few friends to yourself, you will find yourself being pressed down. I have seen many brothers and sisters who have been held down by their friends. They cannot be absolute to God's way; it is hard for them to be good Christians. An unbeliever's standard of morality and conduct will always be that of an unbeliever's. They may not drag you down, but they will surely not lift you up.

B. Not Being Dissimilarly Yoked with an Unbeliever

Second Corinthians 6:14 says, "Do not become dissimilarly yoked with unbelievers." Many people think that this is a word for marriage. I agree that being dissimilarly yoked does imply marriage, but it also describes all other relationships between believers and unbelievers.

1. Being Dissimilarly Yoked with the World Not Being a Blessing but a Suffering

"Do not become dissimilarly yoked with unbelievers." This is a general statement. What does it mean? We have to go on to see the following questions: "For what partnership do righteousness and lawlessness have? Or what fellowship does light have with darkness? And what concord does Christ have with Belial? Or what part does a believer have with an unbeliever? And what agreement does the temple of God have with idols? For we are the temple of the living God, even as God said, 'I will dwell among them and walk among them; and I will be their God, and they will be My people.' Therefore 'come out from their midst and be separated, says the Lord, and do not touch what is unclean; and I will welcome you'; 'and I will be a Father to you, and you will be sons and daughters to Me, says the Lord Almighty'" (2 Cor. 6:14-18). All of these questions issue from the first statement: "Do not become dissimilarly yoked with unbelievers." This is a positive statement. It is the basic premise. After this basic premise, five questions follow. These questions show us that believers and unbelievers are not compatible with one another and cannot be similarly yoked.

I hope you will realize that although we live in the same

society as those in the world today, we cannot build up an intimate relationship with them, whether it be with respect to a business venture, general friendship, or marital union. If an unbeliever and a believer are together, sooner or later they will end up with trouble. Believers have their standard, and unbelievers have theirs. Believers have their ideologies, and unbelievers have theirs. Believers have their views, and unbelievers have theirs. If the two are put together, the result will not be blessing, but sorrow. The two hold different views, opinions, ethical standards, and moral judgments. Everything is different. One pulls one way, while the other pulls the opposite way. Putting both under the same yoke would simply break the yoke. The believer either has to go along with the unbeliever or break the yoke.

I wish all new believers would realize that when believers and unbelievers are put together, the believers always suffer. We should never think that we can pull the unbelievers in our direction. If we want to pull them in our direction, we do not have to do it by making friends with them. I can tell you that I have tried to pull my old friends in my direction, but I did not try to maintain my old friendship with them. We can win our old friends over to our side without trying to maintain our old friendships with them. If we try to maintain our friendships, they will probably win us over to their side.

C. H. Spurgeon once gave a good illustration. A young lady came to him and told him that she wanted to make friends with an unbeliever. She said that she wanted to bring him to the Lord and then become engaged to him. Mr. Spurgeon asked the young lady to climb up on a high table. She did as he asked. By then Mr. Spurgeon was already quite an old man. He told the young lady to hold his hand and try her best to pull him up. She tried very hard but could not do it. Mr. Spurgeon then said, "Now let me pull you down," and with one jerk, she was down on the ground. He said, "It is easy to be pulled down but hard to pull someone up." This answered the girl's question. Please remember that pulling someone up is always hard. It is very difficult to pull an unbeliever up, but it is easy for him to pull you down. Many people have been pulled down by unbelievers. Many brothers and sisters are pulled down by their friends because they have not dealt with the problem of friendships.

New believers should tell all their friends that they have believed in the Lord Jesus. They must open their mouth to testify and confess that they have received the Lord. Whenever they see their friends again, they must bring the Lord to them. I had many friends when I was in school. After believing in the Lord, I would take out my Bible, sit down with them, and talk about the Lord whenever I saw them. My conduct before I was a Christian was very poor. At the least I had learned to gamble and I enjoyed going to the theater. I was easily dragged into these things by my friends. But after I believed in the Lord, I would take out my Bible whenever I sat down with them. After I became known for doing this, my friends began to leave me alone. This was good for me because they stopped including me in their activities. Had I not done that, it would have been unavoidable for me to be dragged away. We would rather not be welcomed by our friends than be pulled away by them. It is best to keep a mild friendship with them, but do not pursue intimate friendship. Be polite and courteous. Do not lose your friends, but do not become deeply involved with them. We belong to the Lord, and we should always bring the Lord to them.

If you serve the Lord faithfully and bring the Lord to your friends in this way, sooner or later they will either turn to the Lord or forsake you. These are the only two possibilities. There is hardly a third possible outcome. They will either follow you and take the same way, or they no longer will bother you. This will work to a new believer's advantage; it will save him much trouble. A person will be dragged away by an unbeliever if the two bear the same yoke, because he has to disobey the Lord in order to maintain his close friendship with the world.

2. Five Questions on
Not Being Dissimilarly Yoked

First, "For what partnership do righteousness and lawlessness have?" You have believed in the Lord and you know what righteousness is. You must deal with your former unrighteousnesses. You must deal with whatever you owe to others. But unbelievers, even the most moral ones, do not know what righteousness means. The two are diametrically the opposite of each other. Righteousness and unrighteousness have no partnership with each other. We cannot take advantage of others in even the smallest way. Perhaps some people like to take advantage of others. In the past you might have thought that this was smart, but now you realize that this is unrighteousness. How can righteousness have partnership with unrighteousness? Your views are basically different now. Thus, righteousness can have no partnership with unrighteousness.

Second, "What fellowship does light have with darkness?" You have been enlightened, and now you see. The other person is in darkness and cannot see. A child of God, who has made some progress on his spiritual journey already and who has some depth in the Lord, will find it difficult even to fellowship with a fleshly Christian who lives in darkness. How much more difficult would it be for him to commune with one who is totally in darkness and sees nothing? At least you have been enlightened by God. Here is a basic contradiction: Light has no fellowship with darkness. Unbelievers can do many things. Their philosophies, ethical standards, and outlook on life are different from those of believers. Believers are in the light, while unbelievers are in darkness. How can they fellowship and commune with one another? They are basically different in nature.

Third, "And what concord does Christ have with Belial?" Belial refers to Satan and contemptible things. Satan is surely contemptible. We belong to the Lord, while unbelievers belong to Belial. We are honorable (1 Pet. 2:9), and they are cheap. We were bought with a high price, with the blood of the Son of God, not with corruptible gold and silver. We have our Christian standing, our dignity as believers. There are many things which we cannot do. I can bargain with a rickshaw-coolie within a reasonable limit. But it would be wrong for me to bargain beyond that limit. We are Christians, and we cannot go beyond certain limits. We cannot bargain too much with others. We must not lose our Christian dignity. We are worth more than the few cents that we bargain for. We cannot lower ourselves to the level of the street hawkers. We have to maintain our Christian standing and our Christian dignity.

Some people belong to Belial. They may do many things. They may take advantage of others or make gain for themselves. But we cannot do the same things. We have our Christian honor and status. How can these two kinds of people be in harmony with one another? One is pulling to one side, and the other is pulling to the opposite side. The two cannot be yoked together. Putting them under one yoke will not work. The yoke will surely break.

Please remember that many people are not that honorable. They are, in fact, rather ignoble. Christians, however, are noble people. The two are totally different; they cannot be yoked together. After one becomes a Christian, he cannot develop strong friendship with unbelievers, because he is incompatible with them.

Fourth, "Or what part does a believer have with an unbeliever?" This is a repetition of the question prior to it. This is another comparison. You have faith, and the other person does not have faith. You know God in faith, but the other person does not believe in God and does not know Him. You find faith in your life, but the other person does not have faith in his life. You trust in God, while he has no trust. You look to God, while he looks to himself. You say that everything is in God's hand, but he says that everything is in his own hand. The two are basically different. We often cannot communicate even with nominal Christians; we cannot fellowship with them. They say that they are Christians, but they have no faith. There is a problem here. Not only is the conduct of the two persons different, but one has faith while the other does not. The conduct is different because the measure of faith is different. With this difference, it is hard to have any communication at all. A believer has nothing to do with an unbeliever. A believer spontaneously trusts in God in many things; it is as natural as breathing. But this is hard to an unbeliever. He would say that the believer is superstitious, backward, or foolish. There is no way for us to make friends with unbelievers. They will pull us down, and the pull will be very strong.

Fifth, "What agreement does the temple of God have with idols?" What is the temple of God? What is an idol? I think this refers to the sanctification of the body. Following this, it says that we are the temple of the living God. In the book of 1 Corinthians, the believers' bodies are considered the temple of God. One group of people were idol worshippers, while the other group of people said, "Our bodies are the temple of God. We cannot defile the temple of God." What we do with our friends is related very much to our body. Drinking, smoking, and other activities all affect the body; they touch the body. But the body is the temple of God. One should not destroy this temple or defile it. We must preserve our body as we preserve God's temple. The living God dwells in us, and we must not destroy this temple. We are the temple of God, while they are the temple of idols. They are related to idols, visible or invisible. They do not care for the holiness of the body, but we do. Do you see the difference here? How can the two be yoked together?

We can never be friends with unbelievers. There is only one result if we befriend them—we are dragged down with them. We should never think that we are strong and steadfast and that it is all right for us to make a few unbelieving friends. Let me say that we have been Christians for many years, but we are still fearful of making friends with unbelievers. A relationship with them invariably brings loss to us. We should contact them only for the sake of bringing them to a meeting or testifying to them. Apart from this, all other contact is dangerous. Once we are in their midst, we will have to sacrifice our standard. It will be hard for us to maintain our Christian standard when we are among them.

C. Evil Companionships Corrupting Good Morals

First Corinthians 15:33 says, "Do not be deceived: Evil companionships corrupt good morals." Having evil companionships means to have improper friends. It is better to translate "evil companionships" as "improper fellowship" or "improper communication." The result of such evil companionship is the corruption of good morals. *Corrupt* means "decay," as the decay of wood by worms. Evil companionship decays good morals.

The expression *good morals* in a milder sense can be rendered "good manners." *Good morals* is a stronger expression. The original meaning of the word lies somewhere between these two words. The word *moral* is too strong, while the word *manner* is too light. It is probably somewhere in between. I think it is better to translate the word as "appearance." This is milder than the word *moral* but stronger than the word *manner.* We can say that improper communication corrupts good appearance. You may be very godly before God, but after you meet an unbeliever who jokes, you begin to laugh. There are some jokes we should not laugh at. But many times we feel that we do not need to be so stifled when we are among them; we feel that if we loosen up a little, they will welcome us more. But this is improper communication, and it corrupts good appearance.

Improper communication and good appearance are opposites. One is good, while the other is bad. The bad will corrupt the good. We must avoid this corruption. Since the Lord's life is within us, we should spend time to cultivate good habits and learn to be restricted in the Lord. We must learn day by day to be godly, careful, regimented, and restricted persons.

Please remember that one contact with unbelievers and one improper communication with them will waste much time. This is a great loss. Each time you communicate with unbelievers, you may need three or five days before you will be recovered to your proper standing, because unbelievers can affect your appearance, habits, and moral conduct before men. This is surely not profitable.

D. Neither Walking, Standing, Nor Sitting

Psalm 1:1-2 says, "Blessed is the man / Who does not walk / In the counsel of the wicked, / Nor stand on the path of sinners, / Nor sit in the company of mockers. / Rather his delight is in the law of Jehovah, / And in His law he meditates by day and by night."

Unbelievers have much counsel to offer. It is most pitiful

for God's children to seek counsel from unbelievers when they have problems. Many children of God ask unbelievers what they should do when they encounter problems. Even when they give you counsel, you cannot do what they counsel you to do. I have many unbelieving friends who offer me advice concerning many things even though I have not asked for it. If you listen to them, you will realize that all their thoughts concern how they may profit themselves. They do not ask whether a matter is right or wrong or whether it is God's will. They have only one motive—personal profit. Can we do something that is purely for our own profit? Some of their counsel not only is for their own profit but even causes loss to others. Some profit does not come at the expense of others, and some does. How can a believer walk in the counsel of an unbeliever?

If you become too intimate with an unbeliever, it will be hard for you to turn his counsel down. As a result, you will be carried away. If you seek counsel from five friends together, it will be hard to reject their suggestion and say no to them, because they are your friends. They have a unified, a unanimous, proposal, and it is good for you. If you talk with them, it means that you are seeking counsel from them. But their advice only comes from their mind. You should not follow this advice.

Moreover, there are many places where you cannot go. Sinners have their own path and their own places. They do not come to church if they want to gamble. They have their own places and their own path. Today, if you communicate with unbelievers, you are taking their path even if you say you are not one of them. This is hard. An unbeliever may want to go to a place that you should not go to. Even if you say that you will not go inside, you are still on the same path. Although you may say good-by and part with them at the door, you have already gone the same way. "Blessed is the man / Who does not walk / In the counsel of the wicked, / Nor stand on the path of sinners." God does not want us to be in their places, and He does not want us to even stand on their path. God wants us to be fully separated from them. We cannot befriend them. Once we befriend them, we will stand on their path or at least touch their places.

"Nor sit in the company of mockers." Almost all unbelievers are mockers. I have seldom found a brother whose friends
did not joke with him or make fun of the Lord's name. I met
many unbelievers during the first few years of my Christian
life who joked about the Lord's name whenever I saw them.
They blasphemed the name of the Lord. If you sit among
unbelievers, they will ridicule you, and the Lord's name will
be blasphemed. They may not mention the Lord's name
before you join them; they may not have the intention to blas-
pheme the Lord's name. But your presence gives them the
opportunity to talk about Jesus and Christianity. They will
carry on with their jokes. If you do not want to sit in the
company of mockers or listen to their mocking, you must not
communicate or fellowship with them or befriend them in any
way.

IV. REPLACING FRIENDS
WITH BROTHERS IN THE CHURCH

A person must settle the matter of friendship during the
first few weeks of his Christian life. He must change all his
friends. You must tell all your friends what has happened to
you. You may still maintain some friendship with them, but
this friendship cannot be intimate in any way. You must
change all your friends. You must learn to be a brother in the
church and replace your former friends with brothers in
the church.

We do not want to go to the extreme. We do not hate our
former friends, and we do not want to ignore them altogether.
But now our contact with them must be on a different level.
Learn to testify to them and bring the Lord to them. We
should be with them for only five minutes, fifteen minutes,
half an hour, or an hour. Do not continue to sit among them.
Do not talk about worldly things with them. Learn to take
your stand and try your best to bring them to the Lord and
the church. Testify to them and preach the gospel to them.
Try your best to make them brothers and sisters in the
church. Do not make friends or have friendship outside the
circle of brothers.

I can assure you that a believer with too many unbelieving

friends will surely be a defeated Christian. Even if he does not sin, he will become worldly. If a person loves the Lord, serves Him, and is faithful to Him and is exercised in himself, he cannot possibly have many worldly friends. If a person has many frivolous friends, it proves that he is sick.

We should not have unclean lips, and we should not dwell among people of unclean lips. In the sight of God, it is wrong to have unclean lips. It is equally wrong and requires equal confession to dwell among people of unclean lips. It is wrong for us to sin, and it also is wrong to dwell among sinners. We need to ask God for grace so that we ourselves do not sin. We need His grace so that we do not cultivate intimate friendship with sinners. You would be angry at someone if he said that you were a thief. Neither would it be a compliment if he said that you were in the company of thieves or that you were a friend of thieves.

The first question a person should ask before the Lord is about himself. The second question he should ask is about his friends. Next to the person himself, a person is represented by his acquaintances. If he wants to remain strong, he must not be careless about his acquaintances and friendships. The minute he becomes careless about his friends, he is defeated. Never be careless in this matter. You must leave all your former friends behind. Learn to make friends with those who fellowship in the church. Your communication with them should be something in the Lord. You should replace all of your former communication with communication that is in the Lord.

V. THE MEANING OF FRIENDSHIP IN THE CHURCH

A. Friendship Being Something That Goes Beyond Normal Relationships

By now you should see that friendship is something very special. It is a relationship which goes beyond social status. It is a relationship that is free from formality. When a communication goes beyond social status and formality, that is friendship. I once said that some fathers are friends to their sons, while other fathers remain fathers for life. I know that some mothers have never been friends to their daughters; the mothers are strictly mothers and the daughters are strictly daughters; they have never been friends to each other. There are many people who never become friends to those in their family; the husband remains strictly a husband, and the wife remains strictly a wife. Many supervisors in offices take a very lofty position, and their subordinates remain inferior to them. There is only an employer-employee relationship between them; they have never been friends to each other. Although some become friends, these are rare exceptions. Being a friend to someone means going beyond the normal relationship. It means to have an acquaintance that extends beyond the normal relationship.

Abraham was a friend of God. If he had behaved strictly as a man and God had behaved strictly as God, they would not have been friends. Abraham forgot his status, and God also set aside His status. Thus, Abraham could be a friend to God.

The Lord Jesus also became a friend to sinners. The Lord Jesus could not have become a friend to sinners if He had remained in His own position. He became a friend because He left that position. If He had not stepped from His position, He could only have been a Savior and not a friend to man. I hope you can see what a friend is. As sinners we could never be joined to the Lord. He is the Judge and we are the judged. He is the Savior and we are the saved. But the Lord laid aside everything to become a friend to sinners. This is why others called Him the Friend of sinners. This is how He leads them to accept Him as their Savior.

I believe that after a person has been in the Lord for a long time and has developed a deep relationship with Him, he will find some brothers in the church to be his friends. He can go beyond the normal relationship. The third Epistle of John is quite clear about this matter. In 3 John, John no longer seemed to be an apostle. He had become an elder instead.

I want to draw your attention to the fact that 3 John was written when John was very old. The letter was written about thirty years after Paul was martyred. At that time Peter also had passed away. Of the twelve apostles, John was the only one left. He wrote as "the elder to Gaius" (v. 1). He was indeed elderly. I like his third Epistle very much. Third John is different from the other Epistles. First John speaks of "fathers," "young men," and "young children." It seems that John was still conscious of clear distinctions there. But in the last verse of 3 John, he had come to a different place; he was standing in a very special position. He was very old by then and could call a seventy-year-old man his son. He was very old, perhaps in his nineties. At such an old age, when he had so much knowledge and had traveled so far in his spiritual journey, he did not address his brothers and sisters as brothers and sisters. He did not use such terms as *children, young men,* or *fathers.* He simply said, "The friends greet you. Greet the friends by name." Do you not sense a certain flavor here? In reading God's Word, we have to touch its flavor and its spirit before we can comprehend the meaning behind the word. If we do not touch the flavor and the spirit, our reading will be fruitless. Here was a man who was so old that he had practically lost all his friends. Peter was dead and so was Paul, but John could still say, "The friends greet you. Greet the friends." Here was a man with so much riches in him. We can say that he had arrived at the pinnacle of his riches. He had followed the Lord for many years and had touched many things. Now he was so old that he could pat the head of a sixty or seventy-year-old man and call him, "My child." But he did not say this. Instead he said, "My friends." I do not know whether you understand what I am trying to say. This has nothing to do with position; John was not speaking in his normal capacity. This kind of speaking uplifts a person. Just as the Lord was a friend to sinners and just as God became a friend to Abraham, John also treated all of God's children, young and old, as his friends. This is altogether different from what we spoke about earlier in this chapter.

B. The Emphasis in the Church Being the Brother Relationship

Some day some of our young ones may arrive at this stage, but today they must behave as brothers in the church. The matter of friendship occupies a very high place in the church. Some day, when we reach a high plane, we may become a friend to little children. We can be far above them, yet can honor them by calling them our friends. Before that day comes, the church must emphasize the relationship of brothers and sisters, not the relationship of friends.

It is interesting to note that the church pays attention to many things, but not friendship. This is because friendship is something that goes beyond the normal relationship. It is something that is beyond the ordinary, something that stands on special ground. Friendship is when a great man honors another man by being his friend. Such a man can be so great that he can call another person his friend. This is not something that any brother or sister can do. Those who are young in the Lord should learn to maintain their relationship as brothers and sisters in the Lord. I hope that you will separate yourself from your former friends and have communication and fellowship with the brothers and sisters in the church instead. If you do this, it will save you from many problems as you go on in your spiritual journey.